White Men Can't Hump
(As Good As Black Men)

Volume II: Sex & Race in America

Todd Wooten

Bloomington, IN   authorHOUSE®   Milton Keynes, UK

AuthorHouse™
1663 Liberty Drive, Suite 200
Bloomington, IN 47403
www.authorhouse.com
Phone: 1-800-839-8640

AuthorHouse™ UK Ltd.
500 Avebury Boulevard
Central Milton Keynes, MK9 2BE
www.authorhouse.co.uk
Phone: 08001974150

First published by AuthorHouse 1/10/2007

ISBN: 1-4259-5976-8 (sc)

Printed in the United States of America
Bloomington, Indiana

This book is printed on acid-free paper.

VOLUME II *SEX* & RACE IN AMERICA

Table of Contents

Chapter 1 Opening Pandora's Box (From VOLUME I)   vii

Chapter 2 Terms / Definitions / Miscellaneous Information   ix

RANT: *A Rose For The Ladies*   *292*

WARNING: FOR MY SELF-RIGHTEOUS READERS   295

SECTION IV W.M.D. (Continued From VOLUME I)

Chapter 3 W.M.D. = **W**eapon of **M**ass **D**esire = Is it True?   296

SECTION V BLACK BALLED

Chapter 1 America's Biggest Myth: "Size Doesn't Matter"   307

RANT: *"The White Male Happy Meal"*   *317*

Chapter 2 "Once you go Black, you don't go Back. Why?"   327

RANT: *"The Serengeti Syndrome"*   *334*

Chapter 3 "Is There a Difference?"   341

Sub-Chapter 'A' "White Folks sing about ***Fallin' in Love***"
"Black Folks sing about ***Makin' Love***"   344

RANT: *"The Decade the Music Died"*   *347*

Sub-Chapter 'B' "Mo Cushion ***vs.*** No Cushion"   357

RANT: *"One-Dimensional **vs.** Multi-Dimensional"*   *363*

Chapter 4 BLACK PORN: "The Proof is in the Chocolate
Pudding"   370

RANT: *"The Death Row Game"*   *381*

SECTION VI RACE CARDS

Chapter 1 Stereotypes   384

Sub-Chapter 'A' 'Cultural Stereotypes'   387

Sub-Chapter 'B' 'Physical Stereotypes' ***vs.*** 'Intellectual
Stereotypes'   394

Chapter 2 The Media   409

Sub-Chapter 'A' "Hate Nigger Radio"   418

    *RANT: Kobe **vs.** Mike (Color Trumps Conviction)*   428

Chapter 3"The Great American Déjà vu" (The Till & Simpson
    Trials)   432

Chapter 4 "**TOM**FOOLERY"   448

    RANT: "Uncle Tonya's Log Cabin Republicans"   460

SECTION VII Closing The Divide

Chapter 1 Closing the Economic & Racial Divide   473

Chapter 2 Closing the Human Divide   481

DEDICATION   484

VOLUME I RACE & SEX IN AMERICA   485

Chapter 1 Opening Pandora's Box (From VOLUME I)

Pandora (*Greek Myth*): The first mortal woman; she opens a box, letting all human evils into the world.

What's evil to one person may be a virtue to another. **White Men Can't Hump (W.M.C.H.)** is going to open America's Sexual and Racial Pandora's Box, and this will allow you the reader to decide what is evil and what is not evil. In America what is considered a virtue when applied to White Men, is usually considered evil when applied to Black Men. **W.M.C.H.** will ask why, and will give possible answers. **W.M.C.H.** will also explore our *differences*, both cultural and physical, and put them in their proper context. Our *differences* should be accepted, respected, and at times celebrated. *Different* doesn't mean ugly, bad or wrong. *Different* means distinct, unique or unlike yourself. Now that we've covered *People Skills 101*, let's get down to business. This book is divided into *two* **VOLUMES**. The *two* **VOLUMES** are broken into *seven* **SECTIONS**, and each **SECTION** has multiple chapters that tie into the next chapter. You can jump around if you like, but to get the full appreciation I recommend you go with the flow and read cover to cover.

I also ask that you don't judge this book by its cover. **White Men Can't Hump** is a book for all Races, creeds, colors and genders; so please sit down and take some time to get to know it. After all, isn't that what we do when we meet someone *different* for the first time? What **W.M.C.H.** will do is help people discuss the uncomfortable subject of Race, by combining Race with a subject that people Love to discuss, Sex. My *first* hope is that by combining the *two* subjects, people will see each of them in a new light, and therefore see each other in a new light. My *second* hope is for this book to create a dialogue that will overshadow its controversial contents. Whenever there's an event that exposes America's Racial Divide, the first thing everyone says is *"We need to have more discussions about Race."* As soon as the event subsides, we ease back into our *"Don't discuss Race because it makes me uncomfortable"* mode. By combining America's Racial past and present, with America's Sexual past and present, there's no escaping the discussion. The truth is, *SEX & RACE* have been interwoven into the fabric of this nation for centuries. **W.M.C.H.** merely exposes where the threads cross paths, that's all. If you're looking to be pissed off, this book will do just that. If you're looking to be entertained, trust me, you'll be entertained. The bottom line is that you're looking, because that's the only way we'll ever learn about each other, and maybe even develop a genuine mutual respect for one another. One thing is for sure, you'll never be *enlightened* if your eyes are closed, and **White Men Can't Hump** is meant to be an eye opener.

"Life is too short to Hate"

Chapter 2 Terms / Definitions / Miscellaneous Information

Usually you'd find this kind of information in the back of a book, but I feel this information would be much more helpful if you got it up front. Because I've been exposed to so many *different* cultures I tend to slip in and out of the King's English, Ebonics, Marine Corps terminology and Slang from the 70's and 80's. I'll also explain a little quirk I came up with that'll allow me to briefly stray off the subject from time to time. I hope you'll find some of these terms humorous, and more importantly, informative. I also hope some of these terms will help you communicate with someone *different* from yourself one day.

(<u>NOTE:</u> Some of the Terms may not be in this VOLUME)

10 % **Rule:** This is a Marine Corps term. This means that every group of people has their *10 %* of fuck ups. No one group has a monopoly on good behavior or poor behavior (i.e., everyone has their *10 %*). I'll give this term an honest re-adjustment for Black Folks. The *10 %* **Rule** will apply to every group of people except for Blacks. Black Folks will fall under the *20 %* **Rule.** I know Black Folks don't want to hear that shit, but that's too damn bad, it's the truth. With Black Folks you've got your standard *10 %* of regular fuck ups, and then an additional *10 %* of fuck ups. Blacks who've been brainwashed into believing that fucking up is cool, fall under the additional *10 %*. Don't get too happy with my candor White America. *20 %* of Black America, roughly *7* Million people, is still considerably less than *10 %* of White America, which would be over *20* Million people. Percentages, per capitas, and the numbers of people incarcerated are very misleading ways to look at crime. The number of people in prison only tells us who's being aggressively investigated, arrested, prosecuted and sentenced. Just because you're *not* in jail, it doesn't mean you ain't fucking up, it just means you haven't been caught yet. If this country pursued White collar criminals and White Male pedophiles, the same way it pursues young Black Males, the Racial make-up of our prison population would change dramatically.

Bizzness: Sex or Good Sex

Black Male Value Meal: Women with *plenty* of titties and *plenty* of ass. This order can also be *Super-Sized.* (Also see **White Male Happy Meal**).

Brothers: Black Men (*pronounced Broth-uz*).

B.T.P.: Back to the point. This tells the reader that a *RANT* is over and the author is getting back on message.

***C.L.R.* Sex:** Consensual, Legal and Responsible Sex. This should be the only kind of Sex.

Cock-Block: When a man impedes or obstructs the efforts of another man to prevent progress. There are countless ways to *Cock-Block*, but the most common way is the use of misinformation to create distrust or fear of the man in question. This type of behavior is not isolated to just men; women also use these techniques against other women. The modern name for this type of behavior is *Player Hating* or *Hatin'*.

Commercial Christians: The Millionaire televangelists, who seem to be more concerned about what people do in their bedrooms, than helping the homeless and the hungry.

Devaluation: *(Slavery's Legacy)* - "A Black Life is Less Valuable than a White Life"

Devaluation Triangle: How Whites apply *Slavery's Legacy* to Blacks. The **Devaluation Triangle** consists of *3*-sides that feed off of each other. The *3*-sides are Hate, Indifference, and Ignorance, also known as H *2* I.

"Double Dose": Two Love interests

Equipment: Penis or Male Genitalia

Female Sexual Anatomy: Groceries, Goodies

Fuck: I will use this word throughout the book in a variety of ways. I'll use it in its standard Sexual context, and I'll also use it as a form of expression (like Vice President Cheney did on the Senate Floor). It's a word that was given to me by my Marine Corps Drill Instructors, and I've carried it with me ever since.

Good Sex: Taken care of *Bizzness*, Droppin' Anchor, Layin' Pipe, 'Hittin' it Right'

Hood: Neighborhood

Jacking-Off: Sorry folks, but this has nothing to do with masturbation. This is a prison term that basically means *Brown Nosing, Kissing Ass* or *Sucking Up*. Examples: **"Man, that Armstrong Williams was always *Jacking-Off* Strom Thurmond"** or **"Man, that J.C. Watts is always *Jacking-Off* Dick Cheney."**

"Language throughout the history of this country": This statement was made by Judge Clarence Thomas during his Supreme Court nomination hearings (i.e., the Anita Hill hearings). What *Language* was Judge Thomas referring to? Judge Thomas would specifically state: **"the *Language* about the Sexual prowess of Black Men, and *Language* about the Sex organs of Black Men, and the *size*."** You'll see this statement throughout the book, because in many ways, this statement is the foundation of the book.

"Life is too Short to Hate": You will find this statement at the ***bottom*** of every page because it's the bottom line if mankind is to peacefully coexist. What do you want your Legacy to be? What is the Legacy of Roy Bryant and J.W. Milam (the murderers of *14*-year-old Emmett Till)? Sure, we know they got away with murder but what is their Legacy? I don't even think David Duke would want to die with that shit on his resumé. As more time passes (*50* years to be exact), old Roy and J.W. look more and more like Lloyd and Harry from the movie **Dumb and Dumber**. They got away with murder because their inbred brethren made up the jury pool (*as well as the gene pool*). They were heroes to many in 1955, but in 2005 they look like two Hate-filled retards. So what do you want your Legacy to be? After all, Life is too short to Hate. Saying this phrase to yourself can also help you avoid road rage situations.

Limbaugh Syndrome: Over-focusing on life in the boardroom (*gettin' paid*), to compensate for short-comings in the bedroom (*gettin' laid*), i.e. the inability to satisfy a woman. This wretched illness afflicts primarily White Males. This illness has existed for centuries, but the modern day poster-child for it is none other than the great Rush Limbaugh. When **Limpbaugh Syndrome** is coupled with **Small-Poleons Complex** (*physically and/or Sexually threatened by Black Men*) the *two* expand to form an intense Hatred of Black Men.

Magnums: Large-*Sized* condoms by **Trojan.**

Male Sexual Anatomy: *Dick*, Equipment, Merchandise, Penis, Tools to get the job done, Weapon

(M.M.L.) - Much More Later. Many of the subjects I'll be covering are inter-woven, so to avoid straying from the main topic, **(M.M.L.)** will tell you there'll be more *info* on a particular topic later.

Motherfuck: It's like the Black version of *Fuck*, but it can be used to describe a person, place or thing. This is my baby. Living in inner-city Cleveland I heard this word in barbershops quite often. I heard this word repeatedly in the Marine Corps. I also heard this word repeatedly when I worked in the prison system. As a Fire Officer I have to be professional and articulate at all times, so it's always nice to come home, relax, and say *Muuutherfuck.*

Multi-Dimensional: Men who are willing to do whatever it takes to help a woman reach **Point 'O' (Orgasm).**

"My Boys": Friends

"My Girl" or "My Guy": Someone whom I have the utmost respect for, but don't know personally (i.e., "My Girl" Halle Berry, "My Guy" Denzel Washington).

N-Bomb: The N-Word.

Nigga(s): Black's usage of the N-word

Nigger(s): White's usage of the N-word

N-Word: Nigger or Nigga. (Also the first *RANT* of **VOLUME I**)

One-Dimensional: Selfish men who only want fellatio (*usually White*) or only want intercourse (*usually Black*).

Packin': Well-endowed or an ***Above Average** size* Penis.

Point '*A*': Foreplay

Point '*O*': Orgasm

"Put yourself in the author's shoes": You'll find this at the ***top*** of every page in this book. This is to remind the reader that even if he or she doesn't agree with the author, there are as many points of view as there are people. It's also my attempt to send subliminal messages to the reader so that he or she will agree with me. I know, I know, people are too smart to fall for some *bullshit* like that. Gay marriage for all men. John Kerry bad man. George W. Bush great man. Gay marriage for all men. John Kerry bad man. George W. Bush great man. Gay marriage for all men. John Kerry bad man. George W. Bush great man. Gay marriage for all men. John Kerry bad man. George W. Bush great man. On second thought, this *bullshit* worked before; maybe I'll give it a try anyway.

Race Card: For Whites, the **Race Card** is similar to crying *Wolf*. For people of color, the **Race Card** is a way crying *Foul*.

Race Test: The **Race Test** is often applied when people of color (*usually Black*) meet someone White for the first time. The person of color simply asks themselves: **"What does this person really think of me?"** It may be done out of paranoia or insecurity, but many people of color do it without realizing it. You can also apply the **Race Test** to someone else by asking: **"How would *that person* be treated by a White Police Officer if they were in the wrong neighborhood?"**

RANT: In life things are rarely Black and White. I like to think of life as an inch of Black on one side, an inch of White on one side, and a mile of Gray in the middle. Those of us who acknowledge the Gray's existence tend to handle the peaks and valleys of life a little better than those who only see life in terms of Black and White or Right and Wrong. ***RANTS*** allow me to stray off topic and briefly explore the Gray areas of life. When it comes to Race, Religion, Politics and Sex, it's all Gray anyway.

RANT Inside of a RANT: Two **RANTS** for the price of one.

Reverse-*Limpbaugh Syndrome*: Over-focusing on life in the bedroom or bedrooms (*gettin' laid*), to compensate for lack of opportunities in the boardroom (*gettin' paid*), i.e. the inability to be employed. This wretched illness afflicts primarily Black Males.

Sex: *Hittin' the skin*

Sexual Power: Sexual Power is the ability to exude Sexual confidence without overtly trying to draw attention to yourself. **Sexual Power** enables a person to Sexually intimidate someone with nothing more than their mere presence. **Sexual Power** is when a motherfucker walks into a room, and everybody clutches their dates arm and asks: ***"What are you looking at?"*** or ***"Who the fuck is that?"***

Sisters: Black Women (*pronounced Sis-tuz*).

Slavery's Legacy: "A Black Life is Less Valuable than a White Life" (i.e., **Devaluation**)

Small-Poleons Button: The **Small-Poleons Button** is pushed when a White Woman falsely accuses a Black Man of rape. There have been countless false charges of rape against Black Men by White Women, and one of the main reasons is that it's a guaranteed attention getter, or a guaranteed attention diverter.

Small-Poleons Complex: White Men who are physically and/or Sexually threatened by Black Men (*derived from Napoleon's Complex*). The *threat ratio* is *75 %* Sexual and *25 %* physical. When **Small-Poleons Complex** is coupled with *Limpbaugh Syndrome* it expands to form an intense Hatred of Black Men. I think it's safe to say that *100 %* of the men involved in the lynchings of Black Men suffered from **Small-Poleons Complex.**

The Small-Poleons Test: The Small-Poleons Test occurs when a White Man sees his woman talking to an unknown Black Man. If he interrogates her like she's a member of Al-Qaida, he flunked the **Small-Poleons Test.**

Takin' care of *Bizzness*: Good Sex

The Tom Charge: When a Black Man is called an Uncle Tom

Tomism: Uncle Tomin'

<u>WARNING:</u> I cover some pretty sensitive subjects with blunt honesty. I'm sure when you see the word **<u>WARNING</u>** you're going to want to read it even more. I guess if I put the word **<u>WARNING</u>** there, I really want you to read it. Whatever the case, if you see the word **<u>WARNING</u>** consider yourself **<u>warned.</u>**

White Boyz: young White Males

White Male Happy Meal: Women who are *super thin,* with large fake breasts, and preferably no ass. (Also see **Black Male Value Meal**)

Wiggers: (*White-Niggers*) White suburban kids who act and talk like urban Black kids.

RANT: A Rose For The Ladies

A wise woman named Madonna once sang a little number entitled **Where Life Begins**, and I think paying proper respect to women is the appropriate way to begin the *2nd* leg of this little journey. Although Madonna was referring to a certain part of the female anatomy being serviced in a certain way, the fact is we all owe women a debt of gratitude, for it is truly with women *Where Life Begins*. It's women who give the gift of life, and what I find to be most disheartening about the world we live in is the fact that women remain our most unappreciated and untapped resource. Over the years I've heard many women refer to God as a woman, and after much soul searching I recently concluded that if there is a God, then God must be a woman. Ladies, I've become a believer. If it wasn't for men fucking everything up, there wouldn't be an *"If there is a God"* question in my heart or mind. I'm sure Sexist preachers and Homosexual priests don't want to hear anything about God being a woman. After all, both Protestants and Catholics actively fight to keep women out of leadership positions in God's house here on earth. You have to admire their consistency. Protestants and Catholics both **Green-Lighted** Slavery, and both closed their eyes during the Holocaust. So whether it be their Sex*ism* of today or their Rac*ism* of yesterday, they don't like to budge when it comes to *ism's*. Throughout history God seems to be handling her business just like your mother. She doesn't punish you as soon as you screw up; she just sits back and lets you build a case against yourself. Then without warning, one day she'll pass judgment on you and firmly lower the boom.

Everything I was taught about God revolved around Love, care and compassion for fellow human beings. I'm aware of a woman's role according to the Bible, but that was written by men at a time when women were considered nothing but property. Among human beings, who's as Loving, caring, and compassionate as women (*obviously* Ann Coulter *doesn't count*). A minister friend of mine once reminded me that God's Love for us (i.e., *his children*) is stronger than anything on this planet, he then inadvertently made my point for me when he said: **"The only Love comparable to God's Love for us, is the Love that a mother has for *her children*."** I rest my case.

I've never had a problem with the Message of religion; my problem has always been with the Messengers, and it just so happens the Messengers have always been men. When you look at the carnage that man has perpetrated against fellow man in the name of their God, why should anyone believe.

Whenever men are looking for ways to justify their *actions* or *inactions*, you can guarantee they're going to fish through the *scriptures* until they find one they can twist or exploit. What was originally intended as a means of providing guidance is instead used as a means to promote self-serving agendas. To list all of the horrifying acts that man has committed against fellow man in the name of their God would be like walking from Miami to Seattle. I've already mentioned Slavery and the Holocaust, and a more recent example would be flying passenger jets into buildings. In each of those *three* high points of human **un-civility**, there were men who actually believed God was on their side. Exploiting the scriptures is just a tool that men use to exploit other men. Most of the time men do just fine exploiting other men without the aid of scripture. Look at who fills our jails, molest our children, pollutes our planet and starts our wars. Do I even need to tell you who? I'll tell you this much, the world would certainly be a better place if women ran it.

As someone who follows politics closely, I find it very disappointing to see women divided into Pro-Life and Pro-Choice or separated as Liberals *vs.* Conservatives. Women should be united in their quest for improving health care for their entire body, instead of divided over their reproductive body. Women should be united in their quest for the same wages as men when doing the same job. Women should be leading the fight to keep all pedophiles and Sexual predators in prison (*instead of in and out of prison*). Women in America have more in common than not, and their goals should reflect their commonality and not their *differences*. What's really sad is that it's men who've created the divisions among women, and then men exploit those divisions for political or financial gain.

A man has no say as to whether or not a woman gets an abortion, so why the hell does a man have any say as to whether or not it's legal. That's just one example of how women let men stick their noses in places where it doesn't belong. Ladies you already know what can happen when a man sticks his nose in a place where it doesn't belong; something usually gets fucked up. Hopefully, as more women become educated and reach positions of leadership, this country and therefore this world, will become a better place to live. As for you men out there who can't fathom taking orders from women, get over yourself. More than likely you're over-compensating for other short-comings in your life, and you should deal with those kinds of short-comings at home, not at work. For now, until the **meek** (i.e., **Women**) inherit the earth, we'll continue to live with the threat of **W.M.D. (Wanton Male Destruction).**

Ladies I'd like to make one more little suggestion that I really wish you would take to heart. Please stop following these societal trends created by men and start establishing your own trends. I want you all to know, men and especially women, as we move forward there are some parts of this book that are pretty graphic. I tell it like it is. The Sex Police will try to tell you that I'm a Sexist, but ladies you know better. Ladies you know I have nuthin' but Love and respect for you. So don't let a bunch of people who've only read this book's cover, tell you what I am, or what I said, or what I meant. Don't let them divide and conquer what you read, what you feel, or more importantly, what you want.

WARNING: FOR MY SELF-RIGHTEOUS READERS

The next *five* chapters are the reason many of you bought this book. ***Don't lie.*** Let's be real, if this book was entitled **"Black Men in America"** no one would be reading it but my family. I promise; you won't be disappointed. I'll be blunt and to the point, but I'll also try to bring some humor to some very *taboo* subjects. I'll try not to come across as filthy, but that'll depend on what you consider filthy. If you're a member of the Sex Police then you've already categorized this book as filthy, so move forward at your own risk. Like I said in **VOLUME I**, this is a book, not a television show. You didn't accidentally flip to the wrong channel. This is in your hands because you chose to put it in your hands. You can put it down, throw it away, or burn it whenever you please. You don't have to cover your kid's *eyes*, because there are *no* pictures. You don't have to cover your kid's *ears*, because this is *not* an *Erectile Dysfunction* commercial or a *Feminine Hygiene* commercial. This is not the *soft-core porn* you see in the *Daily Soaps*, and this is not the *soft-core porn* you see in the annual *Sports Illustrated Swimsuit Issue*. This is just a book. This book will dissect some of America's most *taboo* subjects, and then separate the fact from fiction. This book will discuss these *taboo* subjects like no other book ever has. The next *five* chapters will answer all of the questions that were posed in **VOLUME I** and then some.

If you've already read **VOLUME I,** then I'm sure you realize that *SEX & RACE IN AMERICA* are closely linked and have been for centuries.

So why is it so difficult for people to discuss Race, when many of these same people have no problem openly discussing Sex? The next *five* chapters will examine this mother of all paradoxes, and you the reader will receive the answers to questions that America has always been scared to ask. What you've encountered up to this point, along with the next *five* chapters, will hopefully open up new dialogues and create new discussions about subjects that have always been considered off limits. Regardless of your Race, Sex, creed, color or gender, you've all been **WARNED,** so please enjoy.

SECTION IV W.M.D. (Continued From VOLUME I)

Chapter 3 W.M.D. = *Weapon of Mass Desire* = Is it True?

"Yet just as in childhood I envied Negroes for what seemed to me their superior masculinity, so I envy them today for what seems to me their superior physical grace and beauty. I have come to value physical grace very highly, and I am now capable of aching with all my being when I watch a Negro couple on the dance floor or a Negro playing basketball or baseball. They are on the kind of terms with their own bodies that I should like to be on with mine, and for that precious quality they seemed blessed to me."

Norman Podhoretz
"My Negro Problem – And Ours"
Conservative Columnist/Author
1963

"I'd like to borrow his body for just 48 hours, there are three guys I'd like to beat up, and four women I'd like to Make Love to."

Sportswriter Jim Murray had this to say about the greatest football player of all-time, Mr. Jim Brown.

Like I said in the **Hate** chapter (**VOLUME I**), with men it's about *kickin' ass* and *gettin' laid*. Every man's got some primitive instinct pumping through his veins, but unfortunately some men get a little jealous because other men may have been blessed with a little more. *Physically*, the most beautiful human being on this planet is the Black American Athlete, period. No other group of human beings on this planet comes close. Aesthetic, yet Explosive, Graceful, yet Powerful, you name it and we've got it. The Black American Athlete not only dominates athletics in America, but also dominates athletics on the world's stage. The Black American Athlete was even able to dominate on the world's stage against Eastern Bloc and Soviet athletes who were obviously using steroids. These physical gifts are a blessing and a burden at the same time. It's a blessing

"Life is too short to Hate"

because it's given so many Blacks the opportunity to get out of poverty. It's a burden because too many young Blacks think athletics is the only way out of poverty. One could easily conclude that this is a form of *Limpbaugh Syndrome*. On the surface, over-focusing on *physical* gifts to compensate for supposed *intellectual* short-comings has elements of both *Limpbaugh Syndrome* and **Reverse-*Limpbaugh Syndrome***. But to be honest, neither theory is plausible, because those supposed *intellectual* short-comings were fostered, nurtured and enforced by Whites for centuries, and those supposed *intellectual* short-comings are currently embraced by today's Black Youth. Many Black Youth of today want to be *intellectually inferior*. There's a big *difference* between self-inflicted stupidity and being *intellectually inferior* due to genetics. Self-inflicted stupidity is the same thing as parking in a HANDICAP ZONE when you're not handicap. You know it's wrong, but you do it anyway. That doesn't make you *intellectually* HANDICAPPED, it just makes you voluntarily stupid. These misguided young men help keep the negative perceptions alive, and help reinforce those negative perceptions.

There's no doubt many, many Whites privately believe that ***"Blacks are intellectually inferior."*** That belief was entrenched into the American psyche long before the current hip-hop culture of self-inflicted stupidity. If it wasn't for political correctness, those beliefs wouldn't be private. Those beliefs were openly espoused by both Blacks and Whites for centuries and were passed down generation to generation (*via* Ignorance). So it's safe to say this particular news is *Ancient*, but it's far from *History*. There's no doubt, this form of **Devaluation** was believed by both Races, and there's no doubt about where those beliefs originated (Slavery). Actually, the belief that all people of color are *intellectually inferior* was around well before Slavery in America. That's why the Europeans felt it was necessary to colonize every ***non-White*** hut and village on the globe (*they hit* Africa, Asia, and South America). America took this whole *intellectually inferior* belief to another level. America decided not to take any chances, and decided to enforce *intellectual inferiority*, just in case the whole genetic theory was wrong. That's why a Slave could receive the same punishment for attempting to learn how to read and write, as he received for attempting to escape. That same level of punishment was also dealt out for trying to enroll in *superior* White schools during Jim Crow. Education has always come with a very steep price for Black Folks, and when Black Folks have failed to pay that steep price, they were easily lumped into the *intellectually inferior* category. That's why the ***intellectually inferior*** *Myth* is not *Ancient History*. As long as the *Myth* that ***"Blacks are intellectually inferior"*** is out there, people will be afraid to discuss Black *physical superiority*.

Any boastful-like discussions on Black *physical superiority* could trigger retaliatory discussions on the *Myth* that ***"Whites are intellectually superior."***

I can see why Blacks fear a discussion of this sort. Me personally, I don't fear this discussion, I welcome it. You can pull out ***"50"* Bell Curves** (See **VOLUME I**) and it's a discussion I more than welcome. When we get to the chapter entitled **Stereotypes**, Black *intellectual inferiority* will be one of the main subjects. For now, we're going to examine the Black Man physically, from the neck down. We're going to start this physical examination of the Black Man with the lower extremities. What I meant to say was lower ***extremity***, *not extremities*. The chapter in **VOLUME I** entitled **Punch Line,** gave you Hollywood's perception of the **Black Penis**. In this chapter we're going to take a non-fictional look at the **Black Penis**. After all, don't you want to find out if ***It's True*** before we move on to the next chapter, **America's Biggest Myth: "Size Doesn't Matter"**.

The first time I heard about the **Black Penis** being *different* from other Penises was in the wonderful summer of 1975. The Messenger was none other than the great Black Comedian, Mr. Richard Pryor. Mr. Pryor's classic **"Mudbone"** skit, from the 1975 album **"is it something i said?"** was as much of an eye opening experience, as the movies I mentioned in the **"Fear of the Black Penis"** chapter. Like I said in **VOLUME I,** the summer of 1975 was the summer of growth for me. **The Godfather** and the Emmett Till open-casket photo taught me about Race. **The Exorcist** exposed me to the complexities of religion. I don't have to explain what **Deep Throat** exposed me to. Mr. Pryor was the icing on the cake. With Mr. Pryor, I received additional education on all of the above and then some. Richard covered everything, Race, religion, Sex, drugs and of course, the **Black Penis**. In the **"Mudbone"** skit, Richard told the story of **"The Niggas with the Biggest *Dicks* in the World Contest,"** which was eventually held at the Golden Gate Bridge. The *two* key phrases were:

One Nigga said: *"God damn this water's cold!"*
The other Nigga said: *"Yeah…and it's deep too!"*

Needless to say "My Boys" and I were walking Richard Pryor albums.

You couldn't say anything without getting a *Richard Pryor-like* response. Example: **"Man, this lemonade is ice cold,"** the reply would come in unison, *"Yeah…and it's deep too!"* Then we'd all sit there and giggle. Rest in peace Mr. Pryor, you taught us more than you'll ever know, and you were without question a true genius. I can't tell you how many

Brothers have told me they had to stop and laugh the first time they got *air in the pussy.* The reason for the laughter was because they heard Richard describe the event before they were old enough to know what a *'pussy'* was. The great ones have a way of affecting you, and you carry their words with you for life. Mr. Pryor's big tale about **"The Niggas with the Biggest *Dicks* in the World Contest"** is basically a reflection of what Justice Thomas so painfully described as ***"The language throughout the history of this country."*** Poor Justice Thomas, if only he had married Lorena Bobbit, all would be *White* (*woops*); all would be *right* in his world.

The *Language* that Justice Thomas spoke of goes way back to a time when this nation didn't even exist. There have been a lot of motherfuckers guilty of some major ***B.D.W. (Black Dick Watching)*** over the last **6** centuries. On the surface, I find it very creepy, but I guess I understand. I imagine it's the same mindset that would cause someone to stare at *Siamese Twins.* If you're not used to seeing someone with *two* heads, I guess you'd do a *double-take.* Every place I've worked as an adult, I've witnessed White Guys who were guilty of ***B.D.W.*** I've seen White Guys take this phenomenon a step further and actually give nicknames to Black Men because of their Penis. When I was in the Marine Corps there was ***Big Dick Bob.*** When I worked for the Dept. of Corrections there was ***Hungwell.*** Now, with the Fire Dept., there's ***T.P R.*** ***T.P.R.*** is short for ***Tar Paper Roll,*** which is a reference to the massive Black rolls of tar paper used in the roofing business. There had to be some major ***Black Dick Watching*** going on, judging by the nicknames. To actually put the thought into giving another man's Penis a nickname, speaks to the name of this chapter, **Weapon of Mass Desire**. I am certainly *'not'* implying that all White Men are ***Black Dick Watchers,*** or that all White Men watch *Dicks* of any color. Most guys don't play that ***Dick Watching*** shit, unless you're watching porn. But when a man's watching porn, he's observing what a woman is *doing to*, and *doing with*, another man's Penis. All I'm saying is that it's usually White Guys who notice if someone's Penis is perceived to be *too big* or *too small.* Once the observation has been made, the jokes and the nicknames are sure to follow.

There's no doubt that much of this is just juvenile locker room behavior. There's also no denying that Black Men often adjust their Penis in public, and talk about their Penis as if it were another person, example: **"Yeah..... *Dick* is ready to come out and play toniiight, cos' there's some ladies up in here!"** When it's your Penis, you can do that. White Guys are much more liberal when it comes to other people's *privates.* The White Firefighter who gave the nickname ***T. P. R.*** to a Black Firefighter was not new to this type of behavior. The White Firefighter had earned the department-wide nickname

The Peeker well before he nicknamed the Black Firefighter's Penis ***T.P.R.*** How did he earn the nickname *'The Peeker'* you ask? *'The Peeker'* earned this nickname when he traveled to New Orleans with a group of Firefighters for Mardi Gras several years ago. The story goes like this.

'The Peeker', who I'll call Firefighter *'P'*, became tired during the first evening of Mardi Gras festivities and left the group, so he could return to the hotel and get some sleep. When the rest of the group, who I'll call Firefighters *'A', 'B', 'C',* and *'D'* returned to the hotel many hours later, they observed Firefighter *'P'* sound asleep in a chair, with his head back and his mouth wide open. Firefighter *'A'* then decided to **Tea-bag** Firefighter *'P'*. If you don't know what **Tea-bagging** is, then I suggest you 'Google' it or check out the movie **Soul Plane** for a detailed definition. While Firefighter *'A'* was pulling his pants down and preparing to **Tea-bag** Firefighter *'P'*, Firefighter *'B'* was getting the video camera ready. Firefighter *'A'* then promptly **Tea-bagged** Firefighter *'P'*, and Firefighter *'B'* captured the event on video. Firefighters *'C'* and *'D'* were rolling on the floor in tears of laughter. Firefighter *'P'* slept through repeated **Tea-baggings**, which were all caught on camera. The next day, Firefighters *'A', 'B', 'C',* and *'D'* wanted to view the action that was videotaped the previous evening. After viewing all of the action that occurred on Bourbon St. the previous evening, they suddenly came upon the forgotten video footage from the action that occurred when they got back to the hotel room. Firefighters *'A', 'B', 'C',* and *'D'* huddled around the viewfinder and once again found themselves in tears of laughter as they re-witnessed the repeated **Tea-baggings** of passed out Firefighter *'P'*. Suddenly, Firefighter *'B'* noticed something odd in the viewfinder, so he rewound the footage and paused on the frame in question. Firefighter *'B'* couldn't believe his eyes. As Firefighter *'B'* closely examined the picture on the viewfinder he made an amazing discovery. Firefighter *'P'* had *'one eye open'* the entire time. It was the *one* mysteriously *opened eye* that earned Firefighter *'P'* the nickname ***The Peeker***.

Apparently, due to all of the gut-busting laughter, no one noticed that one eye was open during the numerous **Tea-baggings**. Needless to say, Firefighter *'A'* (the **Tea-Bagger**) no longer thought the whole episode was funny. Firefighter *'A'* also learned a valuable lesson about putting his belongings in places where they don't belong. Firefighter *'B'* (the cameraman, and the only Black Firefighter in the group) and Firefighters *'C'* and *'D'* (the laughers), felt the incident had mushroomed from hilarious to hysterical. After eventually finding out what had occurred, Firefighter *'P'* swore that he had ***both eyes*** closed the entire time, and never seemed to be upset about being **Tea-bagged**. In case you're wondering, Firefighter

'P' also swears he's not a Homosexual, but he's obviously very comfortable around other men's genitalia.

Firefighter *'P'* is not the only White Guy who's comfortable with other men's genitalia. After the Abu Gharib, Iraqi prison fiasco hit the newsstands; I wasn't surprised one bit when I heard Rush Limbaugh's opinion of the incident. Mr. Limbaugh likened the pyramids of nude male Iraqi prisoners, to nothing more than a fraternity hazing. Mr. Limbaugh also repeatedly stated on his radio show, the U.S. Soldiers were just having a ***Good Time***. I repeat, I am not a homophobe, but piles of nude men doesn't equate to having a ***Good Time*** in my book. Mr. Limbaugh obviously reads from a *different* book. As creepy as that may sound, Firefighter *'P'* and Mr. Limbaugh are no *different* from many other White Men over the centuries. The White Male fascination with other men's genitalia can't be denied and certainly precedes the days of the Slavery Auction Blocks. In David Friedman's book **A Mind of Its Own,** he delves into the history of ***B.D.W.*** Mr. Friedman's research into the phenomenon of ***B.D.W.*** netted some very insightful quotes from a number of Europeans who visited the continent of Africa many centuries ago. Here's a sample:

> **"Black Lords (Mandingo tribesman) of this country are furnisht with *members so huge* as to be burdensome to them." Richard Jobson, Treasure-Hunter, Gambia, the year of 1623 "In no branch of the human Race are the *male organs more developed* than in the African. It was among the Sudanese that I found the most developed phallus, being nearly *12* inches in length by a diameter of 2 ¼ inches. This was a terrific machine, and except for a slight *difference* in length, was more like the Penis of a donkey than that of a man."**

> **Dr. Jacobus Sutor**
> *19th* **Century**
> **French Army Surgeon**

I realize this guy was a doctor, but how the hell do you pull this shit off? Excuse me Monsieur; may I measure your member? Excuse me Monsieur, may I observe your member at work? Don't mind me Monsieur, I'll just sit quietly over here in the corner of your hut. Excuse me Monsieur, you wouldn't happen to have any lotion would you? This is mere speculation on my part, but you have to admit this shit is creepy. There were also Black Penis collectors. These men seemed to have the same Black Penis obsession as America's *20th* Century White lynchers. Here's a sample of their *lyncher-like* Black Penis obsession:

"The Penis of an African is larger than that of a European. Preparations of them are preserved in most anatomical museums, and I have one in mine."

Dr. Charles White, English Physician, 1799

"It is said that the Penis in the Negro is very large. This assertion is borne out by the remarkable genitory apparatus of an Ethiopian in my collection."

Dr. Johan Frederick Blumenbach, German Physician, 1806

In many ways, the European fascination with the **Black Penis**, as far back as *6* centuries ago, led to the rationale for Slavery. Obviously, to these gentlemen *Size Mattered*, because they felt the *size* of the **Black Penis** proved that Blacks were sub-human. All they needed was some religious justification to get the Slavery ball (*and chain*) rolling. Man can always count on the good old Bible to supply a *verse* or supply a *curse*, that'll justify his every need. A *verse here* and a *verse there,* a *curse here* and a *curse there*, and **"presto"**, you've got a lazy, shiftless, *intellectually inferior* workforce. This was all done in the name of the scriptures and therefore sanctioned by God Almighty himself. These attitudes were then passed down just like an Italian pasta sauce recipe, generation to generation.

There's no doubt the great European *Black Dick Watchers* of centuries past were convinced they had stumbled onto something big. After all, they had documented, collected, and discussed their findings. I don't care how long ago it was, it still seems creepy to me. You go on a *6* month journey to a foreign land, and you become preoccupied with another man's Penis. You get back home, and you can't wait to kick back with your buddies and tell them about your trip. Then over a *mug of Mead*, you feel the need to tell them about the *massive members* on those *Mandingos.* Then again, I guess it's not really that far-fetched. Only a few decades ago, guys kicked back around an open fire, and over a *cold Pabst Blue Ribbon beer*, they chatted about how exhilarating it was to *hold a* **Black Penis,** and how much fun it was to *cut it off* (*that's right, for it to be cut off, another man had to hold it*). It is certainly a preoccupation with White Men, because there's been a desire to conduct endless studies and endless research. Imagine how many European lives could've been saved if these European doctors would've placed their focus in a more meaningful direction, like Louis Pasteur. Just a thought. European doctors weren't the only doctors guilty of **B.D.W.** Mr. Friedman also pointed out a few American doctors who suffered from this form of *Jungle Fever*. Here's a few more samples from **A Mind of Its Own**:

"Because the genital organs in the African are enormously developed, and his whole life is devoted to matters pertaining to the worships of Priapus, the Sexual centers in his cerebral cortex are correspondingly enlarged."

Dr. William Lee Howard, Baltimore, Md., 1903

"Many years ago I dissected an old Negro man in Washington, D.C. As a subject he was particularly simian in his organization, and one thing I noticed about him, in addition to his immense copulatory organ, was the structure of his toenails, which were marvelously thickened and curved."

Dr. R.W. Shufeldt, Manhattan, N.Y.
From The Negro: A Menace to American Civilization, 1907

I Love that last one. He dissects a cadaver and the primary things he notices are the *Dick* and the toenails. I guess it was truly a head to toe examination. The good doctor may have had a *valid reason* for adding that valuable medical information to his publication, **The Negro: A Menace to American Civilization.** Could this next quote have been the *valid reason?*

"I am informed that the Sexual power of Negroes and slower ejaculation are the cause of the favor in which they are viewed by some White Women of strong Sexual passions in America. At one time there was a special house in New York City to which White Women resorted for these *Buck Lovers*. The women came heavily veiled and would inspect the Penises of the men before making their selection."

Havelock Ellis, British Researcher
Studies in the Psychology of Sex Vol. III, 1913

One must wonder if the **Buck Lover** male escort service had anything to do with Dr. Shufeldt's perception of *"Negroes as a **Menace** to American Civilization."* After all, it was the *same city* and the *same time period.* Dr. Howard and Dr. Schufeldt's focus certainly didn't seem to be on medicine.

When you consider how primitive the field of medicine was in those days, it just seems like a lot of valuable resources and energy was misdirected towards the **Black Penis**. Why? You gotta judge for yourself, but you know what I think. Mr. Friedman's book **'A Mind of Its Own'** is by far the most thorough and objective Penis book out there, for those of you interested in Penile history.

In Maggie Paley's **The Book of the Penis,** she spoke with people who were in a position to know about Penis *sizes*: Gay Men, adventurous women, and an urologist. They all said: **"Black Men are bigger, and Asian Men are smaller."** This seems to be consistent with most of the studies that have been conducted. There have been numerous studies conducted and they usually rank Black Men at # **1**, White Men at # **2**, and Asian Men at # **3**. Don't ask me why Hispanics aren't included, because I don't know. In February of 2004, **The Oprah Winfrey Show** briefly touched on the rankings I just listed. In a show entitled **"Is Your Sex Life Normal,"** Sex expert Tracey Cox asked and answered the following question: **"When it comes to *size*, most people think African-American men are the biggest...True or False? ....True. Research confirms that Asian Men are the smallest, followed by Caucasians, with African-American Men definitely being the largest."**

Ms. Cox's expert testimony created the following exchange between Oprah and an unidentified Black Male in her audience:

Oprah: "Wait a minute. All the Brothers in the audience are going....
No, look....You're blushing. You ever see a Black Man blush?
Did I hear you tell...did I hear you whisper to her...Told you?"
(The audience erupts)

Unidentified Black Male: "I tell her all the time, though."

Oprah: "You tell her all the time."

Unidentified Black Male: "I tell her all the time."

Oprah: "Okay, because...yeah, yeah,...you didn't need a statistical survey."

Unidentified: "Yeah. I didn't...I didn't need that."

Isn't it amazing how easily Race can be discussed when you mix it with Sex? In Anne Hooper's book **'Sex Q & A'** she states: **"Nationality affects Penis *size*. American Men, for example, have been found to have bigger Penises than Thai Men."** I had to laugh about that one because I immediately thought about "My Boy" Tiger Woods. I bet he's not claiming his mother's heritage when the subject is Penis *size*. I think it's a safe bet he's claiming Earl's genes (judging by Tiger's taste in jokes, *I think it's a very safe bet*). I'd certainly claim my Daddy's genes, so I guess I'm right there with you *T.W.*

There seems to be an overall consensus about who's # **1** in the **B.C.S.** (_._._.)**,** (you can fill in your own **B.C.S.** blanks). I told you in **VOLUME I** that I'd let White Folks make the case for me. **According to** *Hollywood / Scientists / Doctors / Explorers / Researchers / Authors / Numerous Studies / the behavior of Lynchers*, and of course **"The language throughout the history of this country,"** It must be True! Brothers are reaching the finish line *first*, but it's only by *a few inches*. **There are no absolutes** and there are always exceptions; so it's not fair to be*little* an entire Race of people, is it? Sound familiar?

There's really no way of ever truly knowing, but one thing we do know is that a lot of men are trying to upgrade their *weaponry*. The **"Language throughout the history of this country"** tells us **who isn't** trying to upgrade their *weaponry*. So **who is** trying to upgrade their *weaponry?* Doesn't attempting to upgrade your *weaponry* cost money?

How much money are American Men spending annually to upgrade their *weaponry?* American Men are spending over a "BILLION **DOLLAR$**" a year on Penis enlargement products. I repeat, American Men are spending over a "BILLION **DOLLAR$**" a year on Penis enlargement products. A BILLION **DOLLAR$** can buy you the following *weaponry*:

70 fully-equipped Apache Helicopters
20 top of the line F-15 jet fighters
One Aegis Class Navy Destroyer
Or you can save your money for **5** years and buy an F-117 Stealth Bomber.

Just think, the men who are spending a BILLION **DOLLAR$** a year on Penis enlargement products could pool their resources, and then buy some real *weaponry*. The question is: **"Who's spending a BILLION DOLLAR$ a year on this bullshit?"** When you're *unemployed* or *incarcerated*, Penis enlargement products probably aren't a priority, so that excludes Black Men from the equation. I doubt if it's Asian Men. There aren't enough

Asian Men in America to total a BILLION **DOLLAR$** annually. Gee, who could be spending a "BILLION **DOLLAR$**" a year on Penis enlargement products? I'm sure you guys can take a wild guess. By the way, none of these herbs, pills, pumps, potions or lotions work. I guess White Men and Black Men have something in common after all. We're both stuck in the skin we're in. Some of us happen to have darker skin and some of us happen to have a little less skin, but we're both stuck. Just think, if we paid less attention to our *differences* and focused more on our common goals, goals like family, education, and jobs, this country could be a much better place. Until that Utopian day comes, you've gotta make due with *what you've got*. The big question now is: ***"Does what you've got Matter?"*** Let's find out.

SECTION V BLACK BALLED

Chapter 1 America's Biggest Myth: "Size Doesn't Matter"

"Everything's bigger in America. We've got the biggest cars, the biggest houses, the biggest companies, the biggest food, and finally the biggest people."

Morgan Spurlock
From the Documentary
"SUPER SIZE ME"

You can't argue with that. America is truly the land of *Bigger is Better*. In America *Bigger is Better* is the primary means of expressing one's personal success. The biggest bank account buys you the biggest purchases. The bigger the price tag on an *item*, the bigger the impression made on those who see it. That's why the Penis is the most amazing *item* in America. In America, the Penis is the only *item* of significance I can think of where *Average* is considered equal to *Above Average*. I'm talking about an *item* that's part of everyday life for more than *two-thirds* of our population. You not only have to factor in men, but you also have to factor in their partners. That means about *two-thirds* of our population handles a Penis on a daily basis and *Average* is still considered equal to *Above Average*. That almost seems *un*-American doesn't it? I'm not talking about the extremes (i.e., *EXTREMELY LARGE* vs. *extremely small*). I'm talking about *Average vs. Above Average*. *Average* is considered equally desirable, equally acceptable, and equal in every way to *Above Average*. If you're a parent and your child told you the *'C'* he got on his math test was equal to an *'A'*, would you accept that bullshit? **Hell No!** Why Not? The answer is, all grades are obviously *not* created equal. When you say *Size Doesn't Matter*, you're saying that all Penises are created equal. The gist of the blanket statement *Size Doesn't Matter* is that all Penises are created equal and therefore *Average* and *Above Average* are the same thing.

I'm sure that's the case for many women. I'm sure many women feel that *"It's **not** what you got; it's how well you use it."* I'm also sure there are just as many women out there who feel the exact opposite. I'm sure there are many women out there who'll tell you that *Average* doesn't do shit for them. I'm sure there are many women out there who feel that *"it's what you got and also how well you use it."* Unfortunately, these women don't have a voice. The *Average* advocates control the airwaves. The *Average* advocates love to make women feel dirty if they desire something that's *Above Average*. The result of this is *half* of women are speaking on behalf of all womankind. The truth is they're only speaking for *half* of all women or maybe less. I'll get right to the point. This whole *Size Doesn't Matter* thing is all about making *Average* Men feel *Above Average*. The initial intent was well meaning, but the end result has actually backfired. What started out as well intended deception has created generations of lazy, selfish men. If honesty had been the policy from day one, men would have entirely *different* attitudes and wouldn't be nearly as selfish in the bedroom. Honesty would've forced *Average* men to expand their playbooks, consult their partners, and be less **One-Dimensional** (See **Terms & Def's.**). If *Average* Men had known from day one that at least *half* of the women out there think *Size Does Matter*, they would work harder at *other things* in order to be competitive. They'd become innovative and they would be forced to become **Multi-Dimensional** (See **Terms & Def's**). Instead, women have let them off of the hook, and then women have the nerve to complain that their partner is selfish. I'm not saying that men who are *Above Average* don't need to work, or don't need to consult their partner, or don't need to be **Multi-Dimensional**. Every man should work at it, every man should consult their partner, and every man should be **Multi-Dimensional**. What I'm saying is, men who are *Above Average* have more upside, so therefore, when properly trained by their partner, bring more to the table. It's like the saying you always hear from NFL scouts, GM's, and coaches: "You can't coach *Speed*, either you got it or you don't, and *Speed* changes the dimensions of the game." Now then, just substitute the word *Speed* with *Size*. This whole thing came about because of flawed medical research, dishonesty during surveys, and an unwillingness to hurt some people's feelings and egos. The result is countless doctors, countless therapists, and countless surveys, all making the same blanket statement on behalf of all women that *Size Doesn't Matter*.

These professionals rarely (*if ever*) say: "To some women *size matters* and to some women *size doesn't matter.*" These blanket statements on behalf of all women do more bad than good because they mislead women into settling for a *Size* that may not suit them, and this could lead to future unhappiness. Wouldn't it be much more beneficial to women if these doctors and therapists made blanket statements such as *Dress Sizes Don't Matter* or *Breast Sizes Don't Matter*. If these doctors and therapists made blanket statements in these areas (*Dress Sizes* and *Breast Sizes*), they could actually save some lives, which is what I thought doctors and therapists were supposed to do. Instead, they mention *offhandedly* that women should be comfortable with their bodies, but they mention with ***absolute certainty*** that Penis *Size Doesn't Matter.* I'll tell you why they do this bullshit later in this chapter. For now I'll let them speak for themselves.

Susan Campbell, Ph. D & Suzie Heumann
From the book **"The Everything Great Sex Book"**

Q- "Does *size* really matter?"

A- "The truth is, *size* doesn't matter- what matters is the man's self-confidence and skill. Much more important than what you've got is what you can do with it."

This is the kind of bullshit I'm talking about. The first thing they mention is the man's self-confidence. Women are being told the initial focus should be to uplift their partner's self-confidence. After building up a man's self-confidence, do you know what women usually end up with? They usually end up complaining that he's selfish and doesn't do shit for them in return. Immediately after answering the *Size* question, this book also mentions that **"Becoming a wonderful, attentive, and caring Lover is far more important than the *size* of your Penis."** The problem is, the majority of this book's readers are probably women. So the statement **"Becoming a wonderful, attentive, and caring Lover,"** merely re-emphasizes that women should help build up their partner's self-confidence. This information was followed with a **warning** about the dangers of *Above Average* Penises. The authors **warned** women of the potential problems that can arise by having Sex with a man whose Penis is *Above Average.* **Warnings** like some vaginas are too small, or the man may not be satisfied if the entire shaft is not stimulated, or deep thrust may cause pain for the woman. The authors then provided an answer for a Penis that's too small for an *Average* vagina. They stated that **"Girth isn't that important, as long as she does her Kegel Exercises"** (*vaginal exercises developed by a **male** doctor named* Arnold Kegel).

This is just a nice way of telling women to *Lower the Bar.* The *Average* Man doesn't have to do shit, because women are told to cater to his self-confidence, and women are then told to do Kegel Exercises to make him feel like he's *Above Average.* Women are even having vaginal surgery to make *Average* Men feel *Above Average.* A new surgical procedure called **Laser Vaginal Rejuvenation** makes the vagina smaller, so both the male and the female get more feeling during intercourse. My question is: **"Why are Kegel Exercises and Laser Surgery necessary if *Size Doesn't Matter?"***

Dr. Betty Dobson, on **ABC'S The View**, September of 2005

Q- "Does *size* matter?"

A- (Laughter, and an *"Oh please-like"* dismissive hand gesture) "I think it matters more to men than to women. I think we're more interested in the *size* of the bank account."

The one constant theme among most of these doctors is they never say: **"To some women *size matters* and to some women *size doesn't matter."*** They always give the blanket answer that *Size Doesn't Matter*, and they usually give the answer in a very dismissive way. Answering the *"Does Size Matter Question"* in a dismissive way has *two* purposes:

 # 1 It's meant to make women who prefer ***Above Average*** feel dirty.
 # 2 It's meant to help men who are *Average* feel good.

What I found most comical about Dr. Dobson's answer was that it completely contradicted the statements that were on the video she was promoting. Dr. Dobson was on **The View** promoting **The *'O'* Tapes,** which is an instructional video on female orgasms. There's a chapter in the video entitled **Penis Size** and it features commentary from *18 different* women. *15* of the *18* women stated that ***Size Matters*** to them. Of the ***three*** who initially stated that *Size Doesn't Matter*, ***two*** eventually stated that ***Size Does Matter*** before their commentary ended. During that *five* minute segment, a whopping *17* of *18* women stated that ***Size Matters***. Remember now, this video is about female orgasms. These women basically stated that even though Penis *size* may not play a major role in their orgasm, it still *matters* to them. This film clip ***wasn't*** shown on **The View**; instead they showed a clip from the chapter entitled **Faking It** (*orgasms*). I wasn't surprised to hear the comments from those *17* ladies, because the shit women tell each other in private is completely *different* from what they say in surveys.

Women have been guilty of political correctness, long before political correctness was fashionable. By trying not to hurt men's feelings women have only hurt themselves, because many men feel they don't have to do the extra work to compensate for their short-comings. This is not entirely the fault of women because they've been bombarded with misinformation and told what's supposed to feel good for years. The fact that an instructional video was produced in order to teach women how to achieve orgasm, tells you there's not just a lack of information, but there's also a lot of bad information. The good doctors, therapists and researchers have invested a lot of time telling women what *doesn't matter*, and have spent very little time telling women to explore and to find what *matters* to them individually.

Anne Hooper, Sex Therapist
From the book **Sex Q & A**

Q- "I am worried that my Penis is too small."

A- Many men get hung up on Penis *size*, believing that bigger is better. Bear in mind that the most sensitive part of a woman's vagina is the lower third- an area that even the smallest Penis is able to penetrate.

Wow! How's that one? She's telling women that a *2* to *4* inch Penis should be enough to get the job done. I found her statement confusing because of the instructional photos in this book. There are photos of fully-nude couples demonstrating Sexual positions that can be used if the man has a smaller than *Average* Penis and the woman has a large vagina. If *Size Doesn't Matter*, and the most sensitive part of the vagina is the lower third, why the need for special Sexual positions that give the illusion of deeper penetration?

Sue Johanson, RN and Sex Expert, **Oxygen TV Channel**, October of 2005

Q- "What's the average *size* for a Penis? Because when me and my wife be doing it...be having Sex...it seems like she be wanting more...and I be giving her all I got...and I don't know whether I'm small, large or average?"

A- The *average* non-erect Penis, non-erect, is *3* to *5* inches long....*3* to *5*. And a guy with a full erection, the average guy is *5* to *7* inches long.... alright. Now....what your wife needs to know, is that most females have no nerve endings in the top two-thirds

of their vagina. So if you had a *12* inch Penis, she couldn't feel it in her vagina, because there's no nerve endings up at the top end. So Penis *size* doesn't really matter. What might make a bit of *difference* is if it was wider at the base. And so.... I don't know.... ask her about that....ask her if it would be pleasurable if it was a little wider at the base, because longer really doesn't make any physiological *difference*. Psychological? Yes. No question. Because if you come out of the bathroom with this humongous erection, your partner's gonna look at that and she's gonna say....*Man, am I good... I really know how to turn him on... I'm a hot little number.* And of course that's good for her self-esteem and ego, but Penis *size really doesn't matter* that much.

I'm still laughing too hard too comment on this one. You had to see this to fully appreciate it.

Dr. Ruth Westheimer, World-Famous Sex Therapist
From the book **Sex for Dummies**

Q- Although you can't deny that men have *different-sized* Penises, does the *size* of the Penis make any *difference* where it really counts – inside the woman's vagina?

A- In most cases, the answer is a very big no-the *size of the Penis makes no difference* inside a woman's vagina. The vagina is elastic; it has to be to allow babies to be born vaginally. So a woman's vagina can accommodate a big or a small Penis. Because most of a woman's nerve endings are concentrated at the entrance to the vagina, the sensations that a bigger Penis may cause aren't all that *different* to her from those caused by a smaller Penis.

These ladies are the most popular Sex experts out there and Dr. Ruth, Dr. Dobson, Sue Johanson and Anne Hooper all have *one* thing in common. They're all between the ages of *60* and *80*. "My Guy" **Jimi Hendrix** used to ask: **"Are You Experienced?"** I'm sure these veteran experts would say *Yes*. *Jimi's* follow up question would be: **"Have you ever been Experienced?"** I wonder if the answer would still be *Yes?* These wonderful ladies are all from the "Masters and Johnson" era. Sex Researchers William Masters M.D. and Virginia Johnson started pumping this shit into women's brains back in the 1960's, when they released their popular book /study **Human Sexual Response**. Masters and Johnson's research concluded that it was **"delusional to relate Penis** *size* **to Sexual adequacy."** The **ABC** News show **20/20** referred to the Masters and Johnson study, when they did a show entitled: **"SEX: Myths, Lies and Straight Talk,"** in November of 2004. This show was hosted by Elizabeth Vargas and John Stossel and focused on the **Top** *10 Sexual Myths in America*. Coming in at # **4** was *"Does Size Matter?"* An on-line poll conducted prior to the show revealed **56 %** of women did not care, i.e. *"Size Didn't Matter"* to them. The *two* experts that appeared on the show had something much *different* to say.

    NOTE: The interviews and commentary were conducted by Chris Connelly.

    Chris Connelly- "Can you reassure the Millions of men who are out there, that *size* **doesn't matter?"**

    Dr. Joy Davidson – "No I can't, because to some women it does."

    Commentary from Chris Connelly: **"Experts like Dr. Joy Davidson, a Clinical Psychologist and Sex Therapist, say the notion that** *size* **doesn't matter ignores the anatomical facts."**

    Dr. Davidson- "Men have been assured that *size* **doesn't matter… women have been told that they only have feeling in the first** *two* **inches of their vagina. We've all been sold a bill of goods about Sex…and now it's time to tell the truth."**

    Chris Connelly- "So what is the truth?"

    Dr. Davidson-"The reason *size matters* **is very simply… that women do have nerve endings deep inside the vagina."**

    Commentary from Chris Connelly: **"Evolutionary Anthropologist Helen Fisher says length isn't the only issue for a woman."**

    Dr. Helen Fisher- "It's the thickness of the Penis that distends the muscles around the vaginal canal and can create pressure on the female genitals that can add to her joy."

Commentary from Chris Connelly: **"There are psychological factors at work too."**

Dr. Davidson- "A lot of women find a larger Penis quite beautiful, more desirable, Sexier... and it can be an arousing psychological experience."

Dr. Fisher- "When women tell you that *size* doesn't matter...
They're either lying to you....
They're either lying to themselves....or,
They haven't had very much experience.
It's one of those *three*, because *Size Does Matter.*"

It's refreshing to hear an expert say: **"To some women *Size Does Matter,*"** instead of the emphatic blanket statements which tell all women what *Doesn't Matter.* I'm not a doctor or an expert or a woman, so the debate about nerve endings in the vaginal canal is out of my league. I think it would certainly be a useful debate, and could also help to dispel *one* of America's biggest Sexual Myths. In the mean time, many women are left in *Does Size Matter Limbo.*

I've read studies that said *40 %* of women have never reached **Point 'O' (*orgasm*)** through intercourse.

I've read studies that said *70 %* of women require clitoral stimulation to reach **Point 'O'.**

I've read studies that said many women prefer both clitoral and vaginal stimulation at the same time, to reach **Point 'O'.**

If any of those studies are true, then I don't see why *size* would be a detractor.

If any of those studies are completely wrong, then I still don't see why *size* would be a detractor.

If *40 %* of women have never reached **Point 'O'** through intercourse, then it's fair to say up to *60 %* have. It also means that *40 %* of women may not have found the right fit. It certainly doesn't mean they don't enjoy intercourse, just because it doesn't help them reach **Point 'O'.** Some women aren't sure what gets them from **Point 'A' (*foreplay*)** to **Point 'O'.** It could be vaginal *one time,* or *one way,* or with *one person,* and clitoral *another time,* or *another way,* with *another person.* Only each individual woman knows, and only each individual woman can search for her own personal answers. Blanket statements from doctors and therapists don't help their search; blanket statements hinder their personal search.

The most objective *Size Matters* information I've found to date is from free-lance writer Karen Fish. In an article entitled 'Size Matters-More to Men', Ms. Fish sums it up like this: **"Obviously Penis *size matters* to a woman. Penises range in *size* from *1* inch to *14* inches on men. The longer and wider and harder the penis, the more friction is created, the deeper the penetration, and the more likely the woman is to achieve vaginal orgasm. However other things are more important to a woman, such as extended foreplay, clitoral stimulation to orgasm, G Spot stimulation to orgasm, and length of time after intercourse before the man hails a cab, generally anywhere from *5* to *7* minutes on average. *Size* definitely matters to women, but it matters far more to men."**

That's an objective and informative assessment that you rarely get from most doctors and experts. These doctors and experts could do a great service for women by providing information that encourages them to explore, instead of providing information that discourages from exploring, by making up their minds for them. You can't tell your partner what you want if you don't know what you want.

My question is: **"*How* can you have *two* opinions so far apart?"** Maybe the better question would be: **"*Why* are the *two* opinions so far apart?"** The opinion that *Size* ***Does*** *Matter (to some women)* is only stating that all women are **'*not*'** the same. It benefits all women because it informs them that everyone is ***different,*** and they should find what specifically fits their needs. *Size* ***Does*** *Matter (to some women)* benefits all women. Who benefits from the *Size* ***Doesn't*** *Matter* opinion? Gee, I wonder who? Who could that be? I'll give you their initials and you'll have to figure the rest out on your own. **White Men** (*woops*, I slipped).

I told you in **VOLUME I**, I wasn't gonna pump Black Men up and I haven't. Most of what I've said about Black Men has come from the lips of Whites, or occurred because of the actions of Whites. I also told you that I was going to bring White Men down a few notches. Unlike many White Men, I honestly *do* believe that all men are created equal. I don't care how much money you have, what your last name is, where you live, or where you went to school. We're all mortal men and we all put our pants on the same fucking way. I believe that, and I believe that because I've walked in too many circles to believe otherwise. We all bring *different* qualities to the table and *different* in my eyes equals unique, not wrong, not bad, and not sub-human. I'm going to be tough on certain types of White Men for the rest of this book. If it doesn't apply to you, then I hope you'll still enjoy the rest of this book. If it does apply to you, then you better do some soul searching my friend. This next *RANT* is entitled, **"The White Male Happy Meal."**

RANT: "The White Male Happy Meal"

America, the land of the red, WHITE and blue, if you're a White Male and you can't make it in America, you have no one to blame but *You*. How's that for a nursery rhyme? It's oh so true. America was established by White Men, for White Men, and has always been run by White Men. America is run by White Men, who take care of their fellow White Men. I'm not mad and I'm not jealous, so please don't think there's any animosity in my heart. Once I figured out who was in charge and why they were in charge, this only made me work harder. Like I said before, I relish being the underdog. I wish more Brothers would relish being the underdog, but I understand that it's tough out here. I know that I'm no *different* from those Brothers who are *struggling*, because I could easily *fit the description* one day and lose what little bit I've got. That said, you can either survive or you can choose to *struggle* to survive. That's the hand the Black Man has been dealt in America. I do have the utmost respect for White Men, but I'll let you in on a little secret. I respect all men, especially good men. No Race has a monopoly on good men or a monopoly on bad men, contrary to popular American belief.

In America, White Men set the standards and establish what's acceptable. That's one of the main reasons I laugh when I hear about this hip-hop Cultural Revolution bullshit. These so-called hip-hop moguls think they've started a Cultural Revolution, and I give them credit because their so-called revolution is definitely being televised. That said, if you think for one second this shit has any relevance in the *Grand Scheme of Things* you're delusional. People are definitely *gettin' paid*, and it's cute to see the little *Wiggers* and all of the Eminem wannabe's, but like I said in **VOLUME I**, fads come and go. The powers that be don't like this hip-hop shit, and whenever they get annoyed they put their foot right on hip-hop's neck like it ain't shit. They won't hire you if you're wearing that bullshit. You're more likely to get arrested if you're wearing that bullshit. You're more likely to *fit the description* and get shot if you're wearing that bullshit. And now the NBA has said we don't want our players (*hip-hop's biggest marketers*) wearing that bullshit. This is solid proof that when push comes to shove, White Men set the standards and establish what's acceptable.

No where is this more evident than the physical appearance of women in America. The majority of trends and fads that are embraced by women in America are done so to please White Men. White Men are the majority, so it's only logical, right. Wrong! Pollution affects all of us; it doesn't choose the majority demographic or the minority demographic. Disease doesn't distinguish between the majority demographic and the minority demographic. I don't care if it's primarily White Women trying to please White Men. If there are problems that reach epidemic proportions in America, then it's an American problem, not a White problem or a Black problem. As a paramedic, I worked on the busiest ambulance in my city, and when my ambulance picked up teenage girls with eating disorders, my concern was for their health and welfare, and not who they were trying to impress. When my ambulance picked up a *19* year-old girl who was having chest pains, and our patient assessment revealed that one of her breast implants was leaking, I was concerned about her health and welfare, and not who she was trying to impress. I was concerned about the *Cause* of their medical condition, and not the *Root Cause.* Since I'm no longer assigned to an ambulance, now I can comment on the *Root Cause*. These young girls and young women were trying to impress White Men, and that my friends is the *Root Cause* of the problem.

The growing epidemic of eating disorders such as bulimia and anorexia didn't come about because the food in America sucks. Hell, we're the only country in the world that's fighting an obesity epidemic. This shit started because White Men started to prefer their women thin, and then *Super Thin*, and then unhealthy thin. Hollywood contributes to this trend by consistently casting the *Super Thin*. The women's magazines contribute by consistently putting the *Super Thin* models and actresses on their covers. The styles of clothing require women to be *Super Thin*, and there's around the clock dieting infomercials to help women squeeze into those *Super Thin* clothes.

In March of 2006, **The Today Show** did a segment entitled **Hate for Overweight Women?** This segment discussed the *three* following statistics:

1 *1/3* of women on television are dangerously underweight.
2 Weight loss products are a *30* BILLION *DOLLAR* a year industry
3 *30* % of women who are overweight are paid less

My question is: **"Overweight by whose standards?"**
We all know whose standards. Hell, I know White Guys who like their women *so thin*; they probably get Sexually aroused by Holocaust footage.

The bottom line is, ladies if you're meant to have some meat on your bones, then you should wear that meat proudly. You can starve yourself to get a man, but what's gonna happen if you put the weight back on? What's gonna happen if you put on weight during a pregnancy? If you've gotta starve yourself to get a certain man, he's probably not worth it. What's happening today is eating disorders have now crept into the psyche of America's children. This current trend of *"Super Thin **equals Super Sexy"*** emanates from White Male Sexual fantasy. There's no doubt that women competing against other women also plays a role in this phenomenon. But what are they competing for? What's the big prize? The big prize they starve themselves for is White Men, period. I'll explain why most White Men prefer *Super Thin* women in the chapter entitled **"Mo Cushion *vs.* No Cushion."** For now, I'm going to finish making the **White Male Happy Meal**.

Let's see, we've got a *Super Thin* figure, how about an order of breast implants. Again I ask, if Penis *Size **Doesn't Matter***, then why does *Dress Size & Breast Size matter?* The answer is simply, that's the way White Men like it. All *three* areas of measurement I just mentioned have been calibrated by American society to meet the approval of White Men. I've always been astounded by this, because women have what men want; therefore, it is women who truly have the power, and therefore it is women who should dictate what look is acceptable. If every woman on this planet wanted to look like William "The Refrigerator" Perry, men would only have *3 options*:

1 Become chronic masturbators
2 Become Gay
3 Learn to Like it

Long-term, those *3 options* aren't very good, and it shows you just how much power women have relinquished.

Super Thin is definitely for White Male approval, but getting breast implants is a little more complicated. Having breasts is part of being a woman, and many women with small or medium breasts, feel the need to upgrade. Upgrading their bra *size* often upgrades their self-esteem. You can't argue with self-esteem or womanhood. But all too often, implants become the immediate option when trying to gain instant White Male attention, and if you've already starved yourself to *Super Thin* status, the only way you're going to have large breasts is if you buy them. Before I begin down this road I want to make one thing perfectly clear, I'm *not* one of those anti-implant guys. I'm a Black Man and when it comes to Brothers breasts aren't for *Show*, they're for *GO*. So to me it's never *mattered* if they were big, small, real or fake. They all taste the same, and I was always happy just to get a *little* taste, or a *medium* taste, or a *big* taste.

I absolutely respect a woman's desire to raise her self-esteem by going from an *'A'* cup to a *'B'* or *'C'* cup, as long as it's in proportion to her body. The same goes for a woman who's a *'B'* or *'C'* cup who wants to upgrade to a *'D'* cup. When it's done in proportion to your body there's no denying their appeal. The questions arise when you go from an *'A'* cup to a *'D'* cup, and you still "starve/strive" for a *Super Thin* figure. It doesn't look healthy, and I just hope it's not done to get a man because a man's not worth it. If you're going to go under the knife to get a man, then beware of what type of man you may catch. You'll reel in plenty of fish, but you may not reel in any keepers. Quite often superficial only attracts superficial, and if the only thing you can bring to the table is breasts, real or fake, you're not going to like the kind of fish you reel in. Have surgery for you, not to get a man. If you've already got a partner, please make sure they're *100 %* on board before you undergo any surgery that's not necessary. These unnecessary surgeries have crept into America's Sexual psyche the same way eating disorders have, because the patients continue to get younger and younger. There are over *200,000* breast augmentation surgeries annually in America, and *2000* of them are performed on women under the age of *18.* Far too many women are going to extraordinary lengths to make a certain segment of our population happy, and this mindset is being developed at younger and younger ages. In April of 2006, **The Oprah Winfrey Show** addressed this topic by showing the following *three* extreme cases:

1 a three-year-old girl who was obsessed with her looks
2 a four-year-old girl who was obsessed with her weight
3 a teen model, who was beautiful to everyone but herself (*she actually felt she was ugly*)

There's no doubt these children were heavily influenced by their mothers. There's also no doubt their mothers were heavily influenced by society. These three cases may be extreme, but somewhere between these *three* cases and the normal concern about one's appearance, is the growing epidemic of *Happy Meal* wannabe's. Women are feeling the pressure to *appeal*, and men just sit back and wait for their *Happy Meal.*

In January of 2006, **The Today Show** did a segment entitled **Better Sex With Plastic Surgery.** The segment featured a plastic surgeon and a psycho therapist, who both stated that plastic surgery, among other things, could lead to a better Sex life. They based their conclusion on a study/questionnaire that was conducted with former patients. The former patients stated:

 # 1 After their surgical procedure, they had Sex more frequently.
 # 2 After their surgical procedure, they had better Sex.

I don't doubt the sincerity of those who participated in the study, because common sense says they're telling the truth. Post-surgery, I'm sure they felt much better about themselves and their improved physical appearance. Psychologically, I'm sure their new appearance boosted their self-esteem and their self-confidence. I'm sure their new appearance and newfound confidence increased the attention they received, and also increased their opportunities to meet new people. None of this was a shock, until they broke down the numbers of who actually participated in the study. *90 %* of all plastic surgeries are performed on women, and *no* men agreed to participate in this study. I repeat, *ZERO* men participated in this study. What does this tell us? It confirms the realness of **The White Male Happy Meal**. It tells us that women are going under the knife in record numbers, at younger ages, to reach an appearance which is acceptable to White Men, and White Men aren't being asked to make any sacrifice whatsoever.

Brothers just don't care about that bullshit. If she's got a little bit of *Tummy*, Brothers say: **"I bet she's got some good *Groceries* below that Tummy."** If she's got some *Hips* and *Ass*, Brothers say: **"Good, cause now I got something I can grab a hold of to *get better leverage.*"** Going under the knife for anything is no joke, because every year thousands of people die on operating tables, or die from post-operation complications, or die from post-operation infections. It would certainly be fucked up to die from a surgery that wasn't necessary. I understand many women get breast implants to enhance their careers (actresses, bodybuilders, cheerleaders, dancers, Hooter's or nightclub waitresses, models, strippers, porn stars, and of course prostitutes at the Bunny Ranch). You can't argue with that. *Gettin' paid* is much more important than getting a man. Technically, it's still being done to get the attention of men, but we all gotta eat, right. Other surgical procedures for the body, such as liposuction and tummy tucks, as well as surgical procedures for the face, are all part of the **White Male Happy Meal *menu***. The hundreds of diets and thousands of diet products are also part of the **White Male Happy Meal *menu***. Large Breasts and a *Super Thin* figure is the new deal, and this my friends is the **White Male Happy Meal**. Then throw in some Kegel Exercises so you can make him feel like he's *packin' heat*, and being a White Man in America is pretty damn neat. For White Men in America everyday must be like one big *Happy Meal.* **Ladies, all I can say is just be careful, just be safe, and always be true to yourself.**

B.T.P.

I don't want to sound like Oliver Stone, but let's be real, the *Size Doesn't Matter* campaign has managed to stay afloat for so long because of necessity. The necessity is to make Black Men in America Sexually irrelevant. As I stated in **VOLUME I**: *"In America, the phrase tall, dark and handsome, applies to anybody and everybody but Black Men."* That's not by accident, and neither is that *Size Doesn't Matter* bullshit. Behind closed doors most people know the real deal. Men certainly know. Men know when they're *gettin' the job done* and when they're puttin' her to sleep. Men know when they're *curling her toes,* and men know what it means to have *fingernails digging in your back.* It all means you're *takin' care of bizzness.* Men aren't spending a BILLION *DOLLAR$* a year on Penis enlargement products so they can look good when they step out of the shower. Men buy BMW's for performance; good looks are just part of the package (*no pun intended*). These Penis enlargement products are all about waking up one morning with the **Ultimate Driving Machine** in your shorts. Men know *why Size Matters.*

Hell, even Lesbians know that *Size Matters.* If the only part of the vagina with nerve endings is the lower third, then why isn't there a market for *2 inch Strap-Ons.* What about Sex toys? I'm not talking about vibrators because that's an entirely *different* ballgame. I'm talking about dildos. I don't think there's a huge market for *Average-sized* dildos. I could be wrong, but I'd bet the *Above Average Size* are the ones flying off of the shelves. There's no doubt that men worry about Penis *size* more than women, because women only have to be concerned about the Penis when it's time to get *bizzy.* Most men see or touch their Penis several times a day, and therefore are more aware of its *size,* or lack thereof. Penis *size* or lack thereof, can certainly affect a man's Sexual confidence. This psychological factor is not just restricted to the *bed*room. Penis *size* also creeps into America's *board*rooms.

HBO's America Undercover series featured an informative Penile documentary entitled **Private Dicks: Men Exposed**. This documentary interviewed over *20* men of several *different* Races, who were between the ages of *17* and *70*. The topics were obviously all pertinent to the Penis, and of course one chapter was dedicated to *size.* One White gentleman who was in his early 50's explained how Penis *size* had a psychological effect on his life:

"In my late *40's* I had gone through a lot of problems and I just needed a boost in my life, you know. And I think the enlargement surgery, the Penis enlargement, it's just something that I said.... *Well, maybe that will make me feel a little bit better,* and it does...about myself. Cause even if you go into a room...it's a *board*room and you got on a three-piece suit, it gives you a little edge....knowing that you probably got a little more."

This gentleman seemed like a nice guy, but you have to wonder how many men out there feel the same way he did before his enlargement surgery. Would White Men who are psychologically preoccupied with Penis *size* outside of the *bed*room, be inclined to hire a Black Man? Just a thought. Penis *size* or lack thereof can certainly trigger **Small-Poleons-like** behavior, which is *bad news* by itself and *double-bad-news* when coupled with **Limpbaugh Syndrome**. Publicly and privately most men believe that *Size Matters*. Privately, many of this nation's women will acknowledge that *Size Matters*. That said, I think it's safe to say most American's would concede that *Size Matters*. The problem is, the *Size Doesn't Matter* crusaders call the shots in America. Occasionally, America lets its true feelings about Penis *size* show. America always admits that *Size Matters* when that *size* is attached to a White Man.

When a White Dude is *packin'* mainstream America loses its fucking mind. The owner of the big White Penis then becomes *Larger than Life* and Legendary in death. John Holmes absolutely revolutionized the porn industry. Mr. Holmes was a bad motherfucker, but if he was *Average* he'd be an afterthought. Mr. Holmes was appropriately nicknamed *The King*, and he wore the crown well. **Deep Throat** opened the door and Mr. Holmes politely walked through and put the industry on his shoulders. In terms of sheer technique and ability, Ron Jeremy was actually better than *The King*. Ron Jeremy could still be performing if he didn't eat himself out of the *bizzness*. Mr. Jeremy's current body *size* doesn't diminish the *size* of his celebrity status one bit. Mr. Jeremy is considered a living legend and the question is why? Mr. Jeremy once stated: *"I'm only 2 inches................short of a foot."* Since *Size* supposedly *Doesn't Matter* in America, Mr. Jeremy's enormous celebrity status must be based on his acting ability and his handsome looks, right? No need to answer that one. Like I said, Penis *size* definitely matters to America, especially when the Penis is attached to a White Male. When an *Above Average* Penis is attached to a White Male it can translate to *Major Green* (*$$$*). A perfect example of this is the resurrection of Tommy Lee.

Just look at how Tommy Lee's career was resurrected after the Sex tape of him and Pamela Anderson surfaced in 1998. Do you really think anyone would be knocking on his door requesting his services for a reality TV show if that Sex tape had *never* surfaced? **Hell No!** In September of 2005, producers of Tommy Lee's reality show got busted after they aired altered footage of a professor giving a lecture on Native American literature. What was the altered footage attempting to depict? The lecture: *"was made into something trivial and stupid about Tommy Lee's Penis,"* said English Professor Frances Kaye. Hello! Hello! People, that's what the fuck the show is about. The show should be called **"Tommy Lee's Penis Goes To College,"** because that's the only reason people are watching. They're hoping to catch a glimpse. If some woman pulled a Lorena Bobbit on him, the show would be cancelled immediately, and would only return if the reattachment surgery was a success. **The Biography Channel** did a special on Tommy Lee which featured veteran Rock columnist/writer Anthony Bozza. Mr. Bozza co-authored Tommy Lee's autobiography **"Tommyland."** This is what Mr. Bozza had to say about Tommy Lee's reality show: **"I think I'd like to see Tommy in Art Class. That would be kinda cool. I also think maybe he could pose nude and the students could draw him and do a whole art show on that."** You can draw your own conclusion on that one. I repeat, does anyone think he'd have gotten a reality show if he'd been *packin'* *Average heat* in that Sex video. Look at all the other Sex videos that have come out since. Don't none of them dudes have reality shows do they? Are the tabloids fucking with any of them guys? They're not on MTV are they? Hell, Collin Farrell, Scott Stapp, and Kid Rock are fighting to keep their Sex tapes from getting out. Let's reflect back to the days of the Paris Hilton Sex tape. Does anyone even remember what the guy's name is who was with her? No. That tape was all about Paris Hilton, and Paris Hilton is the only person who benefited from that tape, in terms of celebrity. The Pamela Anderson and Tommy Lee Sex tape was the complete opposite. The success of the Pamela Anderson and Tommy Lee Sex tape had *nothing* to do with Pam, and *everything* to do with Tommy Lee's Penis. The Pamela Anderson and Bret Michaels' Sex tape is a better quality production, with better action, but created no buzz and created no reality show for Bret Michaels. Apparently *Size Does Matter*.

In November of 2005, comedienne Sarah Silverman was asked by **Maxim Magazine**: **"Do you have any jokes left over from the recent** *Pamela Anderson Roast* **(remember her, the woman in the video)?"**

Ms. Silverman replied: **"All the jokes were about him (*Tommy*) having a huge cock."**

The Roast was for Pam, right? White Dudes out here in the real world absolutely amazed me with their reaction to the Pam & Tommy Sex video.

Here's a sample of some comments I heard:

"Man can you believe the tool on that guy Tommy Lee?"

"Dude, that Tommy Lee's got a crank on him."

"Tommy Lee's got a hell of a rod for a White Guy doesn't he?"

The Brothers I talked to seemed oblivious to Mr. Lee's Penis, instead their focus and their frustration was on the camera work:

"Why didn't he put that motherfuckin' camera on a tripod or somethin'."

"Man fuck that video camera shit. I'da been *rockin' dat ass!*"

"Man if you gonna be videotapin' and shit, then you need to flip that shit around *doggy-style*. Then you can *'hit that shit right'* and still be videotapin."

I never heard one comment about Tommy Lee's Penis from the Brothers. I never heard one comment about *crushin'* Pam from the White Dudes. White Dudes nationwide lost their fucking minds. Late Night talk shows, all of the tabloid papers, MTV, everybody was all over Tommy Lee's jock. Motley Crüe was the shit in their day, but their day was a long time ago. Don't get me wrong, I'm a Tommy Lee fan because he seems like a cool, down to earth motherfucker. He's also a talented musician, and the music business is so unpredictable you gotta *get paid* anytime an opportunity presents itself. But you have to admit the recent Tommy Lee phenomenon has *nothing* to do with Motley Crüe, and *nothing* to do with Pamela Anderson. This whole episode reminds me of the George Michael phenomenon in the late 1980's. Women of all Races lost their fuckin' minds over George Michael's ass. White Women especially lost their minds because they don't get to see a White Man with an ass like a Black Man very often. It was all about Mr. Michael's *Above Average* body part. The resurrection of Tommy Lee has everything to do with an *Above Average* body part. Mr. Lee's *Above Average* Penis has the focus of a nation that says *Size Doesn't Matter.* The only Myth is that people actually believe that bullshit.

Chapter 2 "Once you go Black, you don't go Back. Why?"

"That's White Man's thinking. Always afraid that something Bigger and Better has been there before them."

Ken Norton
From the 1976 Slavery movie "Drum"

This phenomenon only occurs with Black Men. It doesn't happen with anyone else on the planet. I'm sure there are women who have certain Racial preferences, but Black Men are more than a Racial preference if you haven't figured that out by now. When you bet Black, there's a real good chance you won't be welcomed back. Everybody else can go back and forth and then be welcomed back home. Everybody else is welcomed back by their co-workers, their friends, and their family. Hell, a White Man can have a relationship with a Black Woman and go back to his friends and family like nothing ever happened. Any and every Race can do this as long as a Black Man was never part of the equation. Isn't it neat how **History** has a way of coming full circle? Like I said in the **History SECTION** of **VOLUME I,** no one else can push the White Man's Hate-Button like the Black Man can. *"Once you go Black"* is a perfect example of that. White Folks will disown their only daughter for committing this unforgivable sin.

There's no doubt one of the reasons White Women don't *go Back* is because they're not welcomed back (*even if they wanted to go Back).* Quite often they don't want to *go Back*, but we'll get to all of that good stuff later in this chapter. The bottom line is, they're considered damaged goods once they slip to the *Dark Side*. I'm not advocating or discouraging Inter-Racial relationships; you gotta do what works for you. I'm just pointing out one of the many Racial and Sexual double-standards in American society. Any and every Racial and Sexual combination you can think of does *not* carry the punishment of complete banishment from your people. The only time you can receive the ultimate **SENTENCE** of complete banishment from your people is when you bet Black, as in Black Man. Why is that? Maybe Ken Norton's character in the movie **Drum** was on to something? I've overheard White Guys make comments about White Women who've been with Black Men, and I've always found these comments fascinating. Here's a few of the comments I've overheard:

"That *well* has been poisoned, I wouldn't drink from it."

"That *twat* is probably stretched to hell and back."

"I wouldn't go near that shit unless I was *Daniel Boone-in-it* big time."

What's so fascinating about these offensive comments, you ask?
- White Men consider it repulsive to be with a White Woman who's only been with *one* Black Man.
- White Men *don't* consider it repulsive to be with a Black Woman who may have been with *many* Black Men throughout her lifetime.

I find that fascinating because these motherfuckers suddenly forget about a *poisoned well* or a *stretched twat* when they get the opportunity to get some *Brown Sugar.* I'm sure you're wondering what the hell is *Daniel Boone-in-it?* One night I was out with some White Guys after a work meeting, and after many, many drinks I asked one of the guys, *"What the hell is Daniel Boone-in-it?"* The answer was, *"You know, Daniel Boone, the guy who wore the 'Coon Skin Cap'.......it's kinda like a nickname for a rubber, I guess."* I still didn't get it; why would a condom be called a *'Coon Skin Cap'?* The next day I remembered that the girl they'd been talking about had just broken up with a Black Guy (i.e., *Coon*). I couldn't even get pissed. I knew when I overheard the shit that it wasn't meant for my ears, so I shouldn't have asked. But I always like to know shit like this for future reference. I guess it all worked out because I got to share it with you. As Ignorant and offensive as it may sound, I recommend that everyone always *Daniel Boone-in-it* (or **MAGNUM-IT, *WHICHEVER FITS***).

The nuclear weapon of all the possible comments is obviously *Nigger Lover*, and most of the time this one is reserved for a White Female's friends and family. Once they start dropping *Nigger Lover* on you, you may as well pack your shit and get the fuck out, do not pass **GO** and do not say goodbye. As I said earlier, a big part of *"You don't go Back,"* is because you're not welcomed back. White Girls are usually clueless when it comes to this shit. They know that no one approves, but they don't understand the depth of that disapproval until they get spit on, called a tramp, called a slut, called a *Nigger Lover*, physically beaten, and thrown to the street, and that's just from mom, dad, and her brothers. Wait until the rest of the family, friends, and co-workers catch wind of this shit. Kinda reminds you of the story Rosa Parks told in her autobiography **MY STORY**, which I quoted in **VOLUME I**. For those of you who haven't read **VOLUME I**, Mrs. Parks reminisced about a White Lady in Alabama who eventually committed suicide after her affair with a Black Man was exposed. She committed suicide because she was completely disowned by her entire community.

Being booted off of the island by your friends and family is pretty damn severe, but choosing to leave the island and choosing not to return is pretty damn courageous, or foolish, or both. It depends on why you chose to do it and who you chose to do it with. Not being welcomed back is irrelevant if you don't want to go back. Let's take a look at **Once you go Black,** and maybe that'll explain why many White Women choose not to **go Back**. In case you're wondering, I'll touch on Hispanics and Asians at the end of this chapter.

"Once you go Black, you don't go Back" is hardly a Myth, because in most cases it's an easily confirmed reality. The reason the focus of **"Once you go Black"** is primarily on White Women, is because they suffer the harshest treatment for betting *Black*, and they have the hardest time going *Back.* To fully appreciate these occurrences you need to look at the reasons why women, primarily White Women, go Black to begin with. I've read a lot of *different* viewpoints on this subject, and I've witnessed the turmoil and the ups and downs firsthand. The most accurate assessment I've read on this subject is from Emily Monroy, who is a guest columnist for **The InterRacial Voice** and co-editor of the magazine **Urban Mozaik.** Ms. Monroy's editorial entitled **InterRacial Sex** examined the *3 Most Common Stereotypes* applied to White Women who stray from their herd and sleep with men of color. Even though her stated focus was on *why* Whites believe Inter-Racial dating occurs, the result was actually more about *how* White Women who stray from their herd are perceived by other Whites. I still found her editorial very compelling and very applicable to the **"Once you go Black"** phenomenon. Ms. Monroy is a White Woman who only dates men of other Races. She's stated in her writings that she's had a Mexican boyfriend, a Filipino Boyfriend, and a Lebanese ex-Lover to name a few.

She also stated that:

"At this point in my life copulating with a White Man seems about as exciting as eating Wonder Bread for breakfast (boring!!!)."

On that note, I'll let Ms. Monroy explain *how* White Women are perceived when they occasionally stray from the herd, and then I'll explain *why* they strayed from their herd and *why* they usually don't return once they've strayed.

Emily Monroy's *3 Most Common Stereotypes* of White Women who sleep with Men of Color:

#1 The Slut- A White Girl who willingly sleeps with a man of color is a *slut* or so goes the conventional wisdom. It therefore follows that she lacks any Sexual restraint whatsoever. In places like the Old South, such a woman faced public whipping, indentured servitude, rejection from her family and community, and violence from the Ku Klux Klan. Though now the legal consequences of *the slut's* behavior have disappeared, and the social ones diminished somewhat, the *Stereotypes* remain.

#2 The Political Activist- The *political activist* is a left-wing, socially conscious, politically correct woman, who views involvement with a non- White Man (*especially a Black*) as an act of solidarity with an oppressed group and perhaps as a means of thumbing her nose at society, and rebelling against her family. If she and her partner have children, she is further praised in some circles for holding the key to the future of Race relations. But many minorities and left-wingers are skeptical of her actions. People of color rightly doubt whether **Miscegenation** will really sound the death knell for Racism, given the fact that *five* hundred years of Race mixing on this continent and others hasn't achieved that goal yet.

#3 The Ugly Duckling- The *ugly duckling* is a White Woman who might not necessarily get billed as the *'Ugliest Woman in the World'* at the circus but who doesn't turn heads either. In White circles, that is. As soon as she steps out of Fortress Caucasia, she's the belle of the ball. Men of color shower her with attention. In **The Color Complex**, a Black filmmaker humorously describes the allure of the *ugly duckling*: **"Over the years a group of Black Boys grew up masturbating with the White Girls in Penthouse (*adult magazine*)....This caused them to go out and date any 250-pound greasy White Woman they could find, whose only** redeeming quality was that they had blond hair, blue eyes, and White **skin."** The flipside of the *ugly duckling Stereotype* is the implication that she goes out with men of color because she's *not good enough.* If she were, she could do better (i.e., *catch a White Man*). Most *Stereotypes* are ways of simplifying complex behavior so that it's easier to understand.

Anti-miscegenists can explain away the White Woman who consorts with men of color by saying that she's immoral (*the slut*), that she's caught up in hopelessly Utopian ideals (*the political activist*), or that we don't want her anyway (*the ugly duckling*). But in real life things aren't so clear-cut. True, some White female partners of minority men might be seeking a Sexual adventure, trying to fight Racism, or turning to Inter-Racial romance for lack of any other choice. But most of these women have simply found the right person who, as one White Woman interviewed in **The Color Complex** reported, happens to be another color. As with fornication, adultery, and promiscuity, a double standard exists around Inter-Racial Sex. A White Woman involved with a man of color commits the cardinal sin of allowing an **"Other"** male to enter her vagina, whereas a White Man who sticks his *private parts* into those of non-White Women draws little criticism as long as his relationships don't get too serious. White society's outrage over **Miscegenation** has less to do with the purity of the European gene pool than with that of the Caucasian Female reproductive system.

Ms. Monroy tells it like it is and it's hard to disagree with one word. There's just one more thing I'd like to add to her *3 Most Common Stereotypes*. What I'm about to add is not a *Stereotype*, but more importantly, it's the common bond of her *3 Most Common Stereotypes*.

#4 **The Unsatisfied**- The *unsatisfied* woman lives within each of Ms. Monroy's *3 Most Common Stereotypes*.

The Slut is obviously *unsatisfied* and is certainly searching for something. A White Woman can immediately earn the title of *slut* for sleeping with *one* Black Man. At the same time, many promiscuous White Women don't earn the title of *slut* for sleeping with numerous White Men. Is it fair to label a White Woman a *slut* if she's slept with numerous White Men and was *unsatisfied,* and then strayed from her herd *one* time?

The Political Activist is obviously *unsatisfied* and is certainly searching for something. There are a lot of things you can do to fight Racism and spreading your legs is *not* one of them. And just to add to Ms. Monroy's comment about *The Political Activist* deciding to have a Bi-Racial baby. If the *Political Activist* decides to have a Black Man's baby it has nothing to do with making a political statement. If the *Political Activist* decides to have a

Black Man's baby it's because she was hooked on the *pipe*. I'm *not* talking about the *'crack pipe'* either.

The Ugly Duckling; I can't even type that shit without laughing. Every Black Man knows another Black Man who has a White Woman who could fall into that category. That shit about masturbating to **Penthouse Magazine** is absolutely true. **Penthouse, Playboy** and eventually **Hustler** is what most men my age grew up with. You rarely (*if ever*) seen Black Women in those publications. The first time I saw a Black Woman in an adult magazine was in my Grandfather's copy of **Chunky Asses** (he was well over the age of *70* at the time). This magazine featured Women of all Races, and none were less than *300* lbs. The *Ugly Duckling* is obviously ***unsatisfied*** and is also searching for something.

You can label these women with any *Stereotype* you like, but the bottom line is, they weren't ***satisfied*** with their herd, so they decided to stray. Usually ***satisfaction*** or lack thereof, plays a major role with these women. They are either emotionally ***unsatisfied***, Sexually ***unsatisfied,*** or both. Why White Men get pissed off over this shit I'll never know. When a White Woman strays from the herd, White Men have no one to blame but themselves. Just like Black Men have no right to complain when a beautiful, educated, Black Woman is in the arms of a White Man. Black Women routinely have to *tip-toe* through a minefield of Black Men. That minefield consists of men who are Dogs, Players, Unemployed, Incarcerated, Gay/ *on the Down Low* or HIV Positive. Other ethnic groups have many of the same problems; it's just magnified with Black Folks because there's a growing shortage of good Black Men. Black Men who don't fall into any of the above categories are considered a *"Hot Commodity,"* and take full advantage of the *Clean-Cut Brother Shortage*. White Guys help their cause by being selfish spoiled babies. Like I said earlier, Ms. Monroy's editorial examined *how* White Women are perceived by other Whites when they stray from their herd. I'm going to examine *why* White Women stray from their herd to begin with, and *why* they often don't ***go Back***. When a White Girl strays from the herd and hooks up with a Brother it tells you *three* things:

1 She was ***unsatisfied***.
2 She was curious.
3 There weren't any Mexicans available, so it was a last resort.

White Dudes have the world by the **"Balls,"** so they're usually waiting on a **White Male Happy Meal** to come and tap them on the shoulder. So this behavior really puts White Women in a bind. They're not in a bind because there's a shortage of White Men; they're in a bind because there's a shortage of reasonable White Men. They're in a bind because many of the White Men they get involved with just go through the motions. He's going through the motions because he's secretly hoping a **Happy Meal** will eventually come and rescue him. If you're a White Woman, regardless of age, and your resumé is loaded with failed relationships with White Men, you just might stray from the herd. If you're a White Woman and you're tired of selfish White Men who stop showing you respect, and stop showing you attention right after you've spread your legs for the first time, you just might stray from the herd. If you're a White Woman and your White Male Lover is selfish and doesn't get the job done in the bedroom, you just might stray from the herd. Being emotionally and Sexually *unsatisfied* can lower any woman's resistance and peak any woman's curiosity. These are the prime conditions when White Women stray from the herd. For you White Women who are curious about straying from the herd, beware of the **Serengeti Syndrome.**

RANT: "The Serengeti Syndrome"

In case you haven't noticed, I'm all about Syndromes. I can't help it; my formative years were heavily influenced by George Clinton and Parliament Funkadelic. I was taught as a teenager that Sir Nose D'VoidofFunk (aka *The Nose*) is the purveyor of the Placebo Syndrome. The Placebo Syndrome is how Noses everywhere spread fake funk in place of the *P* (the *P* stands for *P* Funk, Uncut Funk, The Bomb). Therefore, I'm always on the look out for Syndromes. When you're always on the lookout for Syndromes, you're more likely to spot other Syndromes. That's how I was able to spot the dreaded *Limpbaugh Syndrome* and the not so dreaded, but equally debilitating, **Reverse-*Limpbaugh Syndrome***.

Serengeti Syndrome is primarily a Black Male affliction because nobody else exhibits the symptoms like Black Men. **Serengeti Syndrome** is the behavior of Black Men when there's a chance that a White Girl may stray from the herd. I can speak to this with absolute certainty because I've had **Serengeti Syndrome** before, and I've waited all night in dive bars for friends who've had **Serengeti Syndrome. Serengeti Syndrome** means that you've spotted one who may stray from the herd, and just like that cheetah or leopard back in the motherland, you're waiting to pounce on the gazelle. The problem is that the rest of the herd (i.e., her girlfriends or *Cock-Blocking* White Dudes) are always there to nudge her back to the herd. The girlfriends aren't really concerned about her *"going Black and not coming Back."* The girlfriends are only doing what girlfriends are supposed to do. They're just protecting her, and usually telling her to be patient. They're telling her she's just as good as a **Happy Meal,** and that eventually some White Guy will notice her. But once she's curious about what's over there in the bushes she can't help herself. This is when Brothers are at their best. I've been in that position before, and like I said, I've waited all night in dive bars for friends who were in that position.

Once you've got it in your mind that she may stray from the herd you're not going anywhere. Brothers will circle the herd continuously, just hoping for that *one* glimmer of daylight and that *one* opportunity to pounce. You're going to wait her out no matter what. If she does stray from the herd and creeps her ass over to see what's in the bushes, look out. BOOOM!!! The panther pounces on the gazelle and the rest is history. The gazelle should've kept her ass with the herd, because it's over now. On the **Serengeti**, all that's left is a carcass for the vultures and hyenas to fight over. Here in the real world, all that's left is memories for friends and family to fight over. Memories about life before *So-n-So* became a *Nigger Lover*. She's now

Put yourself in the author's shoes

considered worthless, just like a carcass on the **Serengeti.** That's alright, because if she got *'hit right'* she could care less.

Don't nothing make a Brother's eyes light up like those magic words: *"I've never been with a Black Guy before."* Ding, Ding, Ding, Ding Jack-*Motherfuckin*-Pot!!! Every Brother who's been in that situation and just read the above passage is grinning from ear to ear this very second. When a White Girl tells a Black Man that she's never been to the **Dark Side,** Brothers get happy as hell because they know *9* times out of *10* they've just landed a damn-near virgin. That applies to every White Woman between the ages of *18* and *80.* You can guarantee that for the first few months she's going to be *drunk.* What's she going to be *drunk* on? You'll have to figure that one out on your own. She's going to be oblivious to the outside world. She's going to be so *drunk*, she's not going to notice if he stops opening the car door for her. She's not going to notice if he's not as sweet as he used to be. She's not going to notice that out of the bedroom he's no *different* than any of the White Guys on her resumé.

The truth is, no Race has a monopoly on Jerks or a monopoly on Good Guys. You've got to know what it is you're looking for. Good Guys and Bad Guys come in all sizes, shapes and colors. You usually find out about a month into the ballgame if he's a genuinely Good Guy, or if all that sweetness early in the relationship was just an act. So you should never judge a book by its color, Black or White. The bottom line is what you're looking for and what you need. What you're looking for and what you need will determine what you'll tolerate. If you find someone who's on the same page, regardless of color, you obviously have a good chance of making it work. If you're not on the same page and you're *unsatisfied*, emotionally or Sexually, there's going to be a *void*. People search (i.e. *stray from the herd*) when they have *voids* that need filled. The biggest relationship *void* is the **satisfaction void.** Being attentive, thoughtful, and sweet, can certainly help cover up deficiencies in the bedroom, but if you're Sexually *unsatisfied*, you won't stay happy. Making her toes curl in the bedroom can certainly mask a lot of selfishness outside of the bedroom. Great Sex is not the *end all* or *be all,* but it can make a lot of **Big problems** much *smaller,* and make a lot of *smaller problems* non-existent. We all know couples who are as happy as pigs in slop, even though they're flat broke. Why are they so happy? Great Sex, period. We live in a nation where the Divorce Rate hovers at *50 %,* and the leading *Causes* for Divorce in America are Financial problems or Sexual problems. Great Sex can make people try to work through their Financial problems. Infidelity usually creeps into the picture when Sexual problems exist, regardless of the Financial situation. Financial problems can be magnified by Sexual problems, and Sexual problems can't be masked by Financial security. Women are more likely to tolerate being broke if their *satisfaction voids* are being filled, and women are more likely to stray from their herd if their *satisfaction voids* are *not* being filled. The bottom line is, a lot of men get away with *not* bringing home the Bacon, because at home they're serving up *plenty* of Tube Steak. So therefore, a lot of women will tolerate *being broke* and will tolerate *opening their own car door* as long as they receive an occasional *earthshaking orgasm*. Hey, once you catch the gazelle you gotta make sure she doesn't escape, right.

There's obviously much more to the **"Once you go Black, you don't go Back"** phenomenon than just Sex. When Inter-Racial Sex blossoms into a full-blown relationship, usually what happens is a unique bond develops. When you know it's just you and that Black Man *against the world*, the emotional bond can be stronger than in most conventional relationships. It becomes a classic case of *Me 'n' You vs. The World*. People who've been involved in team sports can tell you, the *Us vs. The World* attitude can create one hell of a bond. That bond requires all involved to make sacrifices, and when people make sacrifices *for* each other, they're also making a commitment *to* each other. Emotional and Sexual *voids* are being fulfilled simultaneously, and that's what makes many White Women not want to *go Back*. They have no reason to *go Back.* If you've got a resumé full of White Men who were selfish out of the bedroom, who were lame in the bedroom, or both, why would you *go Back?*

The Serengeti Syndrome is normal male behavior that is displayed by men of all Races. All men at one time or another have been out on the prowl looking for someone to stray from the herd. What makes **The Serengeti Syndrome** unique among Black Men is the odds of getting the gazelle are usually very low, and the perceived reward is very high. The conquest is great, but the accompanying headaches could be greater. **"Once you go Black, you don't go Back"** is like the perfect storm. All the ingredients and timing have to be just right, and when they are the outcome is very predictable. I've also seen many White Women who decided that even though things didn't work out with one particular Black Guy, there was something there that made them want to find another Black Guy (*Gee, I wonder what?*). *Not going Back* doesn't necessarily have to happen with the first Black Guy she meets. She may decide the experience was so good, that she'll be like *Goldilocks* and keep searching until she finds one that's just right. Being *unsatisfied* encouraged her to *Go Black*, being *satisfied* encouraged her not to *Go Back*.

The so-called *Slut*, the *Political Activist*, and the *Ugly Duckling* all have *voids*. A Black Man who's a Jerk can fill at least one *satisfaction void*.

A Black Man who's not a Jerk will probably fill both **satisfaction voids**. Women like security, and financial security is a biggie, but Emotional and Sexual security can be just as important if they become major **voids**. So White Men you have no one to blame but yourselves when one of yours strays from the herd. I've heard there are places where you have **"Reverse-Serengeti Syndrome"** (i.e., *White Women actually circling and hunting Black Men*), but I've never personally seen it in America. I experienced it in Norway and it was sheer culture shock. I've got a Black Friend who experienced **"Reverse-Serengeti Syndrome"** in Denmark. A Danish Female that my Black friend met one evening actually locked him in her apartment so he couldn't get away (*while she was at work the next day*). While he was sitting outside on her second-floor balcony, he met another Danish Female who persuaded him to climb down and make a get away. I've also talked to Black musicians who've been to Australia and had similar stories. I've always been mystified by the fact that American Black Men have more appeal abroad than at home. **Voids** and Myths are not the primary reasons for the **Sex Appeal** that American Black Men seem to have overseas. The primary reason American Black Men have **Sex Appeal** abroad is the social environment is not nearly as polluted with *'mis'* and *'dis'* information. The playing field is level and is therefore scaled down to the basics, i.e. the **hunter** *vs.* **hunted**. Just like on the plains of our motherland, **The Serengeti.**

B.T.P.

My old platoon sergeant, the one who told us about the difficulties of Chinese arithmetic (see the **Indifference** chapter in **VOLUME I**), also told us that all women were the same color. He would often tell us: **"Boys, I'm tellin' you, it's all *Pink* on the inside, so it don't pay to discriminate."** He would share those words of wisdom with the platoon when Light-Green Marines (*White*) would complain about Asian Women dominating the strip clubs off base. The Brothers had to take his word for it, because we rarely (*if ever*) found out what color Asian Women were on the inside. We rarely found out because the Asian Women always flocked to the White Guys.

For some reason, we rarely hear about the **"Once you go White, you've done Alright!"** phenomenon. The **'Once you go White'** phenomenon has always been *overshadowed* by the **"Once you go Black, you don't go Back"** phenomenon. **"Once you go White, you've done Alright!"** is much more acceptable and therefore much more prevalent, but you just don't hear much about it. This phenomenon is not controversial because all parties involved have no problem becoming one big happy party. Black Women,

Hispanic Women and Asian Women can freely stray from the herd, and as long as the White Guy says it's true Love, everyone will peacefully co-exist at the same table like it's the United Nations. Throw a Brother into the mix and the shit turns into an Israeli-Palestinian type of conflict. Only the Black Man can push the White Man's Hate-Button, only the Black Man. *There are no absolutes*, but the attitudes towards Black Male Sexuality have been very consistent throughout the history of this country. To give you another example of how far down the food chain Black Men are, I'd bet that a White Son could bring home another White Male as *his* Lover, and receive less ridicule than a White Daughter who brought home a Black Man. The Black Man is not only at the bottom of the social ladder in America, but has also been relegated to the bottom of America's Sexual ladder. So obviously, *"Once you go White, you've done Alright!"* is the way to go in America.

The main reason this book's primary focus is on Black and White, is because there's a long, well-established, often bloody, and usually buried history between Blacks and Whites in America. Another reason the focus is primarily on Black and White is because Hispanics and Asians keep their contact with Black Folks as limited as possible. They've been well-trained by White society on how to perceive Blacks and they strictly adhere to those perceptions. Hispanics often share neighborhoods with Blacks or inhabit neighborhoods that border Black neighborhoods, but contact has never been as positive as it should be. I've always considered Hispanics my Brown Brothers, and I've always gotten along great with Hispanics. I'm sure there's a few Hispanics who read the *RANT:* **America's New Nigger's** in **VOLUME I** and weren't too pleased. I apologize, but you've got to understand, our unsecured Southern border is a National Security concern for all Americans. The people who illegally cross *that* border are an Economic Security concern for all Middle Class Americans. That said, I consider Hispanics our Brothers in the undeclared war against poverty. Unfortunately what's happened is Blacks and Hispanics often become enemies because of poverty. The ridiculous gang epidemic has established geographic, cultural and social boundaries that have magnified our few *differences*, and overshadowed our *one big common bond*, poverty. That said, in America Hispanics enjoy *one* huge advantage over Blacks. They can't activate White Folks Hate-Button like Blacks can (*especially* Black Men). This fact allows Hispanics to stray *to and from* their herd with relative ease.

The truth is, when someone strays from their herd, they usually stray to the *White Side*. Puerto Rican Ladies in New York will give a Brother a peek, but Latinos for the most part don't stray from their herd, and when they do stray they usually stray to the **White Side**. When Asians stray, they definitely prefer to stray to the **White Side**. Hispanics and Asians consider bringing a White Man into the family an upgrade. This is often considered marrying up. The transition is not quite as easy when it's a Black Woman and a White Man, but like I said, if they say it's true Love, everyone will accept their decision. No one gets disowned or banished from the family unless *"you know who"* is part of the equation (his initials are **B. M.**). These are generalizations, and when you're talking about a nation of *300* Million people there will always be exceptions. If *"Once you go White"* is so acceptable, one must assume that certain *voids* are being filled by this phenomenon. What *voids* could these women of color possibly need filled? What do these women of color get when they *Go White?* They usually get at least *one* of the *social trifecta*:

1 *Money*
2 *Status*
3 *Respect*

Sometimes they may only get *one* of the *three* or *two* of the *three*, but it's still going to be considered an upgrade. They may even hit the jackpot and get all *three* in one guy, but they're always going to get at least *one*, and that *one* is *Respect*. They'll get *Respect* right away. I'm sure there are many proud Black Women, Asian Women, and Hispanic Women, who earn more *Money* than their White Husbands or Boyfriends. I'm sure these women feel they bring more to the table than their White Husbands or Boyfriends. I'm also sure when these women walk into a bank, a realtor, a doctor's office, an auto dealership, or a parent teacher conference, the majority of the *Respect* is initially directed towards that White Husband or Boyfriend. The *first* time they walk into these establishments with their White Husband or Boyfriend he'll get the *Respect,* and the *second* time they can walk in by themselves and they'll get their ass kissed. In many cases, a Black Husband may get you the exact opposite. This is the main reason some White Women who've *Gone Black* decide they want to *Go Back* (*home*). They miss that *Respect* they used to get. When they consistently get dirty looks it wears on them. Those dirty looks are meant to wear on them, and meant to remind them of the good old days when car salesmen sprinted to them as soon as they stepped foot on the lot. Now car salesmen act like they don't see you approaching when you're with your Black Man. *Money, Status,* and *Respect,* can fill a *void* that many women of color have *never* had filled. *Money* gives you security. *Status* is all about being *Mrs. So-n-So*. **Respect** is what you get when you're with *that* White Man. What woman wouldn't want at least *one* of those *three?*

This is why it's an absolute Myth that successful Black Men seek White Women. It's the other way around. White Women know that a successful Black Man can give them the **Money, Status,** and **Respect** they've always gotten, and at the same time fill their **satisfaction voids** (emotional and Sexual). The successful Brother may pursue, but I guarantee you the White Girl is going to run just like the White Girls in those **Friday the 13th** movies. She's going to run but *not* very fast, and then she'll trip, stumble, and fall. She'll then sprain her ankle and proclaim: *"Damn, you caught me."* There ain't no **"Serengeti Syndrome"** on this one, if anything it's **"Reverse-Serengeti Syndrome."** When the gazelle simply lies down, hooves up, and says: *"Damn, you caught me,"* what else could it be. I've seen Black pro-athletes in night clubs before and they become the **hunted,** while women of all colors circle and play the role of the **hunter.** These women are hoping for the best of both worlds. They're hoping for good things, *inside* and *outside* of the bedroom. But regardless of who picks who, the perceptions will always remain the same. If a woman of color is with a White Man it's about **Money, Status,** and **Respect.** If a White Woman is with a Black Man, as Denzel Washington said in the movie **Mo Better Blues**, it's a **D-I-C-K Thing,** it's a **DICK Thing.**

"Once you go White, you've done Alright!" is self-explanatory and anyone who's lived in America for about a week certainly understands this. This is understood before you arrive in America. It's often the *difference* between surviving and *struggling* to survive. You can stay with your herd or you can upgrade to a better herd. Neither choice sets you back. *"Once you go White, you've done Alright!"* speaks for itself.

"Once you go Black, you don't go Back" is an entirely *different* ballgame. *Why* is it an entirely *different* ballgame? To ask **why** someone *'Goes Black'* and **why** they don't *'Go Back'* simply doesn't give you the answers you may be seeking, because it's not the correct question. The essence of *"Once you go Black, you don't go Back"* is that it implies there's a *difference* between White Men and Black Men. So the question should be: **"Is there a *difference*?"** **Money, Status,** and **Respect** are superficial *differences*. The physical *differences* that Justice Thomas spoke of when he stated: *"The Language throughout the history of this country,"* only answers *half* of the question because a man's physical make-up only represents *half* of who he truly is. So the true question is: **"Is there a *real* difference between White Men and Black Men?"** Let's find out.

Chapter 3 "Is There a Difference?"

"They are more ardent after their female; but Love seems with them to be more an eager desire, than a tender delicate mixture of sentiment and sensation."

Thomas Jefferson made the above observation
about the Black American Slave.

QUERY XIV
NOTES ON VIRGINIA, 1781-1785

Thomas Jefferson's **NOTES ON VIRGINIA** is probably the best example of how wide ranging the future President's knowledge was. In these writings he showed an in-depth knowledge on subjects such as: (this is the actual list of subjects/queries from his personal writings).

1. Boundaries
2. Rivers
3. Sea ports
4. Mountains
5. Cascades and caverns
6. Productions of minerals, vegetable, and animal
7. Climate
8. Population
9. Military force
10. Marine force
11. Aborigines
12. Counties and towns
13. Constitution
14. Laws
15. Colleges, buildings, roads, religion
16. Proceedings as to Tories
17. Religion
18. Manners
19. Manufactures
20. Subjects of commerce
21. Weights, Measures and Money

22. Public revenue and expenses
23. Histories, memorials, and state-papers

Some of Pres. Jefferson's writings on these various subjects were brief, and some of his writings were extensive and jumped around to even more subjects. There's no denying Pres. Jefferson's incredible intellect. There's no denying the fact that a person must be extremely perceptive to acquire and apply such intellect to everyday life. You'd also expect a person with such intellect to look at things from all angles, and to look at things with a little objectivity. When it comes to judging human behavior Pres. Jefferson was flawed, both personally and perceptively. Maybe it was his personal flaws that clouded his perceptions about human behavior? We'll never know. Maybe his *mis*perceptions fed his personal flaws? We'll never know. What we do know is that it's quite disinguous to say that Slaves were uninterested in Loving one another without looking at the role Slavery played in that perceived lack of interest. I agree with Pres. Jefferson's basic assertion that Blacks are more ardent after their female (i.e., **more Sexual**). I don't agree with how he reached this conclusion. I certainly don't think he's the right person to make any judgments on how someone else displays their Love. Remember, Pres. Jefferson was a Slave-owning married man, who was practicing **Miscegenation** with his wife's *half*-Black, *half*-sister. That said, I can't believe that a man as intelligent as him never understood the role that he (and Slavery) played in creating the behavior he so perceptively observed. I said it before and I'll say it again (**VOLUME I**), you're not going to let yourself get too attached to someone when either of you can be sold at any given second. If that's the situation you faced on a daily basis, would you really put a lot of time and heartfelt effort into a traditional courtship?

If you're a Slave who's been busting your ass in the hot sun for *16* hours, are you going to be able to *wine and dine* females to Pres. Jefferson's standards? It's easy to be a romantic like Pres. Jefferson and focus on the *"delicate mixture of sentiment and sensation,"* when every evening is like a Lovely stroll to the Dairy Queen: *"Do I want chocolate ice cream this evening (Sally) or do I want vanilla ice cream (Martha)."* Pres. Jefferson, like most White Men of his time (*and many White Men of today*), certainly didn't consider Blacks equal to Whites in any way, and his writings bore that out. It's easy to feel *superior* when you're on top, and when you're in charge, and when you make the rules. This can also lead to very narrow *one*-sided observations. That's how you can write one thing in **The Declaration of Independence** and then practice the complete opposite in your private life. Pres. Jefferson was able to write with eloquence about *life, liberty and the pursuit of happiness,* but never understood that the people he owned and so often observed functioned under duress. Even though Pres. Jefferson felt Blacks were *inferior* he still knew Blacks were human beings because he shared a bed with one for four decades. There have been men in certain parts of this country who've fucked chickens, who've fucked pigs, and also fucked cows, but they rarely shared a bed with them. After all, it would be disgusting to share a bed with an animal, wouldn't it?

Pres. Jefferson understood the importance of robbing the Black American Slave of emotion. This practice was a mandatory part of owning Slaves. Rob the Slave of emotion, and then tell everyone that the Slave is a beast, because he doesn't display the same feelings and emotions that White Folks do. By saying the Slave's *desires* were purely physical and *not* emotional (thus proving that Blacks are sub-human), Slavery could then be further justified. It's kinda like walking into a **"Quickie-Mart"** and having the clerk *snatch* the *shoes* and *shirt* off of your body, and then tell you: **"No shoes, No shirt, No Service!"** By *snatching* the Black American Slave's emotion, Sex was often reduced to nothing more than a physical activity that provided a means of psychological escape from bondage. That said, maintaining a healthy Sex drive, even if it was merely a means of momentary escape from bondage, is actually quite admirable. Especially when you consider the horrific living conditions the Black American Slave endured.

Does history tell us there's a *difference* between White Men and Black Men? You bet. Pres. Jefferson's observation: **"They are more ardent after their female; but Love seems with them to be more an eager desire, than a tender delicate mixture of sentiment and sensation"** was a *difference* so profound that one of our founding fathers felt the need to document it. The problem is, Pres. Jefferson's observation completely missed the boat. Pres. Jefferson failed to realize that the real problem has always been the *"eager desire"* that many White Men *lack,* and not the *"lack of sentiment and sensation"* that Black Men *displayed.* The Black American Slave lived in fear, and knew that *"eager desire"* was a much safer bet than *Love.* It was never in the Slaves best interest to *Love,* though I'm sure many did. After all, the music we presently call **The Blues** was born from centuries of heartache that was passed down generation to generation. Sex was the great escape that could free your mind from the hard, long day of work. When Black Folks were finally able to enjoy that magical math equation of **Sex + Emotion = *Making Love,*** they took full advantage of it. Nowhere is this more evident than in Black Music.

Sub-Chapter 'A' "White Folks sing about *Fallin' in Love*" "Black Folks sing about *Makin' Love*"

Here are *10* classic samples of Black *Artists* coming right out and telling you what they want.

 # 1 All Day Music *by* **War (1971)** - "Down at the beach or party in town, *Makin' Love* or just riding around"

 # 2 Close the Door *by* **Teddy Pendergrass (1979)** - "Let me do what I wanna do, all I wanna do is *Make Love* to you"

 # 3 Dream Maker *by* **Rick James (1978)** - "Visions of *Love Making* become so breathtaking"

 # 4 Feel All My Love Inside *by* **Marvin Gaye (1976)** - "When we're *Making Love*, when we're *Making Love,* when we're *Making Love*" (This is the first *3* verses of the song.)

 # 5 Feel Like *Makin' Love* *by* **Roberta Flack (1974)** - Speaks for itself.

 # 6 Let Me Down Easy *by* **The Isley Brothers (1976)** - "More Love and more *Love Making* to fulfill my every need"

 # 7 Let Me *Make Love* to You *by* **The O'Jays (1975)** - Speaks for itself.

 # 8 Love's Holiday *by* **Earth, Wind & Fire (1977)** - "Would you mind, if I *Made Love* to you til I'm satisfied"

 # 9 Lovin' You *by* **Minnie Ripperton (1976)** - "Lovin' you is easy cause you're beautiful, *Makin' Love* with you is all I wanna do"

 # 10 You Know How To Love Me *by* **Phyllis Hyman (1979)** - "You know how to *Love* me, you know how to *Make* it right"

I've got an extensive music library and I grew up listening to everything from **The Blues** to **Polka** and I'm telling you, White People don't sing about *Making Love*, they sing about *Falling in Love* or *Falling out of Love*. Please don't give me that **Get Down Tonight** *shit* by **K.C. & The Sunshine Band,** because *6* of the *9* band members were Black. The White Guys in **K.C. & The Sunshine Band** wrote the 1975 hit song **Get Down Tonight** which gave us the memorable verse: **"Do a little dance,** *Make a little Love,* **Get Down Tonight,** but I'm sure they'd be the first ones to tell you they were playing Black music. Remember, they also had a hit song entitled **(Shake, Shake, Shake) Shake Your Booty.** I rest my case. Black Folks embraced *Multi-Racial bands* such as **K.C. & The Sunshine Band** and **Heatwave,** and adopted *predominantly White groups* such as the **Average White Band** and **Hall & Oates** (*both White*), as their own. We'd say amongst ourselves, *"Damn, them some bad White Boys."* As bad as these White Boys were, they still weren't singing about *Making Love.* **Average White Band's** *School Boy Crush* was pretty damn close though.

I obviously grew up listening to R&B, but due to the lack of Black radio stations in my little town, I was also exposed to every kind of Rock Music. The only White Dudes I ever heard openly express their Sexual intentions was **Led Zeppelin**. **Zep** always got *right to the point* and never minced their words. The success of **Stairway to Heaven** (*from* **Zep's** *4th album*) made everyone run to the record store and buy **Led Zeppelin I, II,** and **III**. It took me a few years to appreciate the beauty of **Zeppelin III**, but **Zeppelin I** and **Zeppelin II** hit me right in my ear hole (*as George Clinton would say*). **Led Zeppelin II** had two songs with very explicit Sexual references that I can remember singing as a *10* year-old, even though I had no idea what they meant. In the classic song **Whole Lotta Love,** lead singer Robert Plant boldly sang: *"I want to give you every inch of my Love,"* and later sang *"Shake for me girl, I want to be your back-door man."* It took me a few years to figure out that Mr. Plant wasn't talking about sneaking in the backdoor of some girl's house. Mr. Plant was much more direct in **The Lemon Song** when he sang: *"Squeeze me baby, til the juice runs down my leg. Squeeze me baby, til the juice runs down my leg. The way you squeeze my lemon, I'm gonna fall right out of bed."* It would take a few additional years before I figured out the meaning of *"every inch of my Love"* and *"squeeze my lemon til the juice runs down my leg."* As you can see, that's a lot more *to the point* than the **Starland Vocal Band's** *Afternoon Delight.* I didn't get my hands on those **Led Zeppelin** albums until 1973, but I'm sure I didn't fully understand them until I was in high school (some *5* years later). I only mention this because **Led Zeppelin II** was originally released in 1969. **Led Zeppelin** was obviously well ahead of their time, and has always stood without peer in more ways than one. Years later I would get my hands on Stephen Davis's **Led Zeppelin** bio-book **Hammer of the Gods**, and I was pleased to read that **Zep** *practiced* *what they preached.* I remember hearing Charles Barkley refer to Larry Bird as *"one bad White Boy,"* and that comment certainly applies to **Led Zeppelin. Led Zeppelin** was without question, *"four bad White Boys."*

Music was really beginning to come of age in the late 1960's and continued to improve throughout the 1970's. I'll admit it, I'm partial to the 1970's because that was the decade of growth for me personally. The 1970's encompassed my childhood, my adolescent years and my teen years. The music from the 1970's stands on its own and can go toe to toe with the music from any decade prior to the 1970's and any decade since. That's why Classic Rock radio stations continue to flourish across the nation. *Artists* whose popularity started in the 1960's like **The Beatles, The Rolling Stones, The Who** and **Jimi Hendrix** carried over well into the 1970's, and they are still popular today. *Artists* whose popularity began in the 1970's like **AC/DC, Aerosmith, Pink Floyd, Queen, Rush** and **Yes** are still popular today. Great groups like **The Bee Gees, Chicago, Crosby, Stills & Nash**, **The Eagles, Fleetwood Mac, Heart** and **Steely Dan** are also still popular today. Solo *Artists* like **David Bowie, Neil Diamond, Billy Joel, Elton John, Carole King, Joni Mitchell, Barry Manilow, Todd Rundgren, Carly Simon, James Taylor** and **Neil Young** remain as popular as ever. What does this tell you? It tells you that great music is timeless. Even though many of these *Artists* are up in years, when they decide to perform they sell out wherever they play. The auditoriums and stadiums are always full, and a large part of those audiences are usually people who weren't born when these *Artists* were at their peak. That doesn't matter because the message within their music is timeless. That's why you see kids who were born in the 1990's wearing **Jimi Hendrix, Led Zeppelin** and **Pink Floyd** tee-shirts. That's also why you see **rap/hip-hop** *Artists* and performers routinely sample from **R&B** music of the 1970's. Since the 1970's ended there seems to be a gradual decline in the quality of music, and that decline became more visible in the mid-1990's. There are still great *Artists* but they are becoming rarer and rarer by the minute. What happened? Who knows? All I know is there is definitely a decade when the music died.

RANT: "The Decade the Music Died"

If you look closely at the *10* songs I listed at the beginning of this chapter, I'm sure you noticed all of them came from the 1970's. I carefully chose *10 different Artists* who were musically *different* from each other, but from the same decade. You could never compare **Teddy Pendergrass** to **Rick James,** and you can't compare anyone to the great **Marvin Gaye,** period. **Minnie Ripperton, Roberta Flack** and **Phyllis Hyman** could never be mistaken for each other or mistaken for anyone else. The four groups I chose, **The Isley Brothers, The O'Jays, War, and Earth, Wind & Fire,** were similar as far as content, but unique in their approach and delivery. You'll never confuse Ronald Isley's voice with Maurice White's voice or Eddie Levert's voice with Philip Bailey's voice. You'll never confuse **Earth, Wind and Fire's** world renowned horn section with the brilliant harmonica of **War's** Lee Oskar. All of these great *Artists* had the ability to give us great ballads as well as songs with great messages, often on the same album. **The Isley Brother's** 1976 album **Harvest for the World** told us *"A nation planted, so concerned with gain, as the seasons come and go, greater grows the pain."* Every year you could count on **The Isley Brothers** to give us a handful of great ballads, and then a message about life. Songs like 1975's **Fight The Power** and 1977's **The Pride** are as relevant today as they were *30* years ago. In 1973, The **O'Jays** album **Ship Ahoy** featured a slew of classic songs, all with *different* messages. **This Air I Breathe** (*a message on pollution*), **Put Your Hands Together** (*a message on unity*), **Now That We Found Love** (*a message on Love*), **For the Love of Money** (*a message on greed*), and the title track **Ship Ahoy** gave you the eerie feeling of being in the creaking hull of a Slave ship swaying on the open seas. **War** gave us the great message album **The World is a Ghetto** in 1972, and **Earth, Wind & Fire** gave us the equally great message album **Head To The Sky** in 1973. In 1971 **Mr. Marvin Gaye** not only gave us a great message album, he also gave us *one* of the *three* greatest pieces of musical *Art* ever painted. I'm obviously referring to **Mr. Gaye's** *What's Going On,* which sits *one* notch above **Pink Floyd's** *Dark Side of the Moon* (1973), and trails *only* **Miles Davis's** *Kind of Blue* (1959) as the most complete recordings in music history. In 1978 **Teddy Pendergrass's Life is a Song Worth Singing** featured the timeless ballad **Close the Door** and the ultimate *hard-times song* **Cold, Cold Word.** **Rick James's** 1978 debut album, **Come Get It!** gave us the great ballad *Dream Maker,* a number of great dance tracks, and the unforgettable **Hollywood,** which vividly described trying to make it from the small time to the *Big Time*. **Roberta Flack** and **Phyllis Hyman** could sing about coping with loneliness with as much passion as they sang about *Making Love*. **Minnie Ripperton's** great song **Memory Lane** embraced the *Art of being sentimental;* which is an emotion that Black Folks are supposedly incapable of expressing according to Pres. Jefferson. In the 1970's music was more about the Message and less about the Messengers. Things slowly started to change with the introduction of Rap music.

Rap music started out as Message music and groups like **Public Enemy** kept the Message alive. The group's unquestioned leader **Chuck D** was *all* Message, *all the time*, and even though *Flavor Flav* would draw attention to himself with the enormous clock around his neck, you still knew that **Public Enemy** was more about the Message than the Messengers. The enormous clock around *Flavor Flav's* neck was strictly for comedic effect, but when you listened to *Flavor* on songs like **911 Is a Joke**, you knew the Message was *not* for comedic effect. By the time the mid-1980's rolled around music gradually became *50/50*. *Half* of the focus was on the Messenger, and *Half* of the focus was on the Message. I know that I've quoted a number of rappers throughout both **VOLUMES** of this book, but if you look closely at the time period of their quotes you'll see there's a definite cut-off. That cut-off is the mid-1990's, and the decline has continued at an alarming rate.

After the death of **TuPac Shakur**, the gradual shift in the direction of music was exposed. There's no doubt **TuPac** sang about a lot of bullshit, but there was still a social awareness that was unmatched by anyone else in music during that time period. **TuPac** said a lot of bullshit in some of his songs, and like every *Artist* before him, he had some great songs, some good songs, and some bad songs. Shit, there are songs on **Jimi Hendrix's** classic album **Electric Ladyland** that I always skip. A few sub-par songs do not diminish **Jimi's** body of work in any way (at least *not* in my mind). And anyone who's ever listened to **TuPac's** CD **Me Against The World** could easily forgive him for the usage of terms such as *bitches* and *ho's* in some of his other work. Even when **Pac** was fucking up, you still felt that he'd eventually get his life together and eventually make a positive *difference*. **TuPac's** social consciousness basically served as window dressing, and masked many greater problems in the music industry. The problem that was being masked was true *Artists* were being replaced with performers. The focus was shifting completely to the Messengers, and the Message was becoming lost. The Message is now about *bling, cribs, cars, bitches, gats,* and *Niggas*. Like I said before, I don't mind these Brothers *gettin' paid* for using the N-Word, but many older folks (*like myself*), would be much happier if they were using it purposefully in songs. Here are a few silly examples just off the top of my head:

- *Niggas* going to School, trying to get their Learn on!
- *Niggas* readin' Books, not bein' Crooks!
- *Niggas* refusin' to Fail, by keeping their asses out of Jail!
- *Niggas* refusin' to be dumb, before they get *bizzy* they put on a **Magnum**!

I would have no problem hearing the N-Word in music or movies, if it was in that context. In **N.W.A's** 1991 song '**Niggaz 4 Life**', Eazy E rapped the following verse: **"Nigga, Nigga, Nigga, Nigga, Nigga, Nigga please, I'm treated like a fucking disease."** You can't really argue with the N-Word being used in that context (especially when Eazy passed away *4* years later of HIV/AIDS).

Many people probably point to gangster rap as the reason for the new focus on the Messengers instead of the Message. I don't agree with that. Gangster rappers primarily sang about what they experienced on a daily basis. Gangster rappers were no *different* than **The Beach Boys**. **The Beach Boys** saw the California beaches, girls, surfing and cars, and that's what they chose to sing about. **N.W.A.** saw the L.A.P.D. cracking Niggas upside the head with nightsticks, and that's what they chose to sing about. **N.W.A.** was a *50/50* group, *Half*-Message and *Half*-Messengers, but they made people take notice. Whether you agreed with their Message or not, you had to take notice. Quite often the Message was in the *ears* of the beholder. Opponents could point to a song like **Fuck tha Police** with outrage, and defenders could point to **Fuck tha Police's** opening verse: ***"Fuck tha police comin' straight from the underground, a young Nigga got it bad cause I'm Brown, and not the other color, so police think, they have the authority, to kill a minority."*** **Fuck tha Police** came out in 1988, which was years before Rodney King, Abner Louima, Amadou Diallo, and the Cincinnati *Race Riots* (i.e., **Unarmed Black Men + Cincinnati P. D. = Dead Black Men**). **Fuck tha Police** sparked nationwide outrage, but no one had any complaints when Gov. Schwarzenegger said ***"I'll be back"*** in 1984's hit movie **The Terminator,** and then promptly shot a couple dozen police officers in less than *four* minutes. It's all in the *ears* or in this case the *eyes* of the beholder. You may consider the Messengers too disagreeable for your taste. You may even completely disagree with their Message. But a Message you disagree with is better than *no* Message at all, which is where we stand today.

In today's music, especially this **hip-hop** stuff, what you hear is the hope of materialism being sold to the hopeless. Music doesn't have to be an educational experience, but it damn sure shouldn't cause people to turn their backs on education. If it's about entertaining then fine, entertain, but don't claim you have cultural clout if you're not talking about anything relevant. Just entertain and perform, and leave the *Art* to the *Artists*. In all fairness to the *Artists* of today, none of the pieces of *Art* created in the 1970's could ever be matched anyway. It would be unfair to expect the *Art* of today, to match the *Art* of yesterday, because the social awareness of today pales in comparison to the social awareness of yesterday.

There will never be another **Stevie Wonder's** *Songs in the Key of Life*. There will never be another **Curtis Mayfield's** *Superfly* (an entire album dedicated to the ills of drug use). There will never be another **Gil Scott-Heron's** *Pieces of a Man* which featured the classic songs *Save the Children* and *The Revolution Will Not Be Televised*. There will never be another **Harold Melvin & The Blue Notes** *Wake Up Everybody*. There will never be another **Bob Marley & The Wailer's** *Burnin'*, which featured the timeless liberation anthem *Get Up, Stand Up*. There will definitely never be another **Jimi Hendrix:** *Band Of Gypsys,* which featured the powerful *Machine Gun.*

Those albums carried serious Messages from serious men during serious times. But don't we have some pretty serious shit going on today? One of the things that made the music of the 1970's so special, was *Artists* could still make their point, even without being serious. They still tried to make you think, even when they were being silly or having fun. **George Clinton's Parliament Funkadelic,** which most people considered fun music or dance music or silliness, could still deliver a powerful Message, in its own unique way. In **Parliament's** 1975 classic song **Chocolate City** (*a reference to Washington D.C.'s overwhelming Black population*), Mr. Clinton painted The White House *Brown* and gave it an administration with Muhammad Ali as President, Rev. Ike as the Minister of the Treasury, Richard Pryor as the Minister of Education, Stevie Wonder as Secretary of Fine Arts, and Aretha Franklin as The First Lady. Comical yes, but **Chocolate City** was also quite telling when you consider the fact that many major U.S. cities were electing their first Black mayors. New Orleans Mayor Ray Nagin echoed **George Clinton's Chocolate City** sentiments in January of 2006, but he probably should've diversified his taste in desserts and requested a *Neapolitan City*. Mr. Clinton was merely dreaming of higher heights and was only trying to inspire Black Folks to do the same (*with the occasional help of special herbs of course*). In 1977's **Funkentelechy** he opened the song with *"Yo…this is mood control, saying you might as well* *pay attention, because you can't afford free speech.*" All of this timeless music was created by people who were more than just great performers. This music was created by great *Artists* who had something to say. They had something to say during a time period when something needed to be said.

There's a gap that's as wide as an ocean, and that gap represents the *difference* between an *Artist* and a performer. Bears in the fucking circus can perform, that certainly doesn't make them *Artists*. *Artists* create *Art*, period. When a true *Artist* has something to say their Message is magnified. The unique ability to magnify the Message is the primary *difference* between an *Artist* and a performer. *Artists* possess the unique ability of communicating their Message by painting a picture with a song. *Artists* are able to accomplish this unique feat because they care. That's what makes a group like **U2** so special. We know they care because they put their time, effort and money where their mouths are. The performer gives you a glimpse. The *Artist* gives you a body of work. The *Artist* music will be listened to decades from now, even if his or her piece of *Art* didn't get a handful of Grammy's. During a time when we still have war, pollution, and a lack of compassion for our fellow man, the **Marvin Gaye** album **What's Going On** is every bit as inspiring and relevant today, as it was when it was released on May 21st 1971. I don't think I need to tell you there'll never be another **What's Going On**.

If you want to know why so many people are stealing music off of the Internet it's because they're tired of paying *$20* for a CD with *one* decent song. In a time when there's plenty to sing about, and plenty of relevant Messages that need to be relayed to the masses, *one* good song for a fee of *$20* isn't going to cut it. The commercialization of music has made music nothing more than a commercial and the lack of consciousness stems from an unconscious generation. The *mid*-1980's gave us *50/50* music, *Half*-Message and *Half*-Messenger, and by the time the *mid*-1990's rolled around, the tipping point had been reached and it pushed music to *all*-Messenger and *no*-Message, and the decline has continued. There is definitely a decade the music died, and we're currently trapped in it. I'd be shocked if there were any radio stations *20* years from now playing music exclusively from the early 2000's. You'd have *three* or *four Artists* from each category of music, a ton of *one* hit wonders, and *ten* tons of over-hyped, untalented performers. There was some good music in the 1990's and a few great *Artists* emerged, but there was so much terrible music from the 1990's, it's not even worth me typing another sentence. In the 1970's we only had a handful of bad songs. We had **The Streak**, **Convoy** and motherfucking **Disco Duck,** but the bad songs from the 1970's centered on silliness. People like to joke about the song **Kung Fu Fighting,** but everyone always sings along word for word when it comes on the radio. The bad music from the 1970's doesn't come close to the 'boy band bullshit' of the 1990's.

The *Artists* of the 1970's gave you the total package. You could listen to **Side *1*** of an album and be ready to go out and protest. You could flip the album over to **Side *2*** and make a baby. Performers today sing about Sexual activity. Black *Artists* of the 1970's sang about *Making Love*, and when they sang about Sexual activity they did it with class. The music of the 1970's lives on, regardless of the music from other decades. Better yet, the music of the 1970's lives on because of the music from other decades.

B.T.P.

Actually, it doesn't matter what decade, if you're talking about Sex, Sexual activity or *Making Love*, the bottom line is that Black Folks sing about it and White Folks don't. Does that mean White Folks are more reserved about Sex or does it mean Black Folks are more expressive about Sex? It may be a little bit of both. People wouldn't sing about it if it wasn't on their minds, and people wouldn't buy it if they didn't want to hear it. Think about the *different* subjects that people have sung about over the years. I bet the **Beach Boys** enjoyed life on the beach. I'd be willing to bet that **Madonna** enjoys dancing. I think it's a safe bet that people who sing about getting high do drugs. I think it's a safe bet that people who sing about having a drink like to get drunk. So therefore, people who sing about........... (*I'm sure you get the point*). Black Male *Artists* of the 1970's came right out and *"told you what they wanted to do."*

James Brown's 1970 classic song **Sex Machine** gets right to the point and lets the whole world know that Black Folks are upfront about *takin' care of bizzness.*

Marvin Gaye made his intentions very clear on the1973 hit **Let's Get It On** and then upped the ante with the unbelievable **You Sure Love To Ball** (*from the same album*). Those two **Marvin Gaye** classics were just two of many that he cranked out in the 1970's. **Let's Get It On** was nearly a full decade before his 1982 hit **Sexual Healing**, which tells you that Marvin never lost his appetite.

People would walk up to **Barry White** on the street and tell him that they made babies to his music. In 1977's **Oh What a Night for Dancing** Barry crooned: ***"And around about 2, tell you what I'm gonna do, girl I'm gonna take you home and stick plenty Love to you, let's get it on, all night long."*** Barry never stopped singing about *gettin' bizzy*, and on his

1991 hit **Put Me In Your Mix** he sang: *"Let me come inside your world.... I can make your toe nails curl!"*

There was also the great **Teddy Pendergrass**, who had to endure women throwing panties at him during concerts. In his 1979 album entitled **TEDDY**, he hit us with the back to back R-Rated classics, **Come Go With Me** and **Turn Off The Lights**.

Isaac Hayes was the voice of Chef on **Comedy Central's** hit show **South Park**. Chef was the show's Dr. Ruth and Mr. Hayes was perfectly suited for the role. After all, Mr. Hayes' music has always been loaded with valuable Sexual information. The soundtrack from the 1971 hit movie **SHAFT** put Mr. Hayes on the map, and *one* single verse in the title track defined the movie in more ways than *one*. The movie opened with the song **SHAFT** and *3* minutes and *30* seconds into the film you hear the verse *"Who's the Black private dick that's a Sex machine to all the chicks? Shaft!"* This single verse set the stage for the rest of the movie. Mr. Hayes translated his **Oscar** winning success into his true passion, which is singing about passion. He displayed that passion in 1973's hit **JOY** and in 1978's classic **Moonlight Lovin'** (*Menage A Trois*).

Isaac Hayes, Barry White, Marvin Gaye, and **Teddy Pendergrass** are without peers, regardless of Race and regardless of the *time period*. **Prince** closed out this *time period* with his second album. 1979's self-titled effort **Prince,** was somewhere between R-Rated and X-Rated. On the beautiful ballad **When We're Dancing Close And Slow, Prince** sang:

"When we're dancing close and slow...
I'm not afraid to let my feelings show
I want to come inside of you
I want to hold you when we're through"

Prince covered *"eager desire"* with the *second* and *third* verses, and then covered the *"tender delicate mixture of sentiment and sensation"* with the *last* verse.

I could continue listing Black Male *Artists* from the 1970's for a few more pages, especially if I started listing One Hit wonders. Black Folks know what I'm talking about because all I've gotta say is **Me and Mrs. Jones (Billy Paul's** only Big Hit). The tradition of Black Men singing about *Making Love* carried on well into the 1980's. **Rick James** got *'right to the point'* in his 1981 song *Make Love To Me*. Here's how **Mr. James** opened *Make Love To Me*:

"Taste so good to the very last drop
You on the bottom and me on top
Rolling around to a saxophone sound
Feel so good, don't wanna come down
Make Love to me baby, do it nice and slow
Make Love to me sugar, sugar, let your feelings show"

Mr. James covered *"eager desire"* with the *first* verse, and then covered the *"tender delicate mixture of sentiment and sensation"* with the *last* verse. Too bad Mr. Jefferson wasn't around to hear *Artists* like **Prince** and **Rick James** because he probably would've appreciated **Prince's** *Do Me, Baby* and **Rick James'** *Fire and Desire.*

The 1980's gave us Black Male *Artists* such as **Babyface, Freddie Jackson, Kashif, Alexander O'Neal, Keith Sweat, Luther Vandross,** and of course more **Prince;** all of whom chipped in with their fair share of *'right to the point'* hits. The number of Black Male *Artists* singing about *Making Love* probably increased in the 1980's. I'm not even counting **Clarence Carter,** who closed out the 1980's with his comical song **Strokin',** which had nothing to do with swimming.

Black Female *Artists* of the 1970's also got *right to the point.* In **Donna Summer's** 1975 hit **Love to Love You Baby** she sings: *"Do it to me again and again, you put me in such an awful spin,"* and then gives you the moans in the background to express the awful spin. **Chaka Khan** got *right to the point* in 1974's **Tell Me Something Good,** and again in 1979's **Do You Love What You Feel**. What do you think **Ashford & Simpson** were singing about in their 1978 classic **Is it Still Good to Ya'**? Even the Queen of Soul, the great **Aretha Franklin,** made it crystal clear what she wanted in 1976's all-time classic **Something He Can Feel.** If I expanded to include the Black Female *Artists* of the 1980's, I could certainly go on for a few more pages. Great ladies like **Angela Bofill,** the late **Phyllis Hyman, Sade, Anita Baker** and the X-Rated **Millie Jackson,** all had unique, but easily understood ways of expressing their desire (*to get bizzy*). And who could forget **Janet Jackson's** 1987 sultry classic *Making Love* **In The Rain?** Then throw in some of the great R&B groups of the 1980's like **Cameo, The Gap Band, Shalamar, Slave, The S.O.S. Band, The Time,** and **The Whispers**, and it seems endless. You also have to remember that most of the Black *Artists* I named from the 1970's continued to pump out *Making Love* songs well into the 1980's and even into the 1990's.

Folks, this is where the fun starts. All of these great *Artists* who sang about *Making Love* were not just singing about *"an eager desire,"* as Pres. Jefferson put it. *Every Black Artist* I've named in this chapter, and I mean *every single one of them*, has *twice* as many songs about *Falling in Love* as they do *Making Love*. Look at the name of every Black *Artist* I've listed up to this point. Now ponder the fact that they've got *twice* as many songs about *Falling in Love* as they do *Making Love* (*excluding Rappers of course*). Obviously Pres. Jefferson didn't know shit about Black Folks. Here's a few Black *Artists* that I haven't listed yet, but have been known to *hum* a damn good *Falling in Love* song: **The Brothers Johnson, The Chi-Lites, The Dells, The Delfonics, The Dramatics, George Duke, Al Green, Michael Jackson, Al Jarreau, Jeffrey Osborne** and **L. T. D., Frankie Beverly & Maze, Smokie Robinson, The Spinners, The Stylistics, The Temptations, The Commodores** with **Lionel Richie,** and of course **Lionel Richie** solo.

Here's a few ladies from the 1970's and 80's that I haven't listed yet: **Diana Ross & The Supremes, Diana Ross** solo, **Natalie Cole, Gladys Knight, Vanessa Williams, Angela Winbush** and **Patrice Rushen,** to name a few. These ladies learned to sing about Love from great teachers such as: **Billie Holiday, Ella Fitzgerald, Lena Horne, Nina Simone** and **Sarah Vaughan.** I don't think anyone would deny that *every single* **Black Artist** I've listed in this chapter can sing a *'Love song'* with a *"tender delicate mixture of sentiment and sensation."* They wouldn't sing it if they didn't believe it, and people of all Races wouldn't buy it if they couldn't feel it.

Black Folks are more than capable of *Loving,* and Black Folks are more than capable of *Making Love.* Being monogamous might be a slight problem from time to time, but like I said in **VOLUME I,** no Race has a monopoly on being *Sexually Irresponsible,* and judging by the current Divorce Rate, no Race has a monopoly on monogamy. *Is there a difference?* I say yes, because we wouldn't sing about *Making Love* so much, and sing about it with such passion, if it wasn't inside of us. Some people are *ashamed* of that passion. I can understand that. Hey, when you're working like a one-legged Nigga on a unicycle, and you're desperately trying to get on the U.S. Supreme Court, you'll use *shame* and even self-castration. Justice Thomas was obviously *ashamed* of the *difference.* Pres. Jefferson failed to see the real *difference* was the *"eager desire"* that many White Men *lack.* Too bad Pres. Jefferson was here in the 1770's instead of the 1970's, because I'm sure he'd have to reassess his little bullshit observations. Don't think for one second that Pres. Jefferson was full of *"eager desire"* just because he had two women. Pres. Jefferson had two women simply because he could, that's all. More than likely Martha was for *Show* and Sally was for *Go.* The question of *"Is there a difference?"* remains, but there's no denying that what Whites and Blacks choose to sing provides a window to the *difference.* What people choose to sing about often provides a window to their *Soul.* Hence the forgotten term *Soul Music.*

What does music tell us? Music is a form of *Art,* and the same theory that applies to movies also applies to music. The theory is *"Life imitates Art and Art imitates Life"* (See **Hollywood**, in **VOLUME I**). So do you really want to know why Black Folks sing about *Making Love?* I'll let one of my heroes sing it to you.

Barry White

I've had my share of Lovers
But some say I'm damn good
And if you think you could turn me out
Baby I wish that you would
Cause you keep telling me this
And telling me that
You say once I'm with you
I'll never go back
You say there's a lesson
That you want to teach
Well here I am baby
Practice what you Preach

That's your answer folks; Black Folks Practice what we Preach. This chapter showed how *Art imitates Life,* the next two chapters, **Mo Cushion vs. No Cushion** and **BLACK PORN: "The Proof is in the Chocolate Pudding,"** will show how *real Life experiences* inspire America's Sexual *Art,* and also influence America's Sexual *Attitudes.*

P.S. I want to send some Love to *Artists* who consistently put out great music throughout the1990's: **Seal, Maxwell, Lenny Kravitz, D'Angelo, Gerald Levert, Prince, Keith Washington, Michael Franks, Erykah Badu, Janet, Mariah, Me'Shell Ndegeocello, Mary J. Blige, Soul II Soul, Public Enemy, TuPac Shakur, Heavy D., Ice Cube, Simply Red, Madonna, Sheryl Crow, Everything But The Girl, Swing Out Sister, Courtney Pine, Pat Metheny, The Cure, Alice in Chains, Pearl Jam, Stone Temple Pilots, Soundgarden,** and of course **U2.**

P.S.S. And some Love to a few present day *Artists*: **Kem, Jill Scott, and Alicia Keys.**

P.S.S.S. As I've gotten older I've come to realize that the 1980's were pretty damn good too.

Sub-Chapter 'B' "Mo Cushion *vs.* No Cushion"

"She's a Brick House, she's the one, the only one, built like an Amazon!"

From the 1977 song Brick House
By The Commodores

Before I get started I want to make a few things perfectly clear. I have absolutely nothing against small women, petite women or thin women (as long as you're *naturally* thin, and not starving yourself to death to get a man). Relationships come in all shades, shapes and sizes, so the most important thing is to find someone who makes you happy. This chapter will focus on the images that are pumped out to society, and *how* White Men and Black Men view those images *differently,* or more importantly, *why* White Men and Black Men view those images *differently.* This goes to the heart of the *"Is there a difference Question?"* **The Commodore's** hit song **Brick House** made it very clear that Black Men prefer women with some meat on their bones. In the spirit of political correctness, what I'm trying to say is Black Men do not discriminate based on *Dress Size.* **99 %** of the Brothers I've met throughout my lifetime do not discriminate based on *Dress Size (within reason).* Why is that? I think it has more to do with Sexual confidence than anything. **Mo Cushion** refers to the saying *"More cushion for the pushin'."* No Cushion refers to the **White Male Happy Meal** (i.e., as *thin* as possible with large fake breasts). The bottom line is most Black Men prefer the curvy voluptuous look, and most White Men prefer the thin look. With White Men, when it comes to their preference in women, *Size Does Matter.*

The song **Brick House** gave us the measurements that often serve as the minimum preferred standard for Black Men (*"36 – 24 – 36"*). **Sir Mix-A-Lot** felt those measurements should be re-adjusted due to inflation. In **Mr. Mix-A-Lot's** 1992 hit song **Baby Got Back**, he stated *"36 – 24 – 36"* is only acceptable on a frame that's *5 ft. 3.* **Mr. Mix-A-Lot** also had a few more gems in **Baby Got Back**:

"I like *Big Butts* and I can not lie, you other Brothers can't deny, that when a girl walks in with an itty-bitty waist and a *Round Thing* in your face.....You get Sprung!"

"My anaconda... Don't! Want! None! Unless you got *Buns*! Hun!"

"I'm tired of magazines saying 'flat butts' are the thing. Take the average Black Man and ask him that? She's gotta pack much *Back*!"

"Yeah baby, when it comes to females, Cosmo ain't got nothing to do with my selection"

"So Cosmo says you're fat, well I ain't down wit that"

When it comes to taste in women, I could literally use this entire song to illustrate the *differences* between White Men and Black Men. I've already explained *why* Black Folks sing about *Making Love*. I think it's fairly obvious *why* Black Men sing about a certain type of female body. Why is the *difference* between the White Male preference in women and the Black Male preference in women important? Our *different* taste in women goes a long way in explaining our *differences* in the bedroom. Obviously discussing these *differences* feeds many of the existing **Stereotypes**. There are always going to be people who don't fall within a particular **Stereotype**; they're the ones who usually get offended (*at times* myself included). That'll all be covered in **SECTION VI (RACE CARDS)**. What I'm about to get into right now is *not* an exact science. I'm sure there are many White Guys out there who prefer voluptuous women, and I even know a few. I'm sure there are many Brothers out there who prefer **White Male Happy Meals**. I'm sure there are many Brothers out there who have naturally thin women, and they Love what they have. I'm also sure that at one time or another they've wrestled with a woman who had some meat on her bones, and they enjoyed every minute of it. My point is, they weren't scared and they weren't turned off.

This is something that is well known throughout American society and shouldn't come as a shock to anyone. I've witnessed White and Black Firefighters switch the TV channel back and forth in the morning because the White Guys wanted to see Kelly Ripa, and the Black Guys wanted to see Katie Couric. The big *difference* between these two women is their *different* body types. I've witnessed White and Black Firefighters basically play musical chairs during an episode of **Will & Grace**. When Debra Messing (Grace) was on the television the Black Firefighters would literally walk out of the room to do something else and the White Firefighters would become transfixed to the tube. When the Black Firefighters heard Megan Mullally's (Karen's) voice they would come back into the room. The White

Firefighters would then step out of the room. This was done with no thought or deliberation; it was completely natural. When the White Firefighters were gone, the Black Firefighters would give the standard Black Male assessments of Ms. Mullally:

"Damn, that girl is thick."
"Damn, that girl got some booty on her."
"Damn, I Love the way she be pushin' them titties up."

For the most part Black Men prefer the *voluptuous* look, i.e. the **Black Male Value Meal**, which means *plenty* of titties and *plenty* of ass. I know a lot of Brothers who prefer their **Black Male Value Meal** *Super Sized (within reason)*. With most Black Men, *Size* truly ***Doesn't Matter***. In December of 2005, **Saturday Night Live** alluded to the Black Male preference in women during their **Weekend Update** segment. **S.N.L's** Rachel Dratch put on a special suit and special make-up to give her the appearance of someone who's heavy-set (i.e., *a fat suit*). Ms. Dratch then went undercover and walked the streets of Manhattan to show how heavy-set people are mistreated in public. She got all of the usual awkward stares and glances until she started running into Black Men. When she started running into Black Men, she started getting *checked-out*. She even got asked out on a date to *Red Lobster*. Was it an exaggeration? Absolutely. Was it hilarious? Absolutely. Was it offensive? Maybe a little bit (only because she was a little too big for the *Average* Brother). Was there some truth to it? There are no absolute truths when you're talking about large *groups* of people, but there are definitely certain preferences within large *groups*. So was there some truth to the skit? **Hell Yes!** There was *plenty* of truth.

South Park also alluded to the Black Male lack of preference in *Dress Size*. In the March of 2006 episode **The Return of Chef,** the boys desperately tried to cure an obviously brainwashed Chef. It would take a trip to a local strip club to snap Chef out of the *cult-like* trance. As soon as Chef's face was smothered by a stripper's massive ass cheeks and massive breasts, he suddenly became normal again.

American society is dominated by White Males and right now they say *thin* is in. If White Men didn't like *thin*, do you honestly believe we'd continue to see it on every magazine cover? Do you really believe all of these *super thin* actresses would be the headliners if White Men didn't prefer that look? There was a time period when being *voluptuous* and having curves was in. The big name stars of that time period had some meat on their bones and had some curves. Dorothy Dandridge had beautiful curves. Marilyn Monroe, Jayne Mansfield, Sophia Loren and Raquel Welch were full-figured, voluptuous women. For some reason, the voluptuous look became extinct in Hollywood. Shortly after it was confirmed by Sex experts that *Penis Size* did **not** matter, a mysterious *psychological* shift occurred within White Men, and then suddenly *Dress Sizes* started **to** matter. I'm not saying that *one* came about because of the other, but there's no doubt the *two* are linked. Who benefits from a society where *Penis Size* **Doesn't** *Matter?* Who prefers a society where *Dress Sizes* **Do** *Matter?* The same people who establish what's acceptable in our society. We all know the answer, don't we?

The truth is, White Men prefer *super thin* women because it *psychologically* boosts their Sexual *physical* confidence. *Thin* makes them feel dominant. *Thin* makes them feel like they're in control. *Thin* makes them feel like they're **Going Deep.** *Thin* makes *Average* White Men feel like they're **Packin' Heat.** This is not an issue for Black Men because Black Men are already Sexually confident. When you're Sexually confident you'll take on all comers: short, medium, tall, healthy, medium, small. After all, we mustn't forget what Justice Thomas said. Justice Thomas said *"The language throughout the history of this country"* tells us that Black Men have **the equipment to do the job,** and **the willingness to use that equipment**. Black Men prefer **Mo Cushion** because it provides leverage. A nice ass is something to hold on to and aids the *bizzness* transaction. That's why Black Men have a healthy respect for healthy asses. I'm appalled when I hear White Guys disrespectfully refer to an *Average size* ass as a *Pooper* or a *Turd-Cutter.* Many White Men have no respect for a nice ass because they can't handle a nice ass. Once you get below the breasts many White Men have no true appreciation for a woman's body, period.

When it comes to breasts, White Men usually only want to look at them anyway. For White Men breasts are for *Show,* and for Black Men breasts are for *Go.* The focus on physical *differences* and physical preferences only tells us *half* of the story. We know what the physical *differences* are, and according to Justice Thomas we've known about the physical *differences* for a long time. Those physical *differences* have been well-documented and heavily discussed for centuries (*mostly by White Folks, I might add*).

We also know that White Men and Black Men have *different* physical preferences in women. These *different* physical preferences are so well-known; they've become fodder for comedians. When it comes to women, what's rarely discussed is the *psychological differences* between Black Men and White Men. The *psychological differences* tell the other *half* of the story, but that *half* of the story is rarely discussed. I personally, have always been more intrigued by the *psychological differences,* because the *psychological differences* are far more telling. The *psychological differences* tell us why Black Men and White Men like what they like, and therefore, do what they do. I'm sure the physical *differences* between Black Men and White Men play a major role in the *psychological differences*, which takes us back to the Sexual confidence factor. The lack of Sexual confidence that many White Men suffer from is the main reason for what I call **Seinfeld-***itis***. Seinfeld-***itis* is when White Men break up with a gorgeous woman immediately after Sex. If White Men don't sense, or don't feel, like they did anything for her, they always come up with a bullshit excuse to get out of dodge. Just like Jerry Seinfeld would do in his sitcom, **Seinfeld**. Jerry would break up with a beautiful woman because she ate her peas one at a time or some bullshit like that. I can't tell you how many times I've heard White Guys say stupid shit like:

"Dude, she just didn't do anything for me"
or
"Man, she just wasn't my type."

All the Brothers would look at each other and say ***"What the fuck are you waiting for, Ms. Universe to fall out of the sky?"*** Women often misdiagnose **Seinfield-***itis* for **Commitment-***phobia*. Just ask yourself if there was a spark in the bedroom. If there was ***no spark*** in the bedroom then it's **Seinfield-***itis*. If a White Dude has a bad night he doesn't want another shot at it. If a Brother has a bad night, or if the *two* bodies didn't mesh, or if it was awkward for some reason, a Brother wants another shot at it. Brothers always want to redeem themselves. You can't have *no* woman out there saying your shit was lame, or saying that you were pitiful in the bedroom. I'm often reminded of a verse from **Ray Parker Jr.'s** 1981 song entitled **All in the Way You Get Down:** ***"She caught me on an off night, but from now on I'm going to make it right! Cause it's all in the way you get down. There's no time for fooling around."*** When you're Sexually confident, it creates a level of Sexual pride that will make you beg for another shot.

White Guys and Black Guys have *different* agendas right from the start. A White Guy wants to know if she's willing to kiss his ass. A Black Guy wants to know how hard he's going to have to work to get some ass. I've always been amazed at the *differences* between White Guys and Black Guys Monday morning (i.e., *post-weekend*) chatter.

White Guys Post-Weekend Chatter:

"Holy shit man, she went down on me right away. I didn't even have to say anything."

"She wasn't my type, so I just got some head and left."

"That chick just wants a husband. I can't deal with her anymore."

Black Guys Post-Weekend Chatter:

"Man I was droppin' anchor, I had that girl callin' my name. I had to tell her to keep that shit down, cause I didn't want her to wake up them damn knuckle head kids she got."

"Four Times! I made her come 4 times in 20 minutes. It was like she was having seizures and shit!"

"I said whose God damn pussy is this!," and she said, "It's your pussy baby, it's your pussy!"

"Dinner, movie, ice cream and she wouldn't let me do nuthin' but suck on them titties. Man I had 'blue-balls' like a motherfucker. That's alright though, I'll be back at it next week and you can believe dat."

As you can see there's a big *difference* in the content of the dialogue. That big *difference* is the result of *different* intentions. Our Sexual intentions are driven by *psychological* factors, as well as physical factors. The *two* factors can feed off of each other, or *one* factor can hinder or adversely affect the other factor. If you're not Sexually confident in your physical make-up, it can certainly have a negative *psychological* impact on your approach to women. If you're *psychologically* over-confident, that can have a negative impact on your physical approach to women. Being *psychologically* over-confident is one of the main reasons so many White Men are selfish and spoiled, they're used to getting what they want when they want it. White Men are intent on getting their way. Black Men are intent on getting *bizzy*. So I guess it's just like **Ray Parker Jr.** said: *"It's all in the way you get down."*

This next *RANT* will take a look at some of the *different* ways to get down, and how those *different* ways apply to White Men and Black Men.

RANT: "One-Dimensional *vs.* Multi-Dimensional"

Def: One-Dimensional- Selfish men who only want fellatio (*usually White*) or only want intercourse (*usually Black*).

Def: Multi-Dimensional- Men who are willing to do whatever it takes to help a woman reach **Point 'O' (Orgasm).**

I stated in **VOLUME I** and it's worth repeating; I grew up with, served with, traveled with, lived with, worked with, partied with, and lifted weights with White Guys from all over this country. I'm light-skinned, I've got a country accent and I listen to Rock music, so in the eyes of many Whites I'm non-threatening. White Guys open up and spill their guts to me. I'm a great listener and the *one* thing great listeners always attract is people who like to talk. Guys talk as much as women do, but guy talk is very *different* from girl talk. Guys just give you the general picture; they don't share every minute detail. Guys focus more on telling you what happened. Women focus more on telling you what happened and how it happened. Guys tell you they went to a party and then tell you what happened at the party. Women tell you where they stopped on the way to the party, who was at the party, what everyone was doing at the party, what everyone was wearing, if there was anyone there they didn't like, and of course, why they didn't like that particular person. My point is guys talk, but it's a *different* kind of talk. One similarity between Guy-talk and Girl-talk is who they choose to talk about. Just like women, men not only talk about the opposite Sex, men also talk about other men. Though it's usually in general terms (i.e., *So-n-So* is an Asshole), there's still a *female-like* critique of the competition. That said, obviously White Guys and Black Guys talk about each other.

I've been in countless conversations with Brothers about how White Guys are *different* from us, and I've been thoroughly questioned by White Guys about the *differences.* I've also overheard conversations between White Guys that weren't meant for my ears. When the conversation is Sex-related, you can often sense the **Small-Poleons Complex** within many White Guys. What gives them away is they're always looking for a *chink* in the **Black Man's Sexual Armor.** Every White Guy I know Loved **Oprah's** show about Brothers on the **Down Low** (Black Men leading double lives, i.e., married to a woman and having Homosexual affairs). Usually the only time these White Guys watched **The Oprah Winfrey Show** was if Julia Roberts or Jennifer Anniston was on it, but they couldn't wait to see the

Down Low episode. I heard jokes about that bullshit for weeks: **"Hey, I wouldn't bend over in front of Wooten. He might be on the *Down Low*, ha, ha, ha."**

White Guys are equally pleased when the *chink* in the Black Man's Sexual Armor comes from the land of fiction. Hollywood always seems to oblige them by finding some kind of comedic way to put a Brother in a dress, or worse. I came to this realization after observing how much White Guys Loved Quentin Tarantino's classic movie **Pulp Fiction. They couldn't wait for Pulp Fiction to be released** on DVD, because it afforded them the honor of watching Ving Rhames get raped, over and over: **"Hey man, rewind that shit, that's hilarious!!!"**

Any *chink* will do, but non-fiction *chinks* seem to have more staying power. I know White Guys who Loved Dennis Rodman's book **Bad As I Wanna Be**, because in their minds it confirmed the Myth that Black Men don't perform cunnilingus. In Mr. Rodman's book he stated that he refused to perform for/on Madonna. I tried to explain to them that Dennis was just being a knucklehead because he didn't want to be bossed around on the first date, regardless of how famous she was. I then realized their beliefs about Black Men and cunnilingus were entrenched, and was actually just part of the *Campaign of Fear and Smear.* I don't know where this Myth originated, but I always look at who benefits from a particular Myth for possible answers. White Men and Black Women both benefit from this Myth because it makes all Brothers look **One-Dimensional,** and therefore less desirable (especially to White Women).

I've read a few studies and surveys that basically stated that Whites engage in oral Sex more often than Blacks. I think it has more to do with your partner than culture. If your partner doesn't do it for you, then you're less inclined to do it for them. I've talked to Brothers who say those studies and surveys are bullshit, and swear that they don't leave the house without their SCUBA equipment (i.e., they're *Down with Diving*). I've also talked to Brothers who come right out and tell you *"Man I don't go down there, but I'll suck the hell out of some titties."* These Brothers are indeed **One-Dimensional**, and if a person is selfish in the bedroom they're usually going to be selfish outside of the bedroom. Many of these same Brothers have a *different* mindset when the discussion is about fellatio.

Brothers are often driven by getting *right to the point*. The problem is, when you think you're good at getting *right to the point*, you tend to forget that you have a partner. Brothers that refuse to be **Multi-Dimensional**, usually make that choice because they feel their intercourse game is strong enough to *get the job done.* These Brothers often fail to realize there are *different* ways to skin a cat, because they feel that their intercourse game is strong enough to skin *any* cat. They fail to understand that women are *different* from men, and therefore may need their cat skinned *differently.* These Brothers fail to understand that a woman may only be able to reach **Point 'O'** one way, and that one way may *not* include intercourse. Brothers often view intercourse as their ***trump card*** and often play that ***trump card*** every hand, so it may require their partner to stress otherwise. It requires communication by both parties. Here's a safe ***Rule of Thumb*** for all of you **One-Dimensional** men out there: **"If you truly want to be Multi-Dimensional, you have to become a Lesbian *trapped* in a man's body."** If you take that ***Rule of Thumb*** at face value you'll miss the point, because the transformation has to be *mental* and *emotional,* as well as *physical.* And just think ladies, if you can teach him the *different* ways to skin a cat, you could have a **Multi-Dimensional** star on your hands (*regardless of Race*).

That said, ladies you can't conclude someone's selfish if you've failed to communicate. Many men don't understand that it's often the build-up that sets the stage (i.e., *mental* and *emotional foreplay*), and they'll never know this unless there's communication. At the same time, you shouldn't expect good service if you're allowing someone to just pass through town. After all, the regular customers always get (*or give*) the best service. If you make it cheap, don't be surprised if that's what you get in return.

Selfishness is a trait that all men share (*regardless of Race*), because most societies on this planet tell us that it's a woman's duty to service her man in the manner that he prefers to be serviced. Not performing a certain service for your partner is a flaw that can be ***rectified***, so this gives Brothers a ton of upside. On the flipside, ***requiring*** a certain service from your partner is a flaw that White Men have been allowed to exploit for personal gain for decades. White Men expect and often demand fellatio, just like they expect to get all of the high paying *jobs* (*no pun intended*). Brothers talk about fellatio the same way they talk about money. When you're poor you talk about money. When you *don't* get fellatio you talk about fellatio. With Brothers the bottom line is still intercourse, so this leaves *plenty* of room for foreplay *(mental, emotional* and *physical),* but it better be early in the ballgame. With Brothers fellatio is nothing more than foreplay, and foreplay is just that, foreplay. Fellatio is often nothing more than selfish *physical* foreplay, because it leaves little room for *mental* or *emotional* foreplay.

With White Guys, fellatio is often the ***end all*** and ***be all.*** I can't think of a better example of this than the *42nd* President of the United States. A thick juicy woman like Monica Lewinsky and Pres. Clinton never wanted anything but fellatio. That's why I laugh when I hear that bullshit about Bill Clinton being the first Black President. If Bill Clinton had some Black in him, there would never have been any evidence on a **Blue Dress.** There may have been some evidence **6** months down the road, but it would've been growing inside of a **Blue Maternity Dress.** If he was Black, there certainly would've been *plenty* of evidence in the Oval Office. Someone would've sat down on a chair and it would've collapsed. Someone would've sat down on the couch, and noticed that it was getting wobbly. Someone would've noticed stains on the couch cushions and flipped them over. Someone would've noticed Ms. Lewinsky leaving the Oval Office looking like she'd just gotten off of the **Tilt-a-Whirl.** Someone would've noticed that President Clinton always ordered the entire White House menu immediately after Ms. Lewinsky left (*or sometimes while she was still there*). I respect Pres. Clinton, but trust me, he's all White.

Like I said, White Guys prefer fellatio over intercourse. They'll Deny it, but fellatio is what they crave. White Guys want intercourse in the beginning of the relationship, just like all guys, but they grow tired of the relationship in a hurry if they don't get fellatio. The *two* main reasons White Guys prefer fellatio are:

1 They're used to being waited on, and served, and taken care of, and catered to (i.e., *they're spoiled*).

2 There is less pressure to perform. It's easy when all you have to do is lay back and let someone else do all of the work. For some men it's tough to perform every time, especially if she requires intercourse to get to **Point 'O'.**

White Guys expect to reach **Point 'O'** when they receive fellatio, so this tells you the importance they place on it. If a man reaches **Point 'O'** first, the woman might find herself shit out of luck. Maybe this is one of the reasons for the explosion in Sex toy sales. A recent study by Berman Center, Elexa by Trojan, and Durex cited the following figures:

- **29 %** of women, ages **25** to **60,** currently use Sexual aids.

- **23 %** of women say they've taken their vibrators along on vacation.

- **60 %** of Sexually active women want Sex more often.

These figures are staggering when you think about it. Let's take one more look at them. Nearly **three** out every **ten** women between the ages of *25* and *60* use Sexual aids. Nearly *one* out of every *four* women takes their vibrator on vacation. Why would a woman ever feel the need to take a vibrator on vacation? Remember now, Black Folks don't work, so we don't go on vacation. *Six* out of every *ten* Sexually active women want Sex more often. Justice Thomas told us that according to our national history, Black Men wouldn't let any problems like this occur. This study tells us there are a lot of White Men who enjoy being **One-Dimensional.** I really thought White Guys were going to turn things around and raise their game when Viagra came onto the scene. First of all let's be clear, Viagra is primarily a White Male drug. Just in case there's any doubt in your mind, here's why Viagra is primarily a White Male drug:

NOTE: Any specific reference to Viagra is meant as a reference to all Erectile Dysfunction Drugs. I figure if I say Viagra you'll know exactly what I'm talking about.

- It was developed by White Men for White Men (according to Justice Thomas, Black Men don't have *equipment* malfunctions).
- Erectile Dysfunction drugs are a multi-BILLION ***DOLLAR*** industry, and Black Men are either unemployed or incarcerated, so we're not the ones buying the shit.
- These drugs require a prescription from a doctor. This means you need to have medical insurance. This means you need a job. Remember, Black Folks don't work.
- Health reasons. Black Men, especially older Black Men, have high rates of cardiovascular disease (*thanks to genetics and all that damn pork we Love so much*). A doctor would be rolling the dice if he prescribed it to someone with cardiovascular problems, and doctors don't like to roll the dice these days (*lawsuits and malpractice insurance*).
- Our government often subsidizes Erectile Dysfunction drugs. Do you really think they'd subsidize a drug that was helping Black Men have Sex? **Hell No!** Can you imagine the outrage if a Black Man raped a White Woman, and he had a bottle of government subsidized Viagra in his pocket? On the other hand, **NBC's** pedophile news show **"To Catch a Predator,"** lures in men who are looking to meet children for Sex, and occasionally these men show up with a bottle of Viagra in their pocket (*and you don't hear a peep from the* Sex Police). Trust me, if Black Men were using this shit in large numbers, there would be restrictions out the ass. Instead, there are free sample giveaways at clinics.

- Viagra is rapidly becoming the most used drug on college campuses. Currently **6 %** of men on college campuses say they use Erectile Dysfunction drugs regularly. As the **6 %** continues to rapidly grow each year, the number of Black Males on campus continues to shrink. Studies have also shown that condom usage is less likely to occur when these young men are popping their erection pills. Wow, a drug that can induce *recreational* unprotected Sex, and still no outcry from the Sex Police. Well, for better or worse, Black Men have proven that they don't need a prescription drug to have *recreational* unprotected Sex.

- The Catholic Church, the Evangelicals, and Conservatives, serve as America's Sex Police, and they've never complained about the use of Viagra. Nor have they complained about the excess advertising of Erectile Dysfunction drugs. These people are staunchly anti-contraception because they believe that contraceptive devices such as condoms and the pill condone *recreational* Sex. Viagra is without question a *recreational* Sex drug, and the Sex Police have been silent from day one. There's no doubt the overwhelming majority of men who take Viagra, do so for *recreational* Sex, and not **Pro-creational** Sex. Can you imagine the uproar if a *recreational* Sex drug was created for women? The uproar over the *Plan 'B' Pill* (LEVONORGESTROL) provides the answer to the above question. The *Plan 'B' Pill* is used as a contraceptive, and is offered to female rape victims at most non-Catholic hospitals. The *Plan 'B' Pill* is slated to receive FDA approval to be sold over-the-counter, possibly in 2006, and I'm sure the Sex Police will be on hand to voice their displeasure. For now, women can obtain a prescription for this medication if they engaged in intercourse and a condom-break occurred (you've got *72* hrs.). Unlike Viagra, which has numerous health risks, the *Plan 'B' Pill* has no such risk. Unlike Viagra, the *Plan 'B' Pill* does **NOT** increase risky Sexual behavior. Unlike Viagra, the *Plan 'B' Pill* has **NOT** gotten a free ride from the Sex Police, but has instead felt their wrath, because they feel it would condone *recreational* Sex. What type of Sexual behavior does Viagra create? The bottom line is, the Sex Police would never dream of biting the hand that feeds their collection plates and their re-election campaigns, and that hand belongs to **White Males**.

Viagra is a White Mans drug, period. I'm not knocking it one bit, because if I ever started having E.D., I'd damn sure get me a prescription. But just think about this shit. Erectile Dysfunction drugs are a multi-

BILLION **DOLLAR** industry, but **60 %** of women want Sex more often. That means there are a lot of men who aren't getting the job done, even with the aid of E.D. drugs. That means there are a lot of **One-Dimensional** motherfuckers out there. That means a lot of White Men must be popping that *little blue pill*, getting their dose of fellatio, and then it's off to sleep *("Fend for yourself baby, goodniiiight...zzzzzzzzz").*

Like I said before, ***there are no absolutes.*** I know some White Guys who know how to handle their *bizzness*, and I know some Black Guys who *don't* know how to handle their *bizzness*. What I find amazing is how White Guys continue to get by, even though they sell themselves short by being **One-Dimensional**. There are also a lot of **One-Dimensional** Brothers out there, but remember what NFL coaches and scouts always say: ***"You can't teach Speed."*** Now replace the word *Speed* with the *'S'*-word that supposedly *Doesn't Matter,* and what you end up with is *more potential* and *more upside.*

B.T.P.

I'm sure you're saying the *differences* I just rattled off are all conjecture and vague generalizations. I'll admit that countless conversations with no more than a few hundred guys is probably too small of a sample to draw any definitive conclusions. These are just witnessed behaviors that can be easily scrutinized and easily criticized, and can't truly be measured. At least that's what critics and skeptics are saying right now as they read this. I'll certainly admit that not everyone falls within the parameters of these vague generalizations and locker room-type comments. But anyone that refuses to admit there are *differences* between White Men and Black Men is simply in Denial. White Men and Black Men prefer *different* types of women physically. White Men and Black Men have *different* agendas once they get a woman. White Men can be selfish because of **what they want a woman to do to them.** Black Men can be selfish because of **what they want to do to a woman.**

There are major *differences* between Black Men and White Men, but how can these *differences* be viewed objectively? After all, you can see many of these *differences* **outside of the bedroom**, but those particular *differences* can be interpreted *differently.* There is *no* ambiguity *inside of the bedroom*, and there are *no different* interpretations *inside of the bedroom.* So for those of you who really want to see the *difference* there's a way, and it's right at your finger tips.

Chapter 4 BLACK PORN:
"The Proof is in the Chocolate Pudding"

"For better or worse, whatever Sexuality an actor has they bring to their part, just like they bring their sense of humor, and their intelligence, and their wit."

Actress Ellen Barkin

I figure if Ms. Barkin's comment applies to mainstream movies (**VOLUME I**), then it would certainly apply to porn. Porn is obviously the extreme end of the Sexual spectrum, but it's still quite telling. First of all, I'm not advocating the viewing of pornography. You gotta do what works for you. All I'm saying is, the premise of **"Once you go Black, you don't go Back"** is *There's a Difference* between Black Men and White Men. If you want to see the *difference* with your own eyes, pornography would be one avenue. Before I start rolling, I want to re-emphasize this book's title.

The full title of this book is **White Men Can't Hump (As Good As Black Men).** I hope my White Readers understand that I'm not saying *'White Men Can't'*, I'm just saying, if **"The *language* throughout the history of this country"** is true, then Black Men must be better. Keep in mind; it is White Men who created the *language* about the Black Penis and the Black Male Sexual prowess. It is White Men who spread that *language* to the masses for centuries. *Unlike* those White Men and *unlike* Justice Thomas, all I'm doing is putting that *language* in its proper context. *Penis Size* and *Sexual Prowess* are negative traits when linked to Black Men, but are much sought after positive traits when linked to White Men. You can't have it both ways White America, at least not in *My Book*. So what does porn tell us?

Saying one group does something better than another group is just another way of saying there's a *difference*. The *difference* must be tangible, and the *difference* must be viewed objectively. Sex or *Making Love* is not a timed event and there's no scoring system, so it may seem difficult to determine if there's an actual *difference*. You certainly couldn't judge Sex like Olympic Ice Skating or Olympic Gymnastics. In those two physical activities, any *differences* are unnoticeable to the untrained eye. Unless there's a major gaffe or a fall, to the untrained eye they all look the same.

Judging those two physical activities is obviously somewhat subjective, but the trained eye is able to detect the noticeable *differences*. Sometimes you can observe something and your senses tell you there's a *difference*. Sometimes your common sense and your ability to reason tells you there's a *difference*. Well folks, I'm here to tell you, you don't need a specially trained eye to see the *differences* between White Male porn stars and Black Male porn stars. The *differences* in terms of performance will slap you right upside the head. Anyone who can't see the *difference* is not only judging subjectively, they're judging based on Denial. Before I delve any deeper into this subject, I want to show you that I'm not the only person in this country who's watched a few dirty movies. Here's some statistics about pornography from some very reputable sources:

The Oprah Winfrey Show (ABC)
November, 2005
Subject: "Porn Addiction"
- Pornography generates *57* BILLION ***DOLLAR$*** annually worldwide.
- Pornography generates *10* BILLION ***DOLLAR$*** annually in the U.S.
- *11,000* new movies are made annually.
- Those *11,000* new movie titles generate *20* BILLION ***DOLLAR$*** annually.
- DVD rentals generate *800* Million ***DOLLAR$*** annually.
- Porn is the # *1* business on the Internet.
- There are more than *4* Million Pornographic Websites.
- ¼ of all Internet search engine requests are porn related (*68* Million per day).
- *70 %* of all Internet porn traffic occurs during the *9* am to *5* pm workday.

Rita Cosby Live & Direct (MSNBC)
December, 2005
Subject: "Porn Valley"
- Pornography generates *57* BILLION ***DOLLAR$*** annually worldwide.
- Pornography generates *12* BILLION ***DOLLAR$*** annually in the U.S.
- *40* Million people visit Pornographic Websites daily.
- *70 %* of men between the ages of *18* and *34* look at porn at least once a month.

- *20 %* of men and *13 %* of women look at porn at work.
- *70 %* of all Internet porn traffic occurs during the *9* am to *5* pm workday.
- Pornography on 'Cell Phones' and 'IPODS' will earn *1* BILLION *DOLLAR$* in 2006 and that figure is expected to double over the next four years.

The availability of porn tells you what role it plays in our society: Good old-fashioned magazines, DVD's, IPOD's, Satellite Dish for your home, access to porn movies in most major hotels, and now Wireless Communications. Don't worry, I didn't forget the 'Crack Cocaine' of Pornography, the Internet. The Internet is the great facilitator, because it not only provides pornographic images, it also provides private accessibility. Consumers now have the opportunity to purchase porn-related products in the privacy of their home. The DVD industry and the Sex aid industry (*magic potions, toys, etc.*) have exploded thanks to the Internet. I think it's safe to say the annual *DOLLAR* figure of *57* BILLION will probably continue to grow. What's the purpose of all of this information? To show how prevalent pornography is in our society. As part of my research for this chapter, I viewed a lot of porn. I'll share my findings in the most appropriate way possible. I won't be *X-Rated,* but I won't be *PG-13* either.

Black Male porn stars exemplify what Justice Thomas so painfully and shamefully described to the Senate Judiciary Committee (see **History**, **VOLUME I**). These men exemplify the physical gifts that Justice Thomas was so embarrassed about, and they also exemplify the willingness and the ability to use those physical gifts. Make no doubt about it, these Brothers have been blessed and any man who states otherwise is in Denial. Can every Black Man perform like the Black Male porn star? Absolutely not. But history has told us Black Men have the tools to get the job done, and the willingness to use those tools. Now take those factors into account, and then read Ms. Barkin's quote again:

"For better or worse, whatever Sexuality an actor has they bring to their part, just like they bring their sense of humor, and their intelligence, and their wit."

It paints a very compelling picture, doesn't it? The picture isn't complete until you have something to compare it to. When you compare the Black Male porn star, to the White Male porn star, you realize there's no comparison at all. If I objectively made a list of the top *10* male porn stars, I'd be hard pressed to place one current White Male porn star on the list.

I'm not saying there aren't any good White Male porn stars, because there are. I'm just saying the Black Male porn stars are *"that"* much better. It's not even close. The Black Male porn stars are better performers physically (i.e., *the tools*), and they're better performers overall (i.e., *the willingness to use the tools*). They also get a more genuine and more realistic response from the actresses. The *difference* is astounding. If you don't believe me, then I suggest you do your own research. If you want to see movies with real sweat, real moans, and *seizure-like* orgasms, then I suggest you check out any of the following Black Male porn stars:

- Mark Anthony
- Mr. BiGG
- Boz
- Shane Diesel
- Byron Long
- Justin Long
- Charlie Mac
- Mandingo
- Sean Michaels
- Mr. Marcus
- Jack Napier
- Wesley Pipes
- Justin Slayer
- Sledgehammer
- Jake Steed
- Lexington Steele
- Ray Victory- Ray was one of the few Black porn stars of the 1980's who actually got to work with many of the top female porn stars, regardless of Race.

These Black Male porn stars can be seen in: **Chasing the Big Ones** (*series*), Lexington Steele's- **Heavy Metal** (*series*), Jack Napier's- **There's Something About Jack** (*series*), Mandingo's- **Mandingo** (*series*), Sean Michael's- **We Go Deep** (*series*), Sledgehammer's- **The Biggest Black Girth on Earth** (*series*), Jake Steed's- **Little White Chicks and Big Black Monster Dicks** (*series*), **I Can't Believe I Took The Whole Thing** (*series*) or the **Brotha Lover** (*series*). I listed these Brothers alphabetically, but if I had to pick a top 5, John Holmes and Ron Jeremy in their primes wouldn't crack the list. The only way to accurately assess the *differences* is to do comparisons. You have to compare the performances of the female porn stars, not just the males. I'm not going to list any female porn stars by name, but I'll tell you what to look for in order to see the *differences* with your own eyes. There are a number of female porn stars (*both Black and*

White), that work with the top White Male porn stars, and also work with the top Black Male porn stars. These female porn stars are the measuring stick that I used to reach my conclusion. Here's the **Judging Criteria** that I used:

- **The Fingers & Toes Don't Lie** - Are the toes curled? Are the fingernails digging in the back or shoulders of the male porn star? Are the fist clinched? Does she have a fist full of sheets? I've viewed female porn stars exhibit these reflexes with Black Male porn stars, and then viewed *the same* females **not** exhibit these reflexes with White Male porn stars. These are spontaneous reflexes and they are not contrived in any way. The Fingers & Toes don't lie. What does this tell you? I believe it tells you *two* things. With many of the White Male porn stars you're viewing people *acting* out Sexual activity. With many of the Black Male porn stars you're viewing great Sex, which doesn't require any *acting* at all.

- **Where Do The Moans Come From?** - Female porn stars are obviously *gettin' paid* to give a performance. To be believable, these girls have perfected the art of screams, moans, and dirty talk. They can all do it, and most of them do it rather convincingly. How can you determine what's real and what's an act? Listen closely and determine where the screams and moans are coming from. If they come primarily from the mouth and throat, she's probably *acting*. If the screams and moans come from the gut, she's probably **not** *acting*. After all, she can create louder screams and moans from her mouth and throat. She can create better sounds and clearer sounds from her mouth and throat. When it comes from the gut it's real, it's not *acting*. The trash talking many female porn stars like to do is often put on the shelf when they're with a Black Male porn star. They don't need to talk trash or scream or moan or act. Quite often you can't understand what these ladies are saying when they're with a Black Male porn star. It's like they're speaking in *tongues* or some shit. When the screams and moans come from the gut, it's real.

- **Reaching Point 'O'** - Female porn stars are no *different* from women out here in the real world. Meaning, I'm sure they know how to fake an orgasm. I'm sure I wouldn't know if a woman was faking an orgasm or not; I'll give you that one. But as a trained paramedic I know when someone is faking a *seizure*, so when I see a *seizure-like* orgasm I know it's real. For one thing, the *seizure-like* orgasm is usually accompanied by moans from the gut, curled toes, and clenched fist. The body convulsions and the eyes rolling back in the head tell you everything you need to know. The absolute proof that it was a real orgasm is when the *"Scene Cuts Away"* and then returns. This tells you it was a real orgasm because she needed a time-out, she was still tingling. My point is, if you can successfully fake an orgasm, why exert all that extra energy to fake a *seizure*. The *seizure-like* orgasms are not fake and you routinely see them with Black Male porn stars. With White Male porn stars, you rarely see the *seizure-like* orgasm. When you do, it's often because there are several female porn stars who tend to have them with everyone they work with.

These are reflexes and reactions that any untrained observer can spot. There's a *difference* between Black Men and White Men, and even though porn is the extreme end of the Sexual spectrum, I again refer you to Ellen Barkin's quote. Whatever qualities you have off of the screen, you'll bring with you on the screen. The Black Male porn stars are bringing **"the language throughout the history of this country"** to the screen. With *90 %* of the White Male porn stars, the female porn stars appear to be *acting*. With *90 %* of the Black Male porn stars, the female porn stars are having incredible Sex. You don't need a trained eye, but if you can't see the *difference* then feel free to use my **Judging Criteria.** Just like the old saying goes, *"The proof is in the pudding."* That said; I want to pay respect to a few current White Male porn stars who know how to handle their *bizzness*:

- Julian
- Rocco Siffredi
- Billy Glide
- Mark Davis
- Evan Stone
- Lee Stone
- Randy Spears
- And the ageless Peter North

I would also like to pay respect to a few White Male porn stars of the past:

- John Holmes
- Ron Jeremy
- Dick Rambone

The White Male porn stars I just listed are very good, they're just not better, that's all. I know that sounds rude, but it's the truth. If I was really trying to be rude I could waste a couple of pages by listing all of the White Male porn stars who are *Average* or flat out suck. There are about *100* guys I could list, past and present, who flat out suck. Physically, they bring very little to the table, and in terms of performance, they *Average 3* to *5* pumps per minute so it's like watching snails mate. They remind me of my old platoon sergeant's favorite saying: ***"They look like a monkey trying to fuck a football** (I'll warn you now, I Love this saying so much that I also used it once in* **VOLUME I.** *My old platoon sergeant had many variations of this saying, and all of them were equally hilarious.)."*

There's not only a *difference* in the abilities of the male porn stars, there's also a *difference* in their on-screen priorities. I don't know if these priorities are established by the White directors or by the White Male porn stars, but there's certainly a *difference* in their on-screen priorities when compared to the on-screen priorities of Black Male porn stars. One possibility for the *different* on-screen priorities could be the White Director's expectations may be limited by the White Male porn star's abilities. Another possibility for the *different* on-screen priorities could be customer satisfaction. Even though most porn scenes start the same way and follow a similar sequence, there is a major *difference* in the time allocated for each Sexual position or each Sexual act. White Male porn stars spend *twice* as much time receiving fellatio, so I guess they're giving their customers what they want to see. Every damn scene in White porn starts off with a *Blow Job* that seems to last an hour. The scene-opening fellatio seems to last longer than the actual intercourse. Scenes with Black Male porn stars also start off with fellatio, but the fellatio is foreplay and certainly doesn't last longer than intercourse. If these directors and actors are merely giving their paying customers what they want to see, then they're also acknowledging there's a *difference* in what Black consumers want to see and what White consumers want to see. Over *30* years ago the success of the movie **Deep Throat** told us that White Men prefer seeing the Sexual emphasis placed on fellatio. **Deep Throat** was made for *25,000 DOLLAR$* and has grossed more than *$600 Million,* making it one of the most profitable films ever made. Before **Deep Throat**, fellatio was considered *taboo* by many. After **Deep Throat**, fellatio was at the top of the White Male Sexual mountain. *Life imitates Art and Art imitates Life.*

When it comes to anal Sex, I don't know if Art is imitating Life. There's no doubt pornography is an inadvertent Sex education tool for Millions, if not BILLIONS of people. When it comes to anal Sex I think pornography has become a trend setter, so maybe *Life is imitating Art.*

This seems to be the new Sexual phenomenon, and it got its big boost from White porn. You see it in practically every scene anymore. The Black porn stars are doing it also, but not as much as the White porn stars. You have to wonder if it's all about finding a smaller orifice. A smaller tighter orifice could make an *Average* man feel *Above Average*. Maybe it's about creating some real screams instead of fake screams. This particular activity has certainly been around as long as mankind has, but currently it seems to be gaining more and more mainstream popularity. Every Sex book I mentioned in the **SIZE DOESN'T MATTER** chapter discussed anal Sex in detail. Anal Sex was even discussed on **Sex and the City**. So which one is it, is *Art imitating Life* or is *Life imitating Art?* We'll never definitively know if the porn industry is just following societies lead, or if society is just following the porn industry's lead. Whatever the case, the porn industry seems to be giving the consumers what they want to see. I guess that in itself is progress, because it wasn't always like that. For a long time people had to watch a lot of boring porn. You knew it was boring, but it was all you had. Now that most of the legal and constitutional barriers have been knocked down by White porn, the door has been opened for Black porn.

Many of the Black Male porn stars I listed earlier are also successful directors and producers. These Black Male porn stars obviously don't make the enormous **DOLLAR$** that mainstream "A-List" Black Actors make. But they do seem to have more artistic Sexual freedom and more entrepreneurial opportunities than the "A-List" Black Actors. Then again, if you're making *8* figures per film, like the mainstream "A-List" Black Actors are, you really don't need to be an entrepreneur. Still, when you consider how far the Black Male porn star has come since the days of VHS and beta-max, it's quite impressive. Back then you could count the Black Male porn stars and the Black Female porn stars on one hand, and still have a couple of fingers left. There were obviously more Black Female porn stars available for White porn than Black Males, (*Black on Black porn was virtually non-existent in those days*). You basically had *4* or *5* Black Female porn stars that every White Male porn star got numerous shots at. You never seemed to have *more than one* Black Male porn star at a time, and you always knew what girl they were going to end up with in every movie. Now that the industry is no longer as segregated as it once was, it's much more colorful so to speak. The Black Male porn stars of today get to work with many of the top female porn stars regardless of their Race. They now get the opportunity to *crush* the top White, Black, Latino, and Asian female porn stars. It's reminiscent of **Prince's** 1980 song **UPTOWN** when he sang: ***"White, Black, Puerto Rican, everybody's just a Freakin."***

That's not to say there's no Racism in the world of porn anymore, because there is. Many of the top starlets and top contract girls refuse to work with Black Male porn stars. Occasionally a top White starlet will creep to the **Dark Side** for a *pay day*, but not too often. **99 %** of the top contract starlets are White, but even the non-White contract starlets avoid Black Male porn stars at all cost. The European Females have been more than willing to pick up the slack. They look just as good as the White American starlets, and they're not worried about fucking up their hair or fucking up their nails. The bottom line is, the European girls don't discriminate and many of the top White American starlets do. Why does this matter? This matters because they prove my point. My point has nothing to do with Inter-Racial Sex. The **Judging Criteria** that I used only considered women who've worked with both groups of men. Withoutnaming names, I can honestly say that every major ethnic group that makes up our nation was represented. All I was looking for was female porn stars who've worked with both Black Male porn stars and White Male porn stars. I then compared their performances. This has nothing to do with Inter-Racial Sex and everything to do with the *differences* between Black Men and White Men, and who's Sexually **better.** Black Male porn stars are better than White Male porn stars, and the women who refuse to work with Black Male porn stars confirm this. What's the first thing female porn stars always say when they're interviewed? They always give you something along the line of:

"It's not really *Sex*."
"It's just a *job*."
"It's only *acting*."

If it's not really Sex, or if it's just a *job*, or if it's only *acting*, then why would you refuse to work with someone based solely on their Race? Are these women trying to bullshit us by sugar-coating their profession? The answer is *No*; they're *not* trying to bullshit us. They're being completely honest because it's not *really* Sex, it truly is just a *job*, and it's only *acting,* when they're performing with a White Male porn star. Can you imagine Julia Roberts outright refusing to be on screen (i.e., *act*) with Denzel Washington in the **Pelican Brief?** Even though there was *no* on-screen contact between Denzel and Julia, there was still *plenty* of *acting* right, it was still just a *job*, right?

I'm sure some of these White starlets are indeed Racists, and they obviously still embrace the Racist ideals they were raised with. You'd often see these girls on **Howard Stern (E! TV),** and he'd always get around to asking them if they've ever worked with a Black Guy. They'd spit out an emphatic **NO** before he could finish the question. He'd ask why and they'd always giggle and give a *half*-assed *"I don't know I just haven't"* type of answer. You could always see the truth right through their giggles. I'm sure some of the White starlets also refuse to work with Black Male porn stars because they don't want to upset their fans. No doubt, the same type of fans that Arnon Milshan referred to in the **Hollywood SECTION** of **VOLUME I**. Racism and Racist fans certainly play a role in their refusals, but bigotry is not the primary reason many of the top White starlets refuse to work with Black Male porn stars. The clear-cut primary reason is these ladies have White boyfriends or husbands, who also act as their managers. Isn't it amazing how everything just sort of wraps itself into one nice neat package? You've got some **Small-Poleons Complex,** and some **"Fear of the Black Penis,"** and some *"Once she goes Black, she may not come Back,"* all wrapped up into one nice neat package. *Fear* is considered the greatest motivator, and when *Fear* makes you turn money making opportunities down, there's more at play than just a *job*.

These White boyfriend/husband/managers often stand there and watch their starlet girlfriend/wife perform with other White Men, and they don't have a problem with it. After all, it's not *real*, they're only *acting*, and it's just a *job*. Many of these White boyfriend/husband/managers are in the business themselves, so they *really* do view it as just *acting*, or just a *job*. That is, as long as their starlet girlfriend/wife is with another White Male. Think about that for a second. These men can stand there and watch their women have Sex with other men, even two or three men at the same time, and it doesn't bother them one bit. It doesn't bother them one bit because they don't consider it Sex; they consider it *acting*, and they consider it just a *job*. At the same time, they won't allow their starlet girlfriend/wife to work with a Black Male porn star. Why is that? The reason is, they know if their girlfriend/wife is with a Black Male porn star she won't have to *fake moan*, and she won't have *act*, because the Sex will be **real**, and their husband/ boyfriend/managers also know that it'll be **real good**, as in *better* than themselves.

These men confirm the *difference* with their refusal. I'm not crying Racism here, I'm applauding in laughter. I'm applauding because their **Fear of the Black Penis,** and their *Fear* of the White starlet *"Going Black and not coming Back,"* proves my point. There is a *difference* and now you don't have to take my word for it, and you don't have to take Justice Thomas's word for it. Now all you have to do is trust the actions of the professionals.

The people who get *bizzy* for a living say **Yes** there is a *difference*.

The people who get *bizzy* for a living say this book's cover is true.

The people who claim it's just a *job*, and claim that it's just *acting*, are acknowledging that when it's done with the best, it's not just a *job*, and it's not just *acting*, it's **real**.

Now let's play a little game.

RANT: "The Death Row Game"

Much of this **SECTION** is based on several of the well known perceptions/*Stereotypes* about Black Men. None of these things are new; I just wanted to put everything in a more positive light. These are things that Black Men deal with practically everyday. White America embraces these *Stereotypes* and considers them to be true, especially when they're applied negatively. I personally have no problem with many of the perceptions, because I've always realized that many of them were based on jealousy. Many of the perceptions also have historical significance, as Justice Thomas reminded us. Many of the *Stereotypes* are factually based and will never go away. When you consider the present day physical perceptions of Black Men, it doesn't take a genius to understand that *Stereotyping* is bound to occur. If *ten* guys were going to start a pick-up basketball game, and *nine* of the guys were *6* ft. *4* in. White Guys and the *tenth* guy was a *5* ft. *11* in. Black Guy, the Black Guy would still be one of the *first* players chosen. If you took those same *ten* guys and wanted to have relay races, the Black Guy would certainly be one of the first guys chosen. Would the same *"pick-up game"* theory apply if the physical activity was Sex? In **VOLUME I,** Gov. Arnold Schwarzenegger explained in the movie **Pumping Iron** that a *Great Workout* was like Sex. The Governor explained that *the feeling of euphoria* you get during and after a workout is like an orgasm. I personally agreed with the Governor, and then developed the following math equation to support the Governor's statement. The math equation was **Sex + Emotion** = *Making Love*. If you believe that equation is true, then you would also agree that **Sex – Emotion** = *A Great Workout (when it's done right)*. So again I ask, would the same *"pick-up game"* theory apply if the physical activity was Sex? Let's play **"The Death Row Game."**

NOTE: I'm writing this in a manner that would appeal to women, but I certainly encourage all of my readers to read along. Okay ladies, I need you to imagine that you're on Death Row and in exactly *12* hours you're going to be executed.

Welcome to Death Row, I'm the warden, and I'm here to inform you that all of your appeals have been denied. Your execution will take place in exactly *12* hours. I want you to know that I'm a fair warden, a kind warden, and a humane warden. I want you to know that I believe your last *12* hours should be a happy *12* hours. It's now noon, and your friends and family aren't scheduled to arrive until *6* pm. Your last meal request will also be ready at *6* pm. The representative of your faith will be here to pray with you after *6* pm. I realize your psychological condition is not very good right now. Knowing that your life will end in a matter of hours has to be an emotional meat grinder. I concur with your sentence, but I also believe being put to death is quite *inhumane*. So what I'd like to do is offer you the opportunity to feel *human* one last time. This offer will help to ease your mind and also help you momentarily escape your fear and anxiety. This offer will allow you to be a free *human being* one last time. I've chosen two of my most trusted guards, and they're here for your pleasure. You're free to choose whichever one you like, and you've got *6* hours of absolute privacy to do whatever you choose. I don't know what you prefer, so the *two* guards I've chosen are completely *different* from each other.

> **Guard # 1-** Is a *25* year-old White Male, *6* ft tall, *180* lbs., and is incredibly handsome, just like one of those young Hollywood movie stars.

> **Guard # 2-** Is a *25* year-old Black Male, *6* ft. tall, *230* lbs., and is incredibly built, just like one of those young NFL linebackers.

Who would you choose ladies? Obviously whoever you chose is basically a personal vote for who you believe would be the best *bizznessman*. Your choice has nothing to do with Love. Your choice has everything to do with enjoying the most natural and the most pleasurable physical activity that humans experience. Your choice is about wanting that experience to be a great experience one last time. Who did you choose? Feel free to go to www.whitemencanthump.com and play **The Death Row Game**.

P.S. - Everyone please remember to always practice *C.L.R.* **Sex.**

B.T.P.

I hope you had as much fun reading this **SECTION** as I did writing it. I'm sure some of you are as uncomfortable reading about Sex as you are talking about Race. My hope is that this **SECTION** and the next **SECTION** help to make these *taboo* subjects a little less *taboo*. Sex & Race have been the backdrop to so much of America's social make-up, that being uncomfortable is merely an excuse for being blind. I'd be willing to bet quite a few eyes have been opened by now. Sex is the one natural activity that shows our common traits as well as our *differences*. Our *Cultural* and *Physical differences* are usually discussed in an *outside of the bedroom* format, under the term *Stereotypes*. *Stereotypes* don't have to be a negative, and if people understood how and when to apply them a lot of hostility could be averted. One of the big problems with *Stereotypes* is they give people an easy way out. *Stereotypes* make people lazy because it's much easier to apply a *Stereotype*, than it is to actually take the time to get to know someone. When people don't know someone who's *different* from them, they often take the *Stereotype short-cut*. This way, they can feel like they know the person without actually talking to them. There are no absolutes when dealing with individuals, and this is how mole hills become mountains. Judging one person based on the preconceived notions of an entire group, is often a recipe for **Devaluation**. The next **SECTION** will take a look at Racial perceptions in America, and will explore America's great Racial Divide. The only time we acknowledge the great Racial Divide is when a major event occurs that has blatant Racial implications. When the Racial implications are dealt, they're referred to as **Race Cards**. Let's play some **Race Cards** shall we.

SECTION VI RACE CARDS

Race relations in America are often like a game of cards. You've got to know when to show your cards (i.e., *your true feelings*) and you've got to know when to hold your cards (i.e., *not over-react*). It can also be like a house of cards and come crashing down on you if you're careless. The **History SECTION** of **VOLUME I** covered America's Racial past. This **SECTION** will cover America's Racial present. **SECTION VII (CLOSING THE DIVIDE)** will touch on America's Racial future. Throughout both **VOLUMES** of this book numerous Myths have been addressed, so now it's time to take a look at the *Cause* of many of these Myths, *Stereotypes.*

Chapter 1 Stereotypes

Def: Stereotype- "A standardized conception or image invested with special meaning, and held in common by members of a *group*"

Stereotypes aren't really a bad thing; it's the application of *Stereotypes* that creates the problems. Once a *Stereotype* has been applied, you'll know if it was the proper application or not, because the person on the receiving end will let you know. We all apply *Stereotypes* to each other everyday. Some *Stereotypes* are somewhat *fair* (i.e., most Black Folks like barbecue ribs). Some *Stereotypes* are *unfair* (i.e., most Black Folks like barbecue ribs, and most White Folks also like barbecue ribs, you just don't hear about it). Some *Stereotypes* are negative and offensive, and we all know what most of them are. Usually *Stereotypes* are nothing more than **assumptions** or **presumptions** applied to an *individual* or a *group*. I personally look at *Stereotypes* like this:

• When a *Stereotype* is applied to an *individual* it's an **assumption,** because every *individual* is as unique as a set of fingerprints.

Example: You can't **assume** the Black Guy who works down the hallway in the Sales Dept. likes barbecue ribs, if you've never even taken the time to get to know him.

• When a *Stereotype* is applied to a *group* it's a **presumption,** meaning there's probably some evidence (*fair* or *unfair*) that supports a particular belief.

"Life is too short to Hate"

Example: It's easy to **presume** all Black Folks like barbecue ribs because every time you drive past Reggie's Rib Shack, on your way home from work, you see a long line of Black Folks. You've based this **presumption** on factual evidence that you've seen with your own eyes. But if you had asked a few questions, you would've discovered that Reggie's Rib Shack is the only fast food joint in the neighborhood, and you would've also discovered that Reggie's Rib Shack has some *good-ass-food* for a *great-ass-price.*

Because America has such a cruel and insensitive past and present, quite often an **assumption** or **presumption** can be deemed offensive. I'm sure all of this sounds pretty basic, but **History** tells us *it's* not. All you have to do is read a major newspaper, or watch cable news, and you'll see that rarely does a week go by in America without giving us an example that *some people just don't get it,* and *some people just don't want to get it.* Here's a story from my childhood that brings together every aspect of how *Stereotypes* affect us, and more importantly, how they should be handled.

In the late 1970's, a White Friend of mine invited me over to his house to play some basketball. He also asked me to bring some other guys along. He stated that his mother was on her way to the store and that he'd have her buy some sodas for everyone. I rounded up *4* guys (*1* White and *3* Black) and we went to my friend's house to play basketball. We played basketball non-stop for an hour, and then we decided it was time for a beverage break. My White Friend then brought out a six pack of ice cold **Grape Crush**. One of my Black Friends then promptly lost his fucking mind and wanted to fight. He said:

"What's up with this fuckin' Grape Crush shit?"
"You must think all Black people drink this shit!"
"I don't drink this bullshit!"

His refusal was based on the fact that White Kids often teased Black Kids when they saw us walk out of a local store with **Grape Crush.** They called **Grape Crush,** *Nigger Juice* and *Monkey Cola.* My White Friend was completely unaware of this. He had walked to a different store with me numerous times and he'd seen me buy **Grape Crush**, so he told his mother to get **Grape Crush**. He figured Todd likes it, so it's a safe bet. It was an honest mistake and I could tell by the look on his face, he had absolutely no idea what my Black Friend was talking about. I knew my White Friend never hung around with the *group* of White Kids who liked to talk that *Nigger Juice* and *Monkey Cola* shit. They used to fuck with him for playing with Black Kids, so he was never around them long enough to hear any of their bullshit. They only said that shit when the numbers were in their favor or when they had older kids with them. A lot of Black Kids were bothered by this and switched to **Orange Crush**. I stuck with **Grape Crush** as a matter of principle. Plus I was a big Oakland Raiders fan, so I wasn't going to switch to *Orange Crush* because it was the nickname for the hated Denver Broncos *Defense*.

I eventually got my Black Friend to calm down, and I also began to wonder if some of his reaction/over-reaction was a little bit of acting. I knew that if it was just us Brothers playing basketball, he never would've said a word, and he would've inhaled that bottle of **Grape Crush**. I began to understand the concept of being in a comfort zone when you're within your *group*. I admired him for standing his ground and refusing to be *Stereotyped*, even though he was denying himself something he truly enjoyed. The end result was an extra bottle of **Grape Crush** was left sitting there all alone and in need of some lovin'. I didn't give a fuck about being *Stereotyped*, and I promptly gave that extra bottle of **Grape Crush** a whole lotta lovin'. What's the moral to the story? There are actually *three* morals to this story and at least *one* them can be applied to just about every *Stereotyping* situation.

1 **Never Assume Anything**. If you're White and you're having some guys over to play cards and some of them are Black, don't **assume** they want Kentucky Fried Chicken. I've seen this shit happen before, and it's an immediate *head-scratcher*. Brothers walk into the kitchen, look at the buckets of Chicken, and automatically switch to *Red-Neck-Alert-mode*. The easiest way to avoid these kinds of misunderstandings is to make some pre-game phone calls. A quick phone call from the host, simply stating: "I was going to get some K.F.C. and a couple pizzas, are you cool with *that?"* eliminates any chances of offending anyone.

2 **Don't Over-React if it was an Innocent Mistake**. Some people may not know any better. Some people make **assumptions.** Some people are just clueless about other cultures. When people are clueless about other cultures mistakes are bound to happen, because their decisions are based on **assumptions.** If it was an innocent mistake, don't turn it into World War III. Find a subtle way to inform the person that their **assumption** was incorrect. If it's done with tact and humor there's a better chance of it not

happening again, versus the damage that's created by losing your mind and over-reacting.

#3 If it's Done with Malice, Do What You Gotta Do. When it's done with malice, then the **Devaluation Triangle** is being brought into play. It could've been done out of **Hate, Indifference, Ignorance** or any combination of the *three*.

Stereotypes are a fine line and you're always better off if you judge people as *individuals* and never assume anything. Many times people will show the exact opposite of what they truly feel, because they don't want to feed into a certain *Stereotype*. Many times a certain *Stereotype* may not even apply to a certain *individual*. I've broken *Stereotypes* into *three* categories: **Cultural, Physical,** and **Intellectual**, so let's look at each category.

Sub-Chapter 'A' 'Cultural Stereotypes'

"So you know what you guys do when he gets in here….. Pat him on the back, say congratulations, enjoy it….. And tell him not to serve fried chicken next year (at the Master's Dinner)……. or collard greens or whatever the hell they serve."

Pro Golfer Fuzzy Zoeller had this to say after Tiger Woods historic win at the 1997 Masters.

It's all in the application. The application of the *Stereotype* is the window into its intent. Mr. Zoeller tried to play this bullshit off as innocent humor, but the manner in which it was applied tells us what his true intent was. Was he making an **assumption?** When you see it on video tape, the answer is **"Hell No!"** Was this an innocent accident? **Hell No!** This leaves you with humor *vs.* malice, and you know where I'm leaning. I won't speculate on which side of the **Devaluation Triangle** applies, but I'm sure at least *two* sides would be applicable. *Cultural differences* are usually applauded within the *Culture*, but often downplayed outside of the *Culture*. Most people prefer to be judged as *individuals* when they're not with their *group*. When I'm at work I don't want to be known as a Black Man or a Black Firefighter, I expect to be known as Captain Wooten, period. When you're outside of your *group* you'd rather not hear any *Stereotypes* at all, especially if the *Stereotype* is negative. Positive *Stereotypes* can also bother people. I know Italian Firefighters who go out of their way to cook non-Italian dishes at work. They don't want to hear comments such as: ***"Man, I knew you were gonna make pasta."*** It may not offend them, but it certainly makes them feel like they have to prove they can prepare other dishes. It certainly upsets me because I Love good pasta. I've always encouraged my men to cook whatever they can cook well. I care more about *quantity* than ethnicity (*quality is a distant 2nd*).

Culture is often a double edged-sword in America. We want to tout our *Cultural differences* and at the same time demand to be judged as *individuals.* I know a Black Female who's deep into African culture, and when she got a cheap replica of an African artifact from a co-worker in a gift exchange, she got pissed off. I told her that next year she should talk about food everyday instead of Africa, and maybe someone would give her a gift certificate to a nice restaurant. When you choose to be identified solely by your *Culture*, you can't get pissed off when those around you identify you solely by your *Culture*.

My short time in the Marine Corps taught me more about our *differences* than anything else I've ever done. *Cultures* can vary dramatically within a particular Race. I mentioned in **VOLUME I** that I've mediated disagreements between Mexicans from California and Mexicans from Texas. Actually these were nothing but drunken arguments and I was the only neutral party available (*though equally drunk*). To show you just how complex the ***Stereotype*** game is, these Latino Marines often displayed their similarities, their unity, and their pride among the rest of the platoon, but amongst each other they would become rivals.

Cultures can vary dramatically by geography. I can tell you, Brothers from the South ain't nothing like Brothers from Chicago, Detroit, D.C., New York or Philly. They may enjoy the same food, the same music, and the same kinds of women, but their *differences* are still very distinct. The language, the clothing, and the demeanor are *differences* that even an untrained eye can notice.

An *individual's* personal experiences can also have an impact on whether or not he falls within a certain ***Stereotype.*** I met a Brother from New Orleans who hates catfish. I was stunned because I had never met anyone Black who didn't like fried catfish. I eventually learned that as a child he choked on a fishbone and never ate a piece of fish again. Little things like this taught me to never **assume** anything when it comes to *individuals*. I was good friends with a White Guy from Oklahoma who hated country music, but always wore cowboy boots. I realize that one has nothing to do with the other, but I still found it odd that he hated country music and practically slept in his cowboy boots. I eventually learned that he was just more comfortable in cowboy boots. He'd worn cowboy boots all of his life and other types of footwear bothered his feet. I can close my eyes and still see those cowboy boots working the dance floor at the 'E' Club (Enlisted Men's Club). It's not very often you get to see cowboy boots dancing to the **GAP BAND'S "You Dropped a Bomb On Me."** Trust me that was some funny-ass shit. I learned to never **assume** anything. Things like food, music, language, and clothing are *Cultural* blankets that can cover the *majority* of a particular *group*, but *majority* doesn't necessarily mean everyone in that particular *group*. *Stereotypes* can certainly be *Cultural* I.D. Cards that can be as blatant as skin color. It's still up to that *individual* to pull out the I.D. Card, and it should never be **assumed** that he or she will.

It's so much easier to **assume**, because then you don't have to take the time to get to know someone. This happens to Black Folks in America more than every other Race combined. Black Folks are partially responsible for this because we're more expressive, and therefore **assumed** to be easier to read. That expressiveness is also easier to mock and imitate. Whether you go back to the days of the exaggerated *Black Face Routines* or to the present day White rappers, Black seems to attract *copy-cats*. The Black look has people getting buttocks implants, shooting collagen in their lips, tanning, getting curly hair or shaving their heads (Jack Johnson was shaving his head a *half-a-century* before Telly Savalas and Yul Brynner). The clothes, the music, and the language have all permeated American society. Black Music is a big factor nowadays because it's teaching the White youth of America a language that their parents don't speak or understand. This is actually pretty scary when you think about it. Little Johnny could be talking about *"Bustin' a Cap"* (i.e., *shooting someone with a gun*), and Mom and Dad are thinking Little Johnny's *"trying to squeeze his head into a hat that no longer fits."* When White America catches itself getting too Black, they just try to find a way to co-opt the idea. They do to Black Folks what the Japanese used to do to them in High-Tech. The only thing is, the Japanese actually improve a product. Nowadays the Japanese don't have to co-opt an idea or a product, because technologically they're probably our equals. They've already surpassed us in electronics and also in the automobile industry, and who knows what's next. When White Folks co-opt shit from Blacks they rarely improve it. I remember when I was in *8th* grade and all of the White Boys ran out and got Afros. They all looked ridiculous, and years later the 1985 movie **Fletch** reminded me of this hilarious time period. Chevy Chase's daydream of playing for the L.A. Lakers took me on a daydream back to the *8th* grade (*Mr. Chase was listed as 6'5 or 6'9 with Afro, but that Fro was every bit of 8 inches*). The Afro-look just didn't work for my White Classmates, and most of them abandoned their Afros before class pictures rolled around. Some things can't be or shouldn't be duplicated, and White America should've realized that the first time **Pat Boone** tried to sing **Tutti Frutti**.

As much as Black Culture is mimicked, it's also often mocked. We've all seen the exaggerated facial expressions in the *"Birth of a Nation-like"* Racist films of the past. The walk, the talk, and the mannerisms are easy to pick up and have fun with. Black Folks often do it amongst each other. Within your *group*, you have that comfort level and this allows you to poke fun at all of your *group's* **Stereotypes**, whether *Cultural, Physical* or *Intellectual*. The joke I remember most as a kid, was when my best Black Friend told his sister: **"When you were a baby Mom never had to get a babysitter for you; she just wet your lips and stuck you to the wall."** If someone outside of the group had said some shit like that, there would've been a fight. What was considered offensive back in the day is often considered explosive by today's standards, because of political correctness. Overall, political correctness is probably a good thing, but I'll be the first person to admit that a lot of good humor has basically been put out to pasture. I personally have never had a real problem with Racist comments because I could verbally cut your heart out and show it to you. I had to have a quick tongue to defend myself, because I was too skinny to fight. Talking about someone's mother was a lot more fun than throwing rocks and running. I would like to see more Black Folks defend themselves with humor instead of playing the **Race Card**.

I read in October of 2005 that White Students at the University of Chicago were having, what they called *"Straight Thuggin' Ghetto Parties."* At these parties they donned all of the typical hip-hop attire, listened to hip-hop music, talked the talk, and drank malt liquor. The Black Students on campus took offense to this and complained about it. More White Kids buy hip-hop music than Black Kids, so I'm sure many of the White Students didn't mean to offend anyone. I'm also sure many of the White Students saw this as a grand opportunity to refer to each other as *My Nigga*. Did the Black Students over-react? Maybe. Then again maybe their reaction was warranted, but humor could've squashed this entire episode. I would've liked to have seen the Black Students throw a *"Minute Man Party."* They should've donned colonial suits and wigs, and passed out flyers announcing a *"Minute Man Party."* The flyers could've explained that a *"Minute Man Party"* is to honor those young White Males on campus who *last no longer* than *Three Minutes* (and that's with the assistance of Viagra), or can muster no more than *Three Pumps per Minute.* I'd be willing to bet there'd be a drastic reduction in the number of *"Straight Thuggin' Ghetto Parties,"* once the word spread about *"Minute*

Man Parties." Political correctness has taken a lot of fun out of life in America. I remember the good old days back in Zanesville, Ohio, when White Guys would make comments about Brothers *ghetto-izing* their cars, or make comments about Brothers loving Cadillacs. We'd always *howl* like huntin' dogs when we'd see a White Guy drive by in his pick-up truck with his girlfriend sitting close to him. We'd *howl* because the girlfriend always looked like an old faithful huntin' dog, proudly sittin' straight as a board, close to her master. Once the White Guys found what the *howls* were about, the *ghetto-izing* comments stopped.

I never liked them silly-ass curb feelers or shiny ass rims on cars, but I never had a car so I had to help defend the guys who let me ride with them. When you're with your own, you're in that comfort zone. When you're with your own you can say: *"Man why don't you get rid of them 'ghetto-ass' rims,"* and everyone laughs. If someone from outside of the *group* said that shit there would be problems. So as you can see, the policy that governs the *N-Word* should also be used to govern the use of *Stereotypes.* These things can only be judged on a case by case basis, because there's always an inch of Black on one side, an inch of White on the other side, and a mile of Gray in the middle. The *Cultural* application of *Stereotypes* is without question the most common, and in America *no group* of people are exempt. I can't even count how many times I've seen drunken White Guys jump into a Karate stance when an Asian Guy walks into a club. It's really hard to believe that people can be so fucking stupid, but you see this kind of stupid shit all of the time. *Stereotypes* are usually applied to others when someone is in their comfort zone (*like Fuzzy Zoeller was*), which usually means in the *majority.* Being in the *majority* makes it much easier to be insensitive, because you're not as concerned about reprisals. Being in the *majority* makes it much easier to directly apply *Stereotypes* to others, especially when they're in the *minority.*

Cultural differences usually work in your favor if you're in the *majority,* and often work against you if you're in the *minority.* I've been in fire stations with *five* other firefighters who were hockey fans, and there were only *two* available televisions (*the television in the officer's room is off-limits*). I'm sure you know what the *majority* chose to watch on both televisions.

When I worked in the prison system, White guards were the *minority* (*80 %* of the guards were Black, *60 %* of the inmates were Black, and *30 %* of the inmates were Hispanic). Being in the *minority* didn't sit too well with most of the White guards and it made them very uncomfortable. For me, this was the first time (*and only time*) in my adult life that I experienced the comforts of life in the *majority,* and I must say it was pretty damn nice (*even though it was in a prison*). One thing I immediately realized was even though my White co-workers were among plenty of Black Folks, they didn't seem to be interested in *Stereotypes*. They never asked any of the standard questions: *"Why do Black people like this?"* or *"Why do Black people do that?"* I always had to endure the *"Why do Black people"* questions in predominantly White environments, because when you're in the *majority* you feel comfortable enough to ask anyone anything you damn well please. In my six years at the prison I never heard one *"Why do Black people"* questions. White employees didn't last very long at the prison, even though it was a decent paying government job with benefits. I suspect that being in the *minority* played a major role in their short stay. I was always amazed at how Blacks and Whites responded when the *minority/majority* roles were reversed. The White employees had a tough time dealing with the lack of respect and the constant threats of violence (*from the inmates and co-workers*). White employees often got frustrated when they didn't get the automatic respect they had always received in the outside world. The White employees who *didn't understand* that respect has to be earned always *struggled*; the White employees who **fully-understood** that respect has to be earned usually survived. Those White Guys are some of my best friends to this day, because the prison work environment is like a war everyday. When you go to war with people who've got your back, you practically become Brothers. Color and *Culture* lose much of their relevance when you depend on each other to survive. The world of team sports and the military serve as obvious examples of this. I have to admit though, the Black employees (*including myself*) always enjoyed watching the White employees who couldn't make it, *struggle*. We always knew which ones wouldn't last very long, and we would sit back and enjoy their frustration before they quit. Here's a few samples of how they were treated:

Here's how they were treated by inmates:

"Hey White Boy! Hey White Boy!
Give me a motherfuckin' cigarette.
You gotta girlfriend?
Let me see a picture of dat bitch.
Damn she's fine!
Hey White Boy, I'm keepin' this motherfuckin' picture.
Go get me a motherfuckin' light for this cigarette and take your time.
Cause I'm fittin' to 'Bust a Nut' to this picture.
What you say this bitches name is again?"

Here's how they were treated by Black employees:

"Hey White Boy!
I'm gonna take a nap.
I was out all goddamn night takin' care of bizzness.
You wouldn't know nuthin' bout that, you probably a Minute Man.
Keep an eye on them motherfuckers and 'don't' open no cell doors for anything.
I don't care if a motherfucker is hangin' or on fire.
You come and tell me first.
Damn, why they always send a sorry ass White Boy to my wing?"

I'm sure many of my White Readers are appalled by what they just read. I'm also sure that at one time or another, many of my Black Readers have been talked to in that tone, or initially treated like that by White co-workers. The language may not have been as harsh, but the intent to belittle was still the same. Talked down to and not given one iota of respect is a tough pill to swallow *8* hours a day and *40* hours a week. White Folks already know this because they invented the *ultimate response* to workplace hostility; that response is called *Going Postal.* When someone goes *Postal*, regardless of Race, it's safe to **assume** that *somehow* they were in the *minority.* The people who go *Postal* are usually referred to as *loners,* and this would certainly put them in the *minority.* That doesn't excuse the use of the *ultimate response*, but it may explain why it sometimes occurs.

Being a member of the *majority* can create an atmosphere of Indifference. Being in the *majority* is a pretty nice gig as long as you never have to leave your bubble. At one time or another, members of the *majority* turn down the wrong street and suddenly find themselves outside of their bubble. Whenever you leave your *majority* bubble, just like when you leave your *Cultural* bubble, all you can do is hope to be judged *fairly.* If people would simply treat others like they themselves prefer to be treated, a lot of the bullshit could be eliminated. We've all heard the verse *"Do unto others as you would have them do unto you."* When you're in the *majority* it's much easier to expect that particular verse than to practice it. When it comes to *Stereotypes* it's usually the application that does the damage, not the *Stereotype,* and usually the application of the *Stereotype* was based on an **Assumption** or **Presumption.** At the same time, if you present your *Culture* before you present yourself, don't get pissed off if that's how you're judged. If you present yourself as an *individual* and you're judged by your *Culture*, then **Don't Over-React,** but certainly watch to see if the **Devaluation Triangle** is in play. There are Millions of people and countless *Cultures*; no wonder all of this stuff is one big shade of Gray.

Sub-Chapter 'B' 'Physical Stereotypes' *vs.* 'Intellectual Stereotypes'

"I advance it, therefore, as a suspicion only, that the Blacks, whether originally a distinct Race or made distinct by time and circumstances, are *inferior* to the Whites in the endowments both of *Body* and *Mind*."

Thomas Jefferson
NOTES ON VIRGINIA
QUERY XIV
1781-1785

'Physical Stereotypes'

"During the Slave period, the Slave owner would breed his Big Black Buck with his Big Woman so that he would have a Big Black Kid….. That's where it all started."

Jimmy 'The Greek' Snyder
Former CBS Football Commentator
Martin Luther King Day, 1988

VS.

'Intellectual Stereotypes'

"Blacks may not have some of the necessities to be, let's say, a field manager or perhaps a general manager."

Al Campanis
Former L.A. Dodgers Vice President
April 6, 1987
On the *40th* Anniversary of
Jackie Robinson's Major League Debut

As you can see, *200* years after Pres. Jefferson's writings, White Men still have many of the same interesting opinions about Black Men. The word *Former* preceded the titles that Mr. Snyder and Mr. Campanis once held. That's because those comments cost both of them their jobs. It may be unfair or unfortunate, but they were old men in a new era. The new era we now call Political Correctness. The *two* comments are always lumped together and replayed whenever someone says something that is considered Racially explosive. It's unfair and unfortunate because the *two* comments are as *different* as night and day. Mr. Snyder's comment might be considered insensitive by some people, both Black and White, but he's factually correct and shouldn't have lost his job. The fact that Blacks over-reacted and Whites Hate to face History, made it convenient to dump Mr. Snyder. *Physical Stereotypes* can certainly be considered offensive, no doubt about it. Whether applied to a *group* or an *individual*, there's a good chance you'll offend someone even if it's true. When applied in a derogatory manner, it's meant to offend.

The application of *Cultural Stereotypes* may be the most common, but *Physical Stereotypes* are the easiest to apply because they're the easiest to see and the easiest to measure. There's no denying the shape of an Asians eyes are *different* from non-Asians. It is what it is and it's the application of the *Stereotype* that causes the problems, not the *Stereotype* itself. *Physical Stereotypes* are measurable and tangible, and often the *differences* can't be denied. There are currently no White cornerbacks in the NFL. That's fact not fiction, and it's a fact for a reason, a *Physical* reason. There are *physical differences* that separate us and they can't be denied. There are distinct *physical differences* that place most of us in a particular *group* and things such as: hair, skin color, lips, nose, and eye-shape can't be denied. We know what the *differences* are, and we use these *differences* as immediate identifiers. Where things get tricky is when people try to apply *Intellectual Stereotypes* the same way they apply *Physical Stereotypes*. Mr. Campanis's comment tears me in half. The widows of Jackie Robinson and Roy Campanella both say Mr. Campanis was not a Racist. I respect those two ladies too much to disagree with them. Mr. Campanis stated that he was tired when he made the comment to Ted Koppel on **Nightline**. Mr. Campanis stated that he meant to say: ***"Blacks lacked the necessary experience."*** It would be easy to give him the benefit of the doubt, until you see the interview in its entirety. A few seconds after the comment, Mr. Campanis hit Ted Koppel with *two* follow-up questions:

"How many *Black Quarterbacks* do you have?"
"How many *Black Pitchers* do you have?"

I don't believe he's a Racist, but he was definitely speaking on behalf of every Racist in America. How else do you explain the fact that HALL of FAME quarterback Warren Moon went un-drafted by the NFL. Mr. Moon went un-drafted even though he led the PAC-10 Champion Washington Huskies to a Rose Bowl victory over *4th* ranked Michigan in 1978. Mr. Moon went un-drafted even though the Tampa Bay Buccaneers drafted Doug Williams, a fellow-Black-quarterback from Grambling, in the first round that same year. Mr. Moon was extremely talented, but he wasn't a *"can't miss" physical* phenom like Mr. Williams. Since Mr. Moon was not a *physical* phenom, he wasn't considered a potential NFL quarterback. Since the quarterback position requires great *intellect*, no teams wanted to take a chance on Mr. Moon, not even with a late round pick. Mr. Moon had to go to Canada and win a handful of C.F.L. titles and several MVP's, before he finally got the opportunity to play in the NFL. Fortunately, he still put up HALL of FAME numbers in the NFL. Unfortunately, the first *6* years of his career were wasted in Canada.

There are definitely many Whites in sports management positions who proudly practice Mr. Campanis's inadvertent Ignorance. The NFL and NCAA Division I Football certainly carry on Mr. Campanis's legacy of Ignorance with their atrocious hiring practices. I'm reminded of the bullshit that happened to former Green Bay Packers Offensive Coordinator, Sherman Lewis. Mr. Lewis couldn't get a head coaching job because he didn't call the plays; Head Coach Mike Holmgren called the plays. Not being the play caller didn't prevent the half dozen position coaches that worked *under* Mr. Lewis from getting head coaching jobs, even though *none* of them had previous NFL experience calling plays.

I've always wondered why former Toronto Blue Jays baseball manager Cito Gaston never got the opportunity to be recycled. White managers often get a *second, third* or even *fourth* opportunity to fail and Mr. Gaston only got *one* opportunity, which was quite successful. Mr. Gaston managed *back-to-back* World Series winners, but never got another opportunity to manage again. He proved that he had the necessities that Mr. Campanis said Blacks lacked, but obviously the rest of Major League Baseball never saw it that way. Mr. Campanis may not have been a Racist, but he certainly spoke on behalf of every Racist in sports management.

In the confusing world of *Stereotypes*, Mr. Campanis's comment marked him for the rest of his life. The one correct comment Mr. Campanis made in his **Nightline** interview was: *"Why are Black Men and Black People, not good swimmers?"* That comment is factually correct. The *difference* between Mr. Campanis's questions about the lack of Black swimmers *vs.* the lack of Black managers, Black quarterbacks, and Black pitchers is answered by the title of this chapter: **Physical Stereotypes vs. Intellectual Stereotypes**. *Physical Stereotypes* can be measured, *Intellectual Stereotypes* can not. Black Folks Love to boast during the Track & Field events of the Olympic Games, especially when there are three Blacks standing on the podiums (*after taking the Gold, Silver, and Bronze*). But you don't see any Black faces on those podiums after the swimming events, do you? *Physical Stereotypes* can be measured, *Intellectual Stereotypes* can not. There are always exceptions and there are no absolutes, but *Physical Stereotypes* are usually fairly accurate and are based on measurable facts. I swim just good enough to survive and that's it. At the same time, if you picked me first in a pick-up basketball game you'd be very disappointed. *There are no absolutes* and it's wise to never **assume,** but when it comes to *Physical Stereotypes* you've got a better shot at being correct than you do when you apply *Cultural* or *Intellectual Stereotypes*.

When the movie **White Men Can't Jump** came out in 1992, it raised a few eye-brows, but for the most part people weren't outraged. There was no outrage because people felt the movie title was somewhat true, even though somewhat offensive. People looked at the NBA and they had an obvious measuring stick. The *physical* activity of jumping could be measured, it was tangible, and you could see it with your own two eyes. The name of this book is **White Men Can't Hump**. Humpin' is a *physical* activity that can be judged and measured (remember, **"The Proof is in the Chocolate Pudding"**). Like I said before, read the full title of this book and please don't judge this book by its cover. I'm not saying **White Men Can't**; I'm just saying that based on what Whites have said about Blacks for centuries, **White Men Can't Hump As Good As Black Men**. Not everything Whites have said about Blacks over the centuries is true. Pres. Jefferson got a lot of things correct in his lifetime, but when it came to Black Folks he was consistently wrong. Pres. Jefferson's judgments about Blacks when it comes to *Love* was incorrect and seriously flawed, because they were made by a seriously flawed man. Pres. Jefferson's judgments about Blacks being **"inferior to Whites, in endowments of both *Body* and *Mind*"** are equally incorrect and flawed.

There are definitely *physical differences* between Blacks and Whites. There are definitely many things of a *physical* nature that Whites do better than Blacks. The # 1 thing Whites do better than Blacks just happens to be the most important thing most of us would ever want to do. Whites live longer. Blacks have shorter Life Spans than Whites for a variety of reasons. Some of these reasons are malicious (*America's biased health care system*), and some of these reasons are self-inflicted (*unhealthy diet and Black on Black crime to name a few).* Whether it is a certain *physical* activity or just plain old living, there are *physical differences* that both sides can point to with pride. I'm sure there are many young White Males who would gladly give up *10* years of Life Expectancy to play in the NFL or NBA. The steroid epidemic has confirmed this. I'm also sure there are a lot of Blacks who were athletic in their youth, but are now in their 50's and 60's, and are fighting for their lives thanks to diabetes or cardiovascular problems. *Physical superiority* is in the eye of the beholder. The point is, things of a *physical* nature, such as Life Expectancy or the Long Jump can be measured. ***Physical Stereotypes,*** even when vague, often have merit. ***Intellectual Stereotypes*** have no merit whatsoever, because there's no truly fair measuring stick or level playing field. The playing field in the world of sports is level. The one place where *physical* activity is meticulously measured is the world of sports. In the sports world everybody plays by the same exact set of rules, and there are officials who enforce those rules. In America, once you leave the world of sports, the playing field usually isn't level. It's unfortunate that sports stories are usually used when attempting to dispel the ***Stereotypes*** about ***"Blacks lacking the necessities."*** There are *three* general reasons why Black ***Intellectual*** ability is usually validated through sports stories:

 # 1 The world of sports is the only true meritocracy for Blacks in America. Winning is money, and in America money is what truly matters. When it became obvious that Blacks had '*the necessities'* to play quarterback, play middle linebacker, play centerfield, and play point guard, the walls slowly came down because winning (*and money*) outweighed bigotry. In the world of sports the best team usually wins, and the best team is usually the team with the best players. At the highest levels of competition, the best players are determined by merit and not by last name, money or inside contacts. The opinion of *Stop Watches* became more important than the opinions of bigots. The *Stop Watch* can't measure *Intellect*, but eventually Blacks got the opportunity to excel at positions that require *Intellect* and leadership. These positions weren't given, they were *earned*. I'm sure many of my White Readers appreciate seeing the word *earned*. I hope my White Readers are equally appreciative of the word *opportunity*. A position can't be *earned* unless an *opportunity* is given. The world of sports is where Black Men are freest to roam. Unfortunately, because the world of sports is the only true meritocracy for Blacks, it has become the only place many Black Men want to roam. Equally troubling is the fact that *opportunities* have been restricted mainly to the playing field. The sidelines and the front offices have been, and continue to be, void of meritocracy.

 # 2 Sports stories are the easiest to see and verify. Myths have been shattered by on-field performances, and you can't deny what you see with your own two eyes. The visual images on the playing field helped to create endless *opportunities* for Blacks.

 # 3 The stories that prove Blacks have *'the necessities'* to excel in any arena outside of sports rarely make it into our history books. We rarely hear about the countless big stories, so you know we'll never hear anything about the countless little stories. The Dr. Vivian Thomas story immediately comes to mind. Dr. Thomas was a key figure in the research and development of the surgical techniques that revolutionized cardiac surgery. Dr. Thomas developed surgical tools with his bare hands, and these tools set the standard for the tools that are used for open-heart surgery today. Dr. Thomas could teach open-heart surgery to White students, and supervise White surgical teams during an open-heart surgery, but was *not* allowed to perform a surgery himself. We occasionally hear stories about the first Black Supreme Court Justice, Thurgood Marshall. We rarely hear about his legal mentor, the great lawyer Mr. Charles Houston. You're not going to hear a lot about any of those gentlemen, because you don't hear about Black *Intellectuals* in America, period. When making a case for Blacks having the *Intellectual necessities*, the case is usually made from the worlds of sports or entertainment. That's sad, but those are the stories that are covered, and that's where the unrestricted *opportunities* currently exist.

Many people in America have a hard time putting the words Black and *Intellectual* in the same sentence. Black *Intellectual* is an oxymoron in the eyes of many White Folks. Many Whites believe there's no such thing as a Black *Intellectual*. This says more about the *clogged* brains of White Folks than it says about the *inferior* brains of Black Folks. The truth is there's a large portion of America that prefers *two* types of Black Folks, **Dumb** or **Quiet,** and preferably **both.** Throughout history there's been a concerted effort to make Blacks dumb and to keep Blacks dumb. Nowadays Whites don't have to work as hard at keeping Blacks dumb, because there's a generation of Blacks doing the work for them. We're *50* years removed from the **Brown Decision,** but many present-day Blacks have adopted the White pre-**Brown** attitude. The White pre-**Brown** attitude revolved around *restricting opportunities* to acquire a quality education. This attitude was as prevalent in the Ivy League schools as it was in the schools below the Mason-Dixon Line (*or as comedian Robin Williams says* "The Manson-Nixon Line"). Nowadays many Blacks choose to *restrict* their own *opportunities* because they lack the pre-**Brown** hunger for education that many Black Folks possessed in those days. Unlike the pre-**Brown** days when Blacks tried to overcome educational obstacles, many of today's Black Youth consider education itself the obstacle. Blacks and Whites have unknowingly worked together quite well at keeping Blacks dumb. White politicians do their part by slashing any and every program that can be slashed (i.e., *head start, pre-school,* etc.), so they can invest in vital programs like corporate welfare, tax cuts for the rich, or pork-barrel projects. Many Whites also seem to find pleasure in the failure of America's public schools. They privately gloat over public school failures, and then offer privatized solutions that exclude Blacks. Thanks to this joint effort, keeping Blacks dumb has become a relatively easy task.

Keeping Blacks quiet has been a much tougher task. In **VOLUME I,** I listed a number of prominent Black Men who were the focus of the federal government because of their outspokenness, men such as Muhammad Ali, Fred Hampton and Paul Robeson to name a few. Refusing to remain quiet has also cost countless Black Men their lives, but I'm not going to list anyone because I don't want to miss anyone. These brave men paid the ultimate price, and deserve the utmost respect, because any outspoken Black Man in America knows that his words can put his life in jeopardy. Nowadays the *felony* charge is the primary weapon used to silence Black Men, because it permanently excludes them from the voting process. At one time, keeping Blacks dumb was the cornerstone to keeping Blacks quiet. That was the primary reason for not allowing Slaves to learn to read or write. Keep'em dumb and they'll stay quiet, keep'em quiet and they'll stay and do our work. Don't just keep'em dumb, but repeatedly tell'em their dumb and eventually they'll believe their dumb. Then repeatedly tell everyone else the Slave is dumb and **"presto,"** everybody believes Black Folks are *Intellectually inferior.* The **L.A. Daily Times** editorial **A Word to the Black Man** gave the nation the *same* assessment of Black Folks that **The Bell Curve** did (see **The Devaluation Triangle (H 2 I)** in **VOLUME I**). The only *difference* is, the **Times** editorial was written *80* years before **The Bell Curve**, and was written without the results of IQ Tests. Obviously the belief that Blacks are *Intellectually inferior* is not new, as Pres. Jefferson so eloquently reminded us over two centuries ago. This belief has been heavily researched because enquiring minds want to know. When it comes to this subject there have never been any blanket statements such as: *"Smarts Doesn't Matter."* You've got people whose research concludes Blacks are *inherently* or *genetically Intellectually inferior*, and you've got people who poke holes in that research. The measuring stick is usually some type of test. You name it, IQ Test, S.A.T. results, G.P.A's or state level standardized tests, and Blacks routinely score lower than all other *groups*. The numbers smack you right in the face. You'd have to be pretty *damn dumb* to argue with all of those numbers. It just so happens, I've always considered myself just a *dumb* country boy from a little town in Ohio, so I'll give it a try.

If someone does something better, I've always been honest enough to admit it. The numbers don't lie, but they also don't tell the complete truth. I'm going to need to see a little more than a bunch of standardized test results before I'd be willing to concede that Black Folks are *Intellectually inferior* to anyone. I don't buy this *Intellectual inferiority* bullshit, and I've yet to read anything by anyone to change my mind. Don't get me wrong, there are definitely some dumb Black Folks out there. Most of them are dumb because they choose to be dumb. Being a dumb ass is an easy life, because you don't have to know shit. I know a lot of dumb White Folks too, and I mean *real* dumb. The *10 % Rule* is in effect because every *group* of people has their fair share of fuck ups (*20 % for Black Folks,* see **Terms & Def's** if you don't remember). To say that one *group* of people is *Intellectually superior* to another *group* is wishful thinking by those who happen to consider themselves *superior*. The fact is we don't know enough about the human brain to make any such claims. These ridiculous standardized tests tell us what someone already knows, but they don't give one iota of insight into a person's *Intellectual* capacity or potential. There's no way an IQ Test can accurately determine a person's *Intellectual* capacity or potential, because an IQ Test can't tell you if there are any factors hindering that person's *Intellectual* development. An IQ Test can only tell you where that person is at; they can't accurately tell you how far that person can go. We don't know enough about the human brain to make ridiculous **assumptions** based on piles of test results. There are still ongoing debates over what stimulates the brain of an infant. We still can't explain why women's brains are stimulated by *different* images than men's brains. Don't worry, I'm not going down the same road as former Harvard president Lawrence Summers, who stated: *"Women are inferior to men in the ability to excel in math and science."* Do women view things *differently?* **Hell Yes!** Does this *difference* cause women to process information *differently?* Probably. Does this *difference* make them

Intellectually inferior in any way? **No,** it just makes them *different*. I think the biggest *differences* between men and women in the fields of math and science are the levels of interest. Women may not be as interested in those fields. What Mr. Summers should have been doing is concentrating on finding ways to encourage women to become interested in math and science. For us to compete with China and India in the future, America will need to tap into every *Intellectual resource available. China graduates 300,000* engineers annually, and the U.S. graduates *60,000* annually. We need to encourage every available mind to help us confront our future challenges, and that should also include minds that function *differently*. We definitely know that men and women are stimulated by completely *different* Sexual images, but we don't really know why. The Sexual images that stimulate men usually don't stimulate women and vice versa. There's also *no* explanation for children who are diagnosed as autistic or mentally retarded, but just happen to be virtuoso pianists or violinists, even though they can't function in society without constant supervision. The human brain is like the ocean because there's a lot of unexplored real estate, and every one of us has our own personal ocean resting between our ears. The field of medicine has mastered every part of the human body except the brain. There's a hell of a lot about the human brain that we just don't know yet, period. But what we do know about the human brain is what stifles it and what hinders it, and IQ Tests don't take that information into consideration. So I'll be willing to concede that all Black Folks are as dumb as *myself* when America levels the playing field, and Blacks Folks still continue to *struggle*.

Like I said, those bullshit tests tell us what a person knows and not what they're capable of knowing. Given the same *opportunities*, I'm quite sure Blacks could hold their own. Being given the same *opportunities* means removing barriers that are exclusive to Black communities. Ill-funded and ill-managed public schools are an overwhelmingly Black problem. These schools are usually in terrible *physical* condition, which also takes away from the learning experience. Terrible environmental conditions are exclusively found in predominantly Black areas. Places like East St. Louis, Illinois, which is *97 %* Black, and is so polluted that *half* of its citizens have asthma. There are high lead levels in the soil where children play, and raw sewage that spills into homes, streets, and even high school cafeterias. What affect does this pollution have on the brain of an infant or a toddler or a child? For those of you who like to sing about the rights of the unborn, what affect do these horrible environmental conditions have on the development of the fetus? In the state of Illinois, East St. Louis ranks:

#1 *in fetal deaths*
#1 *in premature infant deaths*
#3 *in infant deaths overall*

East St. Louis has a population just over *30,000,* which may not seem like a lot of people, but every state with a large Black population has at least one East St. Louis. How does this poisonous air affect the development of a child's brain? The early years are the most important years in the brain's growth and development. The need for fresh oxygenated blood is crucial for growth and development of all the vital organs, especially the body's maestro, the brain. How much fresh oxygenated blood is the young brain getting when the lungs are *struggling* due to asthma? The toxic air triggers the asthma that reduces the amount of oxygen in the blood. The toxins in this air are also absorbed into the blood stream when inhaled. So these children get the *triple whammy* of:

- the lack of oxygen (*because of asthma*)
- the lack of quality oxygen (*because of the pollution that also triggers the asthma*)
- the introduction of toxins into their bloodstreams (*because of the pollution*)

Poor pre-natal care, plus no adequate health care post-birth, multiplied by toxic living conditions, equals a slim chance for a quick *Intellectual* start. I'm amazed at how the polluters are always allowed to set up shop within a stones throw of a Black community. To add insult to injury, these places don't even hire any Black Folks. Tavis Smiley's National Bestselling book **"The Covenant with Black America"** listed the following *Environmental factors* that IQ Test fail to measure, much like the EPA (Environmental Protection Agency):

- Nationally *3* out of *5* African and Latino Americans live in communities with abandoned toxic waste sites.
- The U.S. General Accounting Office (GAO) estimates that there are between *130,000* and *450,000* brownfields (*abandoned waste sites*) scattered across America's urban landscape from coast to coast. Most of which are located in or near low-income, working class, and people-of-color communities.
- Over *870,000* of the *1.9 Million* (*46 %*) housing units for the poor (*mostly minorities*), sit within a mile of factories that reported toxic emissions to the EPA.
- More than *600,000* students (*mostly African-American*) in Massachusetts, New York, New Jersey, Michigan, and California attended

nearly *1,200* public schools located within a ½ mile of state-identified contaminated sites.

Now let's factor in sub-standard housing with lead paint and bad drinking water, and it just doesn't seem like an environment that encourages the growth of a child's *Intellectual* capacity, as **"The Covenant with Black America"** also pointed out:

• Lead poisoning continues to be the **#1** environmental health threat to children of color in the U.S., especially poor children and children living in inner cities.

• Black Children are *five times* more likely than White Children to have lead poisoning.

These statistics are not meant to illustrate Black excuses; these statistics are meant to illustrate problems that are Black exclusives. Then when you factor in poorly funded and poorly managed public schools, the recipe for disaster is nearly complete. The icing on the cake is the Black parent factor. We've got parents who aren't financially ready to be parents, parents who lack the maturity to be parents, and parents who are woefully uneducated themselves. There are Millions of young Black parents who don't know how to stimulate their child's brain because no one ever stimulated theirs. I'm not making excuses for Black Folks; I'm just stating the facts. I'm sure I've got some White Readers right now who are saying: *"Excuses are like assholes, everybody's got one."* I couldn't agree more, but what would happen if we played a little game of **Trading Places**. Remember the movie **Trading Places**, which showed how Eddie Murphy and Dan Akroyd changed as people when their environments were switched. I know it was just a movie, but what would happen if you took some White Kids out of their comfortable suburban environment, and placed them in the *Hood?* What would happen to their test scores? How good would they sleep at night with gun shots and the constant sounds of sirens? How good would they feel coming home to an empty refrigerator everyday? A brain that is positively encouraged, continually stimulated, well-nourished, and well-rested, functions remarkably better than one that isn't. I found this out in the *4th* grade, and I've never forgotten it.

I lived with my Grandparents at the time, and one night I was dreaming that groundhogs were digging a hole in the yard. I eventually woke up because my dream stemmed from the fact that something was digging a hole in the left side of my brain. I woke my Grandmother up and told her that something was digging in my brain. She took me in the bathroom where she had good lighting, and she told me to hold still. She held my head over the sink and told me to close my eyes and mouth. She then began to poor **Witch Hazel** into my left ear which only made the digging worse; it felt like something was digging a hole in my brain. She dug her fingernails in the back of my neck and told me: ***"Damn it boy! Hold still!"*** She then began to poke in my ear with a sharp object and the digging stopped. She then grabbed some tweezers and suddenly the pressure in my brain was released. She had just pulled a big juicy cockroach out of my ear with those tweezers. She had to stab the roach to death with a nail file because drowning it with ***Witch Hazel*** didn't work. Needless to say, I didn't sleep too well that night. I put balls of toilet paper in both of my ears but I still couldn't sleep. That morning I didn't feel like eating either. I promptly went to school and bombed a Spelling Test. Spelling was my favorite subject, and I couldn't believe the silly mistakes that I had made. I eventually got over it, but it took about a week before I could get a good night's sleep. I used to tease my Grandfather for having more hair in his ears than on his head. After the cockroach incident I considered him lucky, because his bushy ear hair could keep the roaches out.

What happened to me was trivial compared to all of the kids who walk to school in total fear everyday. There are also Millions of kids who go to school hungry everyday and depend on school to provide the best meal of their day. There are Millions of kids that view school as nothing more than a temporary refuge from a troubled home life. The troubles at home can have a cumulative effect that can suppress that inner-spark that every child possesses. Even when there are two parents in the home, in Black America both parents usually have to work. In White suburbia, it's often optional. When both parents are working, you often have a *12* or *13* year-old running the household. When I moved in with my parents at the age of *11*, I was suddenly responsible for feeding my brother and three sisters, keeping the house clean, and making sure everyone's homework was done. At times I found myself too mentally and physically exhausted to do my own homework. I realize these are burdens that many people are forced to endure, regardless of Race, but I think it's safe to say that Black Folks deal with more than their fair share. The bottom line is, in order to reach its fullest potential, the brain must be *well*-stimulated, *well*-nourished, and *well*-rested. To achieve the three *wells* I just listed, a somewhat stable environment would be more than helpful. To achieve a stable environment, the living conditions outside of the home are just as important as the living conditions inside of the home.

Like I said, play **Trading Places**, but not for a day and not for a week; let's try it for a few years. What kind of test scores would we see? When Blacks get out of these harsh environments, they still routinely trail other *groups* on every standardized test. Many people point to *Cultural* bias. I don't know, I'm not an expert, but I'll tell you what I do know. Black parents that make it out of the *Hood* usually go overboard and spoil their kids. They strive to give their kids a material life that they themselves never had. Blacks who get out of the *Hood* often get complacent, and their attitude becomes *"Hey, I made it, I can relax now."* They want to give their kids everything that they never had, but by giving their kids everything, they fail to give them the hunger for success that helped them (i.e., **the parents**) get out of the *Hood* to begin with. I've seen numerous studies that show Black Kids watch more television than any other group of kids. I've recently seen a study on **CNN** that stated *30 %* of Black Kids watch more than *6* hours of television per day *vs. 8 %* of White Kids who watch more than *6* hours of television per day. Television and video games often become the babysitter in Black households, so after *6* hours with the low-cost babysitter there's very little time left for studying (i.e., *brain stimulation*). White Kids and Asian Kids are being groomed to meet the challenges of our ultra-competitive society as soon as they hit pre-school age. Black Kids are watching hours of **BET**. The White brain is being challenged and stimulated. The Black brain is often stymied by factors outside the home, and of course factors inside the home. Parents have to lead the way by continually stimulating their child's brain, but too many Black parents are clueless when it comes to this because it was never done for them. The Uneducated attempting to lead the Uneducated is basically the Blind leading the Blind, and this is the *Intellectual* Mt. Everest that Black America faces. Standardized Test will never tell us the true height of this mountain, because in America some people get to start their climb at the mountain's half-way point, while others continue to dwell at the bottom.

The beauty of the human brain is that a person's *Intellectual* potential is limitless, so it's all about stimulation. I will never concede genetic or *Intellectual superiority* to any *group* of people unless there's a level playing field. I've read all the bullshit about backwards ass African countries, and I've even read unpleasant comments about the African continent from former Pres. Richard Nixon. What people always seem to forget when it comes to Africa is none of those countries were fucked up until Whites decided to go in and colonize. The Africans were happy hunting and dancing, and singing and fucking, and were *not* seeking anyone's help. When you've got everything you need at your fingertips, there's no need to innovate. Innovation is born out of necessity. They may have appeared to be backwards and not very progressed as a people, but you have to remember whose measuring stick was being applied. The Native Americans were doing just fine and they never asked for anyone's help either. The people of India and other parts of Asia never asked for anyone's help either. The measuring stick for a civilization's progress has always been the White measuring stick, which doesn't make it the right measuring stick. People are *different* and that doesn't make one *Culture superior* to another. If technological advancement is always going to be the measuring stick for *groups* of people, then vision or lack thereof, should also become part of the judging criteria. Whites Love to come up with ways to make life easier, but always seem to overlook the long-term ramifications. Easier or cheaper is not always better. If there's a profit to be made, you can guarantee that any long-term vision will be thrown out the window, and the mass production will commence. Their motto is: ***"We'll deal with the problem when it gets here, for now, let's get paid and kick back in the shade."*** Whether it is the institution of Slavery or our dependence on fossil fuels, it's always the same *Short-Sighted Formula*:

- **Create an easier way or a short cut.**
- ***GET PAID FOR IT.***
- **Disregard the long-term ramifications along the way.**
- **Deal with it when you've run out of alternatives.**

Look at any of the problems our nation faces today, and I'm sure you'll see the *Short-Sighted Formula* has already been activated. Look at our current energy crisis, look at our current immigration crisis, look at our growing outsourcing crisis, look at our impending China crisis, and within each crisis you can see the *Short-Sighted Formula* just humming along. Applying the *Short-Sighted Formula* certainly requires *Intellect*; only about *half* as much *Intellect* as imagining what the long-term ramifications are. It's been nearly a century and a half since Slavery ended and its effects are still being felt, especially when its effects are Denied. We're just beginning to feel the effects of our dependence on fossil fuels, and we can no longer afford to Deny. *It's not what you create that matters; it's what your creation creates that matters.*

Intellectualism cannot be measured objectively, because man tends to view things through a very subjective prism. I've always been amused by the fact that when Black Folks exhibit extreme greed that causes pain to others, like the ridiculous Hurricane Katrina looters, it's considered animalistic behavior.

Can you honestly conclude that White Men who work on Wall St. are *Intellectually Superior* to the Black Men that looted during Hurricane Katrina?

The White Men on Wall St. may be more educated, but are they truly *Intellectually Superior?*

If they are truly *Intellectually Superior*, then what's their excuse for looting?

If they are truly *Intellectually Superior*, then shouldn't they be able to control those animalistic urges? Their advanced education and life of privilege has only taught them how to mask behavior that's ***no different*** from the Black looters in New Orleans. Can someone be considered *Intellectually Superior* when their soul is consumed with greed and their vision goes no further than the next pay day? Surely *Intellect* is required if a man is to see beyond what's directly in front of him, isn't it?

Hey, what the hell do I know? I'm just a ***dumb*** country boy from a little town in Ohio.

Chapter 2 The Media

"When I go to the money machine at night...I ain't looking over my back for the 'Media'...I'm looking for Niggas!"

Chris Rock
'BRING THE PAIN'
1999

"The thing I Love about this country of mine is that whether you're a psychotic killer or running for President of the United States..... The one thing you can always count on is White America's Fear of the Black Man."

Michael Moore
'BOWLING FOR COLUMBINE'
2002

Who's right? They both are. I definitely agree with Mr. Rock, I'm scared of Niggas at night too. The fact of the matter is, there are places in every city where you shouldn't go at night and a lot of times it's because of Niggas. Is this over-publicized? Sometimes it is, but sometimes the *over-publicity* is deserved. That said, *sometimes* doesn't have to equate to *all the time*. Mr. Moore astutely pointed out in **Bowling For Columbine**, that even though crime has gone down, the Media coverage of crime has increased. This gives the impression that crime is on the rise, and this automatically keeps the spotlight on Black Men. Black Men have become the primary face of America's Criminal Justice System. With the Media's help, Black Men are the primary face of an incident even when they're the victim. Most people have heard of the Rodney King Trial, the Abner Louima Trial, and the Amadou Diallo Trial, but seem to forget that those men were not the ones on trial. More than *10* White Men were on trial in those *three* cases and I bet the average person on the street probably couldn't tell you the names of more than *one* of them. The primary face is usually going to be a Black face once the Media gets involved. We've all heard the unofficial motto of the news business: **"If it bleeds, it leads."** That motto has become the norm because today's news coverage is more about entertainment than information. Black Folks still can't complain about *over-coverage* because

Black Folks are still shooting each other and still knocking each other upside the head. It is what is, so what can Black Folks do about it?

Like I said in **VOLUME I**: *"Black Folks can demand the same treatment as White Folks, Nothing More and Nothing Less."* Meaning, if you're going to continue to *over-cover* what is essentially Black on Black crime, then start *over-covering* White on White crime with the same passion. The best place to start is with the White Male pedophile.

The Media, with the help of Black Men, have made certain crimes synonymous with Black Men. When the Media says carjacking, mugging, rape, armed robbery or drive-by shooting, everyone immediately pictures a young Black Male. These crimes have a Black face attached to them, and this causes every young Black Male to continually *fit the description*. It's unfair, but life is unfair. The Media is just doing its job, but unfortunately they're only doing half of their job. When I hear that *liberal* Media bullshit I want to puke. There ain't nothing liberal about the Media when it comes to Black Folks. The Media considers Black Folks a major source of entertainment and I don't see anything liberal about that. What this tells you is their newsrooms and boardrooms lack diversity, and are therefore quite conservative, not liberal. I mentioned the Hurricane Katrina news coverage in **VOLUME I** and I think it's a perfect example of how the newsrooms of America lack diversity. The main message from many of America's Media outlets was *"Black Folks loot and White Folks just look for things."* Katrina exposed the biased coverage that Black Folks have been sodomized by for years. The problem has gotten worse because there are so many *different News Mediums* today. The wide variety of Media outlets has created a culture of competition. This culture of Media competition has blurred the lines between entertaining the public *vs.* informing the public. Nowadays it's quite easy to see who's winning the battle. Entertainment and sensationalism continue to trump good old fashion information. In its quest to entertain the audience, the Media is hurting the general public by failing to inform them. They've completely failed to inform the general public about the White Male pedophile, because that's not as entertaining as the young Black Male with a gun. When the Media says child molester, child pornography, pedophile or Internet Sex predator, everyone should immediately picture a middle-aged White Man.

The Media just doesn't want to make that type of commitment. Suddenly the Media has a conscious and doesn't want to *Stereotype* anyone. They don't want to *Stereotype* middle-aged White Men, because the vast majority of Media decision makers just happen to be middle-aged White Men. Shouldn't the public's interest and the public's welfare be placed ahead of the personal interest of the Media's membership? Do Black journalists *under-cover* Black crime because they don't want it to reflect poorly on them personally? No, because they know its part of the business. What do Black Folks want? We want White criminals to receive the same *over-coverage* as Black criminals. Black Folks want to see the mug shot of the White Male pedophile blown up and plastered on the front page of the newspaper, just like the mug shot of the young Black Male. The face of pedophilia is a White face and the coverage should provide the same ominous mug shots and create the same level of public outrage. Don't rush through the fucking news segment because it's uncomfortable. Leave the mug shot on the screen, full-blown for the entire segment, just like the mug shot of the young Black Male, *Nothing More and Nothing Less*. I suggest you begin this practice immediately, because thanks to the Internet the problem is only getting worse.

What's so sad is the Media's failure to inform the public is actually contributing to the problem. *Over-exposure* and *over-coverage* would be an excellent way to continually remind the White Male pedophile that the public is watching him, and that his urges are unacceptable. Pedophiles need to be continually reminded, because this helps them control their physical urges. The Media should be trumpeting this information to the masses, to law enforcement, and to law makers. The Media is always a day late when it comes to the White Male pedophile, because it's just not as entertaining. An armed robbery at a liquor store in the **Hood** is much more entertaining than a middle-aged White Man that abducted and repeatedly raped a *12* year-old girl. Whites are much more comfortable branding the young Black Male as **public enemy # 1**, even at the expense of their own children. There should be continuous Media reports and news specials on pedophiles and Internet predators. I've yet to see a Media report which tells the public that pedophiles require constant treatment because they can never be cured. I've yet to see any Media reports explain that pedophiles always have those urges and their treatment focuses only on curbing those urges.

The Media doesn't give this kind of information because American society places no importance on this current crisis. In January of 2006, **MSNBC** reported on a treatment facility in Florida that doesn't do a whole lot of treating. The **MSNBC** report cited the following incidents occurred at the **Civil Commitment Center** treatment facility:

- Pedophiles received child pornography
- Rapists got drunk on homemade alcohol
- A man was killed over a bag of 'Cheetos'
- Sex offenders received less than *8* hours of treatment per week

- *60 %* of the offenders at the facility were allowed to refuse treatment
- The facility was poorly funded, poorly staffed, and security was unbelievably lax

This type of fiasco is not new but the **MSNBC** report on it certainly was. The **MSNBC** report unknowingly showed a much greater problem; the lack of serious concern by all levels of government, and therefore all of society. Florida has had numerous high-profile child abduction/Sexual assault/murder cases, and they still don't take this shit seriously. This isn't a regional problem, it's a national problem. The White Male pedophile not only gets a free ride from the Media and society, but also routinely gets a free ride from the Criminal Justice System. This shit has gotten to the point where it's almost comical. Here's a few ridiculous examples of what I mean by comical:

Hey, did you hear the one about the Vermont judge who chose to sentence a White Male pedophile to *60* days of treatment, instead of *3* years in prison? This man confessed to raping a *6* year-old girl repeatedly over a span of *four* years, and his options were *60* days of treatment or *3* years in prison.

Hey, did you hear the one about the Nebraska judge who sentenced a White Male pedophile to *10* years probation for Sexually assaulting a child? The judge felt that prison life would be too harsh for the convicted child molester because he was only *5* foot *1* inches tall.

Now compare those sentences to the decades of prison time that Black Men routinely receive for *fitting the description*, or for a bullshit drug arrest. If you want to know why Black Folks have absolutely no trust and no respect for the Criminal Justice System, the Vermont and Nebraska cases are perfect examples of why. The Vermont and Nebraska cases are just two of *too many to count*, because when White Male pedophiles are arrested, it's usually not the first time. Due to the fact that America's jails are full of young Black Men with ridiculous sentences for harmless drug offenses, the prison system is a revolving door for the White Male pedophile. I can't believe no one has figured this shit out yet, but eventually someone will. The current outrage over liberal judges is being directed solely at Gay marriage, and once again the White Male pedophile is getting a free pass. Every time there's a child abduction that makes the national news and the predator gets caught, his record is always a grocery list of Sex offenses. Everyone is always outraged because the pedophile was out of jail early, but no one ever asks why. The jails are full of mandatory sentenced Black Male drug offenders, and there's no room for the men who prey on America's children. When the White Male pedophile gets out of jail early, he has the ability to become a suburban chameleon. White Male pedophiles are then aided by police departments and concerned citizens who are on the constant *look-out* for *hip-hop-looking* young Black Males (*which just happens to be the same exact look emulated by suburban White Youth, minus the Black skin of course*). The lack of law enforcement focus and the lack of concern over Sex offender's lists (*until after the fact*) further aid these suburban chameleons. In the spring of 2006 the state of California actually aided the chameleon process by housing paroled High-Risk Sex offenders in hotels just blocks away from Disneyland. How can some ridiculous shit like this happen? It happened because the White Male pedophile is *not* as threatening as the young Black Male.

I've yet to see any Media reports explain that pedophilia is an inherent Sexual preference. Some men prefer a nice ass, some men prefer breasts, some men prefer other men, and the pedophile prefers children. The pedophile's preference happens to be the one that's against the law. There are a number of shows that use **"America's Most Wanted"** techniques and warn us that a Sex offender is on the loose. This is great, but it doesn't educate the public on how to protect themselves from the pedophiles that have yet to be exposed. **The Oprah Winfrey Show** has been on a *John Walsh-like* mission, and she's been successful at getting some of these guys off of the street, but it's still small potatoes. **NBC's** news show **Dateline** actually lures pedophiles into staged meetings via the Internet. **Dateline's** **"To Catch a Predator"** series is the only show on television that truly informs the public of the seriousness of this problem. They've been pulling in *Double-Digit* numbers of predators per show and the predators just keep coming. **Dateline** made it a point to inform the viewers that these men were from all walks of life, all ages, and all Races. Yes, it's absolutely true these men were from all walks of life. There have been teachers, husbands, an actor, a Rabbi, a police officer, a New York City Firefighter, and an employee from the Dept. of Homeland Security (in other news, several months later the Deputy Press Secretary for the Dept. of Homeland Security was arrested for trying to solicit Sex from a minor on the Internet). It's true the predator's ages ranged from *18* to *68*. It's only partially true that these men were from all Races. If *80* to *90 %* of the men who show up to have Sex with a *14* year-old boy or girl are middle-aged White Men, any talk of diversity is simply misleading the public. Then again, it's easy to be misled when you're in Denial.

I'm not saying all of America is in Denial-mode like the Catholic Church. I'm saying America only focuses on the pedophile or the predator after he commits an offense, and the focus is usually very brief. The only pedophile or accused pedophile that I've seen take a prolonged beating in the Media is Michael Jackson. Catholic Priests have skated past the Media and skated past criminal prosecution, and the Church didn't take this shit seriously until they had to start opening their pocketbooks. I'm sure the victims of Priests would've liked to seen some jail time handed out, but the victims always lose in these situations. The victims are the big losers because they carry the scars for life and unfortunately some of them join the pedophile club when they become adults. After all, many pedophiles say they were Sexually abused as children, thus creating a new cycle of abuse. I've yet to see any thorough Media reports on **NAMBLA (North American Man/Boy Lovers Association).** The White Male pedophile has gotten such a free ride he's become emboldened and has actually formed an organization. **NAMBLA** openly promotes what they call *"intergenerational intimacy."* Now that's some pretty bold shit right there. The only people I've seen shine a light on **NAMBLA** are Trey Parker and Matt Stone, the creators of **South Park**. In June of 2000 **South Park** addressed the existence of this organization in the episode entitled **Cartman Joins NAMBLA**. As usual, **South Park** was ahead of the pack. I certainly don't question the right of pedophiles to form an organization. I question the Sex Police and the so-called moralists in this country for allowing pedophiles to have the *"Balls"* to form an organization. Like I said in the **"Busta Test"** (in **VOLUME I**), the moralists don't give a fuck about children after their born. I guess we'll have to wait for pedophiles to say they want to marry victims the same Sex as themselves for the Sex Police to finally step in.

Please don't think that I'm implying all middle-aged White Males are pedophiles. That would be like implying all young Black Males are carjackers, muggers, rapists, armed robbers or gang members. That simply wouldn't be fair would it? That could cause women to clutch their children in the presence of middle-aged White Men, the same way they clutch their purses in the presence of young Black Males. That would be rude wouldn't it? Black Folks only want the same treatment as White Folks, *Nothing More and Nothing Less.* If you're going to *over-cover* crime, then do you're civic duty and *over-cover* everyone's crimes. The public deserves to be truly and completely informed. I repeat, I am not saying all middle-aged White Men are pedophiles or Internet predators or Sex offenders. All I am saying is those particular offenses should have a White Male face attached to them. Here are a few general characteristics that pedophiles share and then you can decide whose face should be attached to these crimes.

"In America, who should be the face of Sex crimes against children?"

- They appear to be trustworthy and respectable.
- They have a good standing in the community.
- They have no criminal record.
- They are primarily family men.
- They are usually well educated.
- They can be very religious.
- They choose jobs and activities that allow for access to children.
- Their relationships with women are often troubled by Sexual dysfunction.

I repeat, **"In America, who should be the face of Sex crimes against children?"** At night, if you've gotta go to the money machine you might be watching for Niggas, but during the day I hope you know who you should be watching for when your kids go to the park. The truth is White Males have cornered the market when it comes to Sex crimes against children. All of the statistics say these crimes are committed overwhelmingly by White Males and I've seen statistics that have ranged from *60 %* to *80 %*. The child-pornography industry is flourishing on the Internet, and pulls in an estimated *20* BILLION *DOLLAR$* a year. How much of that *20* BILLION comes from the pockets of uneducated, unemployed Black Men? *Three*-figures? *Four*-figures? I'd bet it's not over *Five*-figures (in case your wondering, *20* BILLION is *Eleven*-figures). I'm sure White America would *Love to Believe* that Black Men sell drugs, do drugs, make babies, commit violent crimes, and still put in a good *six* to *eight* hours a day stalking children on the Internet. I'm sorry White America, but that's a little too much for the inherently lazy Black Man. There just aren't enough hours in a day for the dumb lazy Black Man to pull all of this shit off. After a tough day at the office, or church, or school, or the Dept. of Homeland Security, White Men seem to have a little more free time on their hands. At any given *minute* there are at least *50,000* predators hunting for children on-line. The White Male pedophile no longer has to cruise the playgrounds or parks, he can prowl for his victims while sitting in the comfort of his own living room. When asked about the high tech pedophiles that have been arrested, FBI Chief Spokesman, Special Agent Pete Gulotta stated:
"They're almost all White Males between the ages of *25* and *45*."

Author Nsenga Warfield-Coppock states in his book
'Advances in Adolescent Rite of Passage':
"The prison population of gruesome

Sexual crime is *97* % White, with sometimes as many as a third of incarcerated White American Men, in any given prison, being there for Sexual offenses."

I hope my White Readers don't think this is too harsh. If I really wanted to be harsh, I could've said *"White Male pedophiles like 'em young, because it makes them feel like they're Going Deep, and it makes them feel like they're Packin Heat"* (sorry folks, there's nothing Happy about this Meal). If I really wanted to be harsh, I could also get into the *Serial Killer* phenomenon. The *Serial Killer* phenomenon happens to be another area of Sex-related crime that's dominated by middle-aged White Males. I'm not a harsh person, so I'm not going to make harsh statements. All I'm going to say is Black Folks want the same Media treatment as White Folks, *Nothing More and Nothing Less.* If the Media wants to *over-cover* Black crimes for the sake of entertainment, then *over-cover* White crimes as well. Even if Blacks committed *50* % of all crimes, this means somebody else is committing the other *50* %. But you don't seem to hear as much about the other *50* % who also knock motherfuckers upside their heads (*or just molest children*). We know who else commits a large percentage of the crimes, but they're not as aggressively investigated, prosecuted or incarcerated. Maybe that's why they're not as aggressively televised. Then again, maybe the lack of Media coverage is the reason they're not as aggressively investigated, prosecuted or incarcerated.

White America has been pre-conditioned to sleep better at night when young Black Males are being incarcerated in record numbers. The Media feeds the bullshit to the masses, and the masses influence the Criminal Justice System via elected judges, elected prosecutors, jury pools, and legislation. This helps to create the continuous cycle of *over-focusing* on the Black criminal, and of course, *under-focusing* on the White criminal. When I was a mall cop, I was always called to **Payless Shoes** whenever a *group* of Black Women entered the store. It seemed like every time I was stuck at **Payless Shoes** watching Black Women, White Guys would walk out of **SEARS** with power tools. The Black criminal gets more TV time, so therefore the Black criminal gets most of the security focus. In the meantime, the White criminal gets less security focus, and therefore gets away with the crime. The slanted Media focus on the Black criminal has also slanted the public's perceptions on *"who is committing crimes against whom."*

In December of 2005 **The Oprah Winfrey Show** featured the cast from the movie **CRASH**. The movie **CRASH** centers on Racial *Stereotypes*, and featured a number of complex Racial situations involving members from most of the ethnic *groups* that make up America. Ms. Winfrey wisely had an expert in the audience to answer the complicated questions on Race relations. The Race expert was Prof. Ray Winbush from Morgan St. University, and he stated the following: **"The fact of the matter is, most crime in this country is *Intra*-Racial** (*within the Race*), **rather than *Inter*-Racial** (*against a person of another Race*). **Meaning the fear….the American fear…is that White Women for example…will be raped by Black Men. In fact, only *3* % of rapes are *Inter*-Racial."** Ms. Winfrey was astounded by that figure and even more astounded when she did the math, because she replied: **"Which means that *97* % of the White Women in this country who are raped… *97* %… are raped by White Men?"**

Most people probably think that *97* % of *all* rapes are committed by Black Men, and the Media has played a major role in those perceptions. Their reporting is certainly Indifferent towards Blacks, but more importantly, their biased reporting creates Indifference among the masses. It's a vicious cycle because the biased reporting feeds the masses and the masses then demand action from the Criminal Justice System. This results in a lot of Black Men *fitting the description* for shit they didn't do, or receiving *over-exposure* for the shit they did do. To this day, the Black Male rapist is *one* of White America's greatest fears. Fear of the Black Male rapist has *over-shadowed* centuries of *under-exposed* White Male rapists. The standard Media practice of *over-focusing* on one *group* and *under-focusing* on another *group* is one of the driving forces behind Racial profiling.

If America didn't have such a Racist past (*and present*), Racial profiling could be done without offending anyone. Skin color is an I.D. Card that every man possesses. The problem is, people of color are the only people routinely asked to show some form of I.D. I understand and appreciate Racial profiling because we practiced it in the Prison system. Whenever an inmate was assaulted we could tell by the methods and weapons used, if a Black inmate, a White inmate, or a Hispanic inmate was responsible. This wasn't with absolute certainty, but it was a great starting point. The key was to maintain an open mind, look at every possibility, and to avoid working with blinders on. Even though we started our investigation with the obvious **assumptions,** we never **assumed** anything. I remember one time a box of ink pens was stolen from a prison classroom. Most people would've **assumed** that Black or Hispanic inmates took the pens so they could make shanks (*home-made knives*). We knew the White inmates stole the pens and sure as shit, after a thorough search, that's who we busted. We went right to the White inmates because we knew they needed the pens for home-made tattoos. Did we Racial profile? Absolutely. What I don't like about Racial profiling is that it only applies to Black Men. Don't give me that Hispanic shit, because if a Hispanic Male is clean-cut he'll get a pass. Clean-cut Black Men still get pulled over routinely in America. America's perceptions of what a criminal looks like, and who commits crimes against whom, have become so psychologically embedded, I fear these perceptions will never change. The only good thing about the attacks on **9/11** is now someone else is getting Racial profiled. I absolutely Love hearing Middle-Easterners complain about getting Racial profiled. *Welcome to the Club guys!* As many times as I've had taxis fly past me in New York and Chicago, I certainly have no sympathy for you. My only hope is that people like Dinesh D'Souza (a conservative from India who thinks he's a White Guy from Indiana) gets stripped searched every time he goes to an airport. I can't stand it when someone comes to America, reads a few books, hangs out with people of privilege, and then tries to tell everyone how the Race game is played. Mr. D'Souza looks Middle-Eastern, and therefore *should* be strip searched every time he goes to an airport. Then he'd truly be qualified to write a book about Race in America. People like Mr. D'Souza come to America and believe they're better than others because American society tells them who belongs at the bottom of the barrel. Now, thanks to **9/11**, a new *group* of people are considered as ominous as Black Men and I personally welcome that. I say profile on.

Profiling, just like reporting, needs to be balanced because anytime you *over-expose* one entity, you're bound to *under-expose* another. The *over-focus* on the Black Male criminal pretty much guarantees the *under-focus* on the White Male pedophile. The *over-coverage* of missing White Females has guaranteed the complete *lack of coverage* when women of color are missing. Isn't it funny how that works? Diversity in the newsrooms and boardrooms could certainly make a *difference*, but as long as the public enjoys news coverage that's like the show **COPS** (*i.e., entertainment instead of information*), we know who'll be the face of crime. There's not only a lack of diversity in the regular newsrooms, there's also a lack of diversity in the sports newsrooms. The Entertainment Media excludes Blacks from the Sexual conversations of America. The regular News Media exploits Blacks for entertainment purposes. The Sports Media spreads contempt for Blacks, even though it needs the Black athlete in order to survive. Nowhere is this more evident than sports radio. Let's take a listen.

Sub-Chapter 'A' "Hate Nigger Radio"

"Physically, **the most beautiful human being on this planet is the Black American Athlete, period. No other *group* of human beings**

on this planet comes close. Aesthetic, yet **Explosive**, Graceful, yet **Powerful**, you name it and we've got it. The **Black American Athlete** not only dominates athletics in America, but also dominates on the world's stage."

Sound familiar? That was part of the opening to **W.M.D. = _Weapon of Mass Desire_ = Is it True?** In America, both pro and college sports have become big money businesses, and the Black athlete is a major reason why. This doesn't sit too well with a lot of people in this country, and some of those people just happen to be in the Sports Media. I know that I have a bad habit of repeating myself, but like I said in the _Stereotypes_ chapter, America prefers _two_ kinds of Black Folks, **Dumb** or **Quiet**, and preferably **both**. The Sports Media considers many Black athletes **dumb**, but to survive they can't afford for them to be **quiet**. Men like Jim Brown, Bill Russell, and Muhammad Ali, to name a few, weren't dumb and weren't going to be quiet for anyone. These men were products of their time and their time required them to use their _Intellect_ and their voices, as well as their athletic ability. They still created tons of resentment among the bigots of our nation and also among the Media that covered them. The White Media's resentment in the past stemmed from the fact that Blacks had the audacity to demand equality. Today's resentment comes from a number of _different_ sources, but many of the same attitudes towards Blacks remain.

One of the _sources of resentment_ is **Intellectual Stereotypes** continue to be applied to young, poorly educated, Black athletes. I'll be the first person to admit that many of these young Brothers don't speak too well. Many of these young men were encouraged to focus on nothing but sports during their high school years, and also during their brief college experience. By encouraging these young men to _over-focus_ on sports, they've been allowed to _under-focus_ on the opportunity to learn how to speak in complete sentences. Then when you factor in their upbringing, whether from rural America or urban America, you'll see that they didn't have to speak any other language than the language of their community. That doesn't make them dumb; it just makes their language skills less developed. Of the _three_ major sports baseball is the most complex, and poorly educated Blacks have still excelled in baseball, on the field and in the dugout. The teams that go the deepest in the NBA playoffs are the teams that play the smartest, and as we know, every team in the NBA is predominantly Black. If you've ever seen an NFL playbook or talked _X's_ and _O's_ with a player, you realize that you can't be a dumb ass and play pro football. There's much more to athletics than running, jumping and throwing, so if you're a dumb ass, you're usually not going to last very long. Unfortunately, because of poor language skills, many Black athletes are considered dumb asses and this is where the journey of journalistic contempt begins. What really cracks me up is that when you look at the situation objectively you realize the journalists are the real dumb asses. How the fuck can you go to college for at least *4* years and not be able to muster up anything more thought provoking than:

"How did it feel **to hit the game winning shot?"**
"How did it feel **to give up the game winning hit?"**
"How did it feel **growing up poor in the inner-city?"**
"How did it feel **to grow up without a father?"**

The *"How did it feel"* questions are the dumbest fucking questions you can ask, because everyone knows what the answer is. The people that consistently ask these kinds of stupid ass questions do so because they're lazy dumb asses. They want the athlete to do their jobs for them, and if the athlete gives them a *three* word answer like *"It felt bad"* or *"It felt good,"* they'll label him as dumb or uncooperative. If you think it's unlikely that educated journalists could be dumb asses, just remember that a journalist actually asked Doug Williams: *"How long have you been a Black quarterback?"* I rest my case. The poor language skills feed the **Intellectual Stereotypes** and help to create resentment.

Another *source of resentment* stems from journalists seeing the money these athletes make. Journalists see the money via homes, cars, jewelry, clothing, and public discussions about contracts. You know as well as I do, many of these White journalists are saying to themselves: **"This dumb, Black *"So-n-So"* is making *10* Million *DOLLAR$* a year to run up and down the floor and he can't even talk."** The big money Black athletes are getting pisses a lot of people off, period.

Another *source of resentment* stems from the fact that many White journalists wanted to play the games they now cover, but weren't good enough.

Another *source of resentment* stems from the fact that many of these White journalists see Brothers nude in the locker room all of the time. One must wonder if this has created some form of journalistic **Small-Poleons Complex.**

Regardless of the *reason for the resentment*, it all gets vented on good old sports radio or in the daily newspaper columns. Sports radio is where White Men get to share their contempt for Black Men and not be called Racist. No one comes right out and says **"I Hate them fucking Niggers,"** but these radio commentators paint the picture and set the tone for these types of discussions. They list everything under the sun and repeat it over and over and over. You can see and hear the fruits of their labor when you go to a live sporting event. When you see and hear the Racist venom at live sporting events, it doesn't take a genius to know where much of it comes from. The radio commentators tell the audience that a certain athlete is terrible or sucks or is a big jerk, and the audience takes that information to the game with them. The only problem is that after a few beers the words *Big Jerk* evolve into *Black Nigger.*

When you listen to sports radio, teams rarely win. What usually happens is someone on the losing team was a *quitter* or a *choker.* It's rarely a matter of the best team won, because that's not as much fun. It's rarely a matter of the best man won, because then you'd have no one to blame for the loss. It's much easier to stir the emotions of the public when you label someone a *quitter* or a *choker.* It's much easier to create a villain than to give credit to the better team. It's much easier to create a bad guy in the world of sports because of the prevalence of Black Males. Now factor in sports gambling and you've got another *source of resentment.* The radio commentators basically tell the listeners (*many of whom just lost money gambling on sporting events*) that their team lost because a rich, spoiled athlete (*code for no-good Nigger*) *quit* or *choked.* Calling Black athletes *quitter* or *choker* is definitely not a new phenomenon. In the early 1900's, the White Media and White boxers routinely called the first Black Heavyweight Champion, Jack Johnson, *yellow* (i.e., *quitter, choker* or *coward*). It's actually quite ridiculous when you think about it. You've got a bunch of guys, who have no more strenuous activity on their resumé than a **Girl Scout**, calling the world's premier athletes *quitters* and *chokers.* If an ex-athlete says it I'll listen, but occasionally ex-athletes choose to follow the journalistic pack. The ex-athletes who don't follow the pack are usually somewhat objective and remind us that the best team or best man won. I'm sure there have been times when athletes didn't give or couldn't give *100* % because they were physically injured. I'm sure there have been times when an athlete was overcome by the pressure of the moment and made a crucial mistake. I'm also sure that *99 %* of the time, the better team or the better man won the battle on that particular day.

I'd like to believe these commentators are just trying to entertain their audience, but there's a very noticeable bias in their commentary and the Racist connotations are more than obvious. A White athlete who celebrates after a score is exhibiting a Love for the game, a Black athlete who celebrates is ruining the game. Trust me, I grew up watching teams coached by Woody Hayes and Bo Schembechler, so I'd rather not see excessive celebrations, but emotional expression can raise the level of performance. The Sports Media's double-standard commentary on celebrations is beyond bias. Brett Favre pumps his fist and jumps up and down after a touchdown pass, and he's exalted for his Love and passion for the game. Is the *Lambeau Leap* any less contrived than a *cell phone* or a *Sharpie* celebration? If it's Love and passion when Mr. Favre does it, then it should be Love and passion when anyone else does it. White athletes who refuse to cooperate with the Media are labeled as *not friendly* or *surly.* Black athletes who refuse to cooperate with the Media are labeled as *jerks, malcontents, troublemakers, poisonous or immature. Surly* by definition is just as harsh, but why don't they call the White athlete a *jerk*, just like they do the Black athlete? Because they know their audience is used to being served **Dark Meat** for lunch, that's why.

The Sports Media also Loves to talk that bullshit about *"today's athlete isn't outspoken enough."* Yet whenever an athlete comments on something outside the field of play, the columnists and commentators chop his head off. They did it in the past and they do it today. The outspoken athletes of the past weren't well received and were usually lambasted by the White Media. The only person who had the *"Balls"* to consistently say Muhammad Ali was getting fucked over by the U.S. Government was Howard Cosell. Brent Musburger called Tommie Smith and John Carlos *"a couple of Black-skinned Stormtrooper's"* for their raised fist at the 1968 Olympics. So for the present day Media to act like everything was rosy between the outspoken athletes of the past and the Media, is bullshit. They want these Brothers to stick their necks out and comment on things outside the field of play, so they can put the noose around their necks in the next day's columns and on the airwaves. When Black athletes do speak out, the focus is usually on *"whether or not he should've said it"* or *"how will his comments affect the team."* The least amount of focus is placed on whether the athlete's comments have merit. That attitude goes right back to the kind of Black Folks America prefers (i.e., **Dumb, Quiet** or **both**). The basic attitude becomes: *"Shut up Nigger, you get paid to run, not to think or have an opinion."* So you're damned if you do and you're damned if you don't. Brothers like Barry Bonds and Tiger Woods drive them crazy because they don't kiss anyone's ass, and they don't talk to anyone unless they want to. How dare they? Who the hell do they think they are? That's why anytime the Sports Media gets the opportunity to pounce on someone who doesn't fully cooperate with them, they'll pounce in a hurry.

I'll give the Sports Media a little bit of credit for fairness. They're definitely equal opportunity offenders. They'll fuck over a Black athlete who's shown them the utmost respect, just as quickly as they'll pounce on guys who've shown them no respect at all. They're definitely equal opportunity in that regard. Men like Walter Payton and Barry Sanders found out the hard way. Mr. Payton had to have a humiliating press conference, so he could tell the world that he did nothing wrong to contract the rare liver disease that eventually took his life. Members of the Media, whom he always treated with the utmost respect, were spreading rumors that he may have contracted AIDS. How's that for respect? Barry Sanders was always absolute class, both on and off the field, and when he retired he was labeled a *quitter* by the Sports Media. That sentiment immediately took root within White fans. Mr. Sanders was always soft spoken, humble, unselfish, and never celebrated or brought attention to himself, on or off of the field. Mr. Sanders probably would've broken Walter Payton's all-time rushing record had he played just one more season, but records meant nothing to him. Forgoing the opportunity to break the all-time rushing record was the ultimate act of unselfishness, but he was still labeled as selfish for retiring. When he decided to retire, the Media and the public's attitude was basically: ***"Nigger, who do you think you are? You can't retire until we say you're washed up."*** Shortly after Mr. Sanders retired, the coach that he didn't want to play for quit on his team in the middle of the season, and the word *quitter* was never mentioned. Men who always treated the Media with dignity and respect were treated with no dignity and no respect by the same Media. It truly makes you wonder if there is more to it than just providing entertainment. It's the little things that keep the **Devaluation Triangle** alive, it's the little things.

Have you ever noticed the *different* tone when a White athlete displays greed *vs.* when a Black athlete displays greed? Here's an example that for some reason didn't stir the public's emotion. After Super Bowl XL in February of 2006, it was reported that former San Francisco 49er's Hall of Fame Quarterback Joe Montana refused to participate in the pre-game festivities. It was reported that Mr. Montana didn't want to participate because the NFL wouldn't pay him a *$100,000* appearance fee. Needless to say, if this was a Black athlete he would've been burned at the Media's stake, and lynched by sports radio's Hate. A Black athlete would've been called every kind of greedy Black expletive you can think of. He would've been accused of having a drug addiction, or accused of being broke due to financial incompetence, or accused of having too many mouths to feed, or accused of being selfish, or accused of having no respect for the game that put him on the map, and on, and on, and on. Joe Montana and Terry Bradshaw were both absent and the harshest word I could find was *unfortunate*. Often you can learn a lot from what isn't said, and the lack of outrage after Super Bowl XL said a lot.

Well before the revelations about Barry Bonds using steroids hit the papers, there was a major *difference* in how the Sports Media covered drug use. A Black athlete busted with marijuana or cocaine was ostracized. A White athlete busted for steroid use just made a mistake. Marijuana and cocaine hinder performance and steroids enhance performance, but you'd think it was the other way around. A Black athlete busted with a gun in his car is ostracized. A White athlete or coach or General Manager gets a D.U.I. and it's just a mistake. Alcohol is responsible for as many deaths annually as hand guns, but you'd never know from the news coverage. The bias in the Sports Media is actually no *different* than the bias in the News Media, but the effect is *different*. The biased reporting in the News Media is meant to entertain, and is also meant to create fear. The bias in the Sports Media is meant to entertain, but more importantly, is also meant to create anger. Sports Media, especially the radio, often becomes **Hate Nigger Radio**. Then when you throw in the **Hate Nigger Columnists**, you basically end up with modern day lynch mobs. Nowadays the anger and Hate is measured with daily on-line polls. The commentators incite the anger, and then measure how effective they were at the end of the show by sharing the poll results with their listeners.

We've all heard the Sports Media criticize athletes when they make statements such as: **"Money had nothing to do with my decision."** The Sports Media always replies: **"When an athlete says money had nothing to do with it, then you better believe money had everything to do with it."** When it comes to money, in most cases the Sports Media is right. This same theory also applies to Race, and it should come as no surprise that the Sports Media usually gets it wrong on this one. Usually when White Folks say *"Race has nothing to do with it, then you better believe Race has everything to do with it."* No journalists apply the Race Disclaimer (i.e., *Race has nothing to do with it)* as often as sports journalists. This is actually quite laughable when you consider the fact that no group of journalists are more Racist than sports journalists. They trumpet Hate on a daily basis, but immediately tell us *"Race has nothing to do with it."* Go back a few pages and check out the *sources of resentment* one more time and draw your own conclusion.

In July of 2005 **ESPN** got right to the point when they conducted an on-line poll that allowed people to vote for the athlete they **Hated the Most.** *Eight* of the *thirteen* athletes listed were Black, *three* were White, *one* was Latino, and the last athlete was Vijay Singh. When the voting was finished Blacks made up *three* of the top *five*, and *six* of the top *ten*. I wasn't surprised by the number of Blacks who ranked high on the list. I wasn't surprised that Barry Bonds was # *1*. I'm not a Barry Bonds apologist, but

I'm not *Tommy* either (i.e., *deaf, dumb & blind*). 2006 is the year White America gets to crucify a **"Black Jesus"** and then tell us that *"Race has nothing to do with it." Black Jesus* is not a reference to Barry Bonds the individual, it's a reference to the fact that Mr. Bonds is paying for everyone else's sins. *He's paying for:*

- His own competitive and egotistical sins (*there were Roid users breaking records and winning MVP's all around him*)
- The sins of the hundreds of ballplayers who were never exposed
- The sins of the fans (*after all, fans dig the long ball*)
- The sins of the Managers, the General Managers, the Owners, and Major League Baseball's front office (*they all closed their collective eyes*)
- The sins of the Sports Media (*they too closed their collective eyes*).

NOTE: What would've been the Sports Media's reaction if Barry Bonds had been the man chasing Roger Maris's single season home run record in 1998, and a bottle of *ANDROSTENEDIONE* (**a substance banned by the NFL and the Olympics**) had been spotted in his locker?

Do you think there would've been a little bit of Media scrutiny?

Do you think he would've received a little more scrutiny than Mark McGwire received (*that's not a question, because we all know the answer*).

And of course, *"Race has nothing to do with it."*

This steroid shit could've been squashed a long time ago, but everyone I just listed took the *"Don't ask, Don't tell"* approach. In a nation where half of the people cheat on their taxes, cheat on their wife, or both, suddenly cheating became a capital offense. In a game that thrives on cheating, suddenly cheating became the world's greatest sin. And of course, *"Race has nothing to do with it."* Baseball will forever be tainted by the Steroid Era, and rightly so, but Baseball's Segregation Era is still considered its Golden Age. And of course, *"Race has nothing to do with it."* Steroids have had less of an impact on Baseball's hallowed records than Segregation did, but you'd never hear that from the Sports Media. In 1941 Joe DiMaggio hit safely in *56* straight games, and Ted Williams finished the season with a *.406* batting average. Would these *two* all-time greats have been able to pull off those *two* amazing feats if they had to face the great Negro League pitcher Satchel Paige *two* or *three* games that season? The entire nation was complicit in Baseball's Segregation Era, and the entire nation was complicit in Baseball's Steroid Era. **No** *one* individual was the face of the Segregation Era. Unfortunately, only *one* individual is the face of the Steroid Era. And of course, *"Race has nothing to do with it."*

It's easy to make blanket statements that *"Race has nothing to do with it"* when you're not getting the Hate mail that Mr. Bonds gets (*"YOU BLACK APE"*). It's easy to make blanket statements that *"Race has nothing to do with it,"* when you're not the one being called Nigger in the outfield. The members of the Media (*both Black and White*) who make these blanket statements may be sincere when they say that *Race has nothing to do with their personal contempt* for Mr. Bonds, but they don't speak for the public. They speak their contempt to the public and then play dumb. They revel in the level of Hatred they help to create. When a certain segment of the population is repeatedly told that a certain Black Man is a bad person, they don't care if he cheated, or if he was rude to fans, or if he was disrespectful to reporters, that's just superficial excuses to apply attitudes with a much deeper and much more relevant **History.** The only thing they care about is reveling in the Hatred and then piling it on. Just like in the days of lynching when the noose, the shotgun, and the bon-fire weren't enough to get the job done. The job wasn't considered complete unless the Nigger was *castrated.* I admire Barry Bonds because he reminds me of Cicero from the movie **Mandingo.** Every time Barry hits a home run, he's quoting Cicero: *"After you hang me, kiss my ass!"*

This is all about Race and it has been about Race from day # **1.** The seed was planted many years ago when Barry got tired of answering the stupid ass *"How did it feel"* questions. How dare he show contempt for the Media? Of course, there have *never* been any White athletes who had contempt for the Media. Legendary White athletes like Joe DiMaggio and Ted Williams were *never* rude to the Media, right?

The Sports Media knew exactly how to raise the level of Hatred to the boiling point; just introduce a White Woman into the equation. The book that served as judge and jury for Barry Bonds was **Game of Shadows**. **Game of Shadows** chronicled Barry's steroid journey in great detail and one of the key sources was Mr. Bonds ex-girlfriend, who just happened to be White. **Game of Shadows** gave White Men the juicy details they needed in order to raise their level of Hatred to the boiling point, and there's absolutely no doubt the *two* White authors knew exactly what they were doing. According to the book, Mr. Bonds was controlling and verbally abusive to his White girlfriend. Wow, imagine that. A spoiled athlete being controlling and verbally abusive, that's unheard of. The White girlfriend attributed this behavior to steroid use. The White girlfriend never called the police or had Barry arrested, but the book's authors knew the information about a Black Man being abusive towards a White Woman would lead to windfall profits. The authors felt the implied steroid connection made this a print-worthy fact. I guess this means that Atlanta Braves manager Bobby

Cox was *Roid Raging* when he was arrested for allegedly punching his wife in 1995. And of course, no book about a Black Man would be complete without an attack on Black Male Sexuality. The book accused Mr. Bonds of dating a number of *different* White Women, but also stated that he suffered from Sexual dysfunction. The authors quickly put *two* and *two* together and pointed out that Sexual dysfunction is a common side effect of steroid use. The Sports Media cracked jokes when Raphael Palmeiro became a spokesperson for Viagra, but few bothered to put *two* and *two* together until Mr. Palmeiro flunked a steroids test. The opportunity to Sexually belittle Mr. Bonds, and the opportunity to introduce a scorned White Woman, created the left and right *Bloody Gloves* of the book. This information allowed the authors to frame a guilty man in the *court of public opinion.* And of course, ***"Race has nothing to do with it."***

I wasn't surprised to see Terrell Owens was *# 3* on the **"Most Hated Athlete"** list. I was definitely surprised by the Black athlete who came in at *# 2*. The athlete who was voted as the *# 2* **Most Hated Athlete** in America was Kobe Bryant. I can understand why his endorsers dropped him. That was purely a business decision. Why did the fans drop him? I thought the charges against Kobe had been dropped? Kobe may have won in the *court of law*, but he's been destroyed in *the court of public opinion.* Someone obviously spoke to the masses and the masses obviously agreed with what they heard. What the **ESPN** on-line poll tells us is that **"Hate Nigger Radio"** is very alive and its effectiveness is very well. What I always like to do is compare America's reaction to similar situations, and then focus on the inconsistencies. I could compare the Kobe Bryant situation to the Woody Allen situation, but that wouldn't be an accurate comparison. I needed to find a star who's as big as Kobe Bryant, and who's also been charged with a similar offense. Wow, how about Mike Tyson? Let's compare the Kobe situation to the Tyson situation. Let's see if **"Hate Nigger Radio"** played a role in Kobe Bryant being crowned the *# 2* **Most Hated Athlete** in America.

RANT: Kobe *vs.* Mike (Color Trumps Conviction)

If ever there was a man who could claim he received a *High-Tech Lynching,* its Kobe Bryant. That shit Justice Thomas was crying about was nothing compared to what Kobe has endured. Obviously from a historical perspective Kobe's situation would certainly be deemed lynch-worthy. Kobe was accused of raping a White Woman, need I say more. The lynch mob was the News Media, the Entertainment Media, and of course the Sports Media. The American public anxiously waited to see Kobe Bryant swing from the tree known as the Criminal Justice System. There's no doubt Kobe is *100 %* responsible for putting himself in that situation, but he's not responsible for the aftermath. The Media turned Kobe Bryant into **Strange Fruit** for the airwaves and newspapers, and like crows they gleefully plucked away (see **VOLUME I**). First of all, let's dispel a few Myths about why Kobe is the *# 2* **Most Hated Athlete** in the country.

> **# 1 The Adultery Myth-** This country lauds its celebrity adulterers. For some reason everyone got a sense of morality when they found out a Black celebrity cheated on his wife. Why? In America adultery has never adversely affected the image of a public figure. This country can't get enough of Hollywood's adulterers. The Entertainment Media needs celebrity adultery to stay afloat. Hell, adultery has even made many stars even more popular. Adultery had no negative effect on the image of Spencer Tracey and Katharine Hepburn, and this was during a time period when marriage was considered sacred. Accusations of adultery certainly haven't had any negative affect on the popularity or image of Brad Pitt or Angelina Jolie. Two of the most popular Presidents in our nation's history are confirmed adulterers, and adultery hasn't hurt their image one bit. For some reason, a Black athlete and an unknown hotel employee from a little town in Colorado were held to a higher standard than fucking Priests. Believe me, adultery has absolutely nothing to do with this nation's Hatred of Kobe Bryant.

> **# 2 The Disloyal Teammate Myth-** The Hatred for Kobe has nothing to do with him squealing on Shaq for supposedly committing adultery. You can't Hate a guy for committing adultery, and then also Hate for him squealing on someone else for supposedly committing the same sin. The Hatred for Kobe was entrenched

well before the revelations that he *squealed* on Shaq hit the papers and airwaves.

 # 3 The Break-Up of the Lakers- The Hatred for Kobe has nothing to do with him supposedly breaking up the Lakers. The L.A. Lakers have always been one of those teams that you either Love or Hate. The Lakers are like the Dallas Cowboys, the New York Yankees, the Duke Blue Devils (*college basketball program*) or Notre Dame (*football*). You either Love them or Hate them. The Laker Lovers who turned on Kobe were offset by the Laker Haters who were thrilled when the team broke up. The truth is, true Laker fans never really turned on Kobe when the team broke up, because they knew the team's owner made the final decision.

Kobe Bryant was accused of raping a White Woman, that's the **# 1** reason he's the **# 2 Most Hated Athlete** in America, period. No one knows what happened in that Colorado hotel room except Kobe and the accuser. What we do know is there was never a trial. Now let's take a look at the Mike Tyson situation. First of all, I'm a Mike Tyson fan and I'm always rooting for Mike inside of the ring, and more importantly outside of the ring. I've always felt that Don King is a despicable human being for the way he's ripped off so many young Black Men. Mr. Tyson is without question, Don's biggest victim. Don never has any problem being a financial mentor, but outside of that he's absolutely worthless. Then when you see what kind of financial mentor he is, he's worse than worthless. That said, Mike is *100 %* responsible for the situation he found himself in. Mr. Tyson was convicted of rape and served *3* years in prison. Just think, if he'd molested a *6* year-old girl for *4* years in the state of Vermont, he could've gotten off with just *60* days of treatment. Mr. Tyson is known for many, many things in the Media and rapist usually doesn't even crack the top ten. Here are a few things that Mr. Tyson is known for:

- Biting off Evander Holyfield's ear
- Great knockouts
- The youngest Heavyweight Champion in boxing history
- Great Quotes (*I'll eat his children!*)
- Great pre-fight press conferences
- The interview he and wife Robin Givens did with Barbara Walters
- His loss to Buster Douglas is considered the biggest upset in sports history

- The demolition of Michael Spinks
- The late night demolition of Mitch 'Blood' Green
- The decline of his career after hooking up with Don King

I'm not saying Mr. Tyson *should* be known as a rapist. I'm asking *why* Mr. Bryant is known as a rapist. Mr. Tyson didn't even make the **Most Hated Athletes** list. Many people feel that Mr. Tyson was innocent and received terrible legal representation. I don't disagree with either theory. No one knows what happened in that Indianapolis hotel room except Mike and the accuser. The one thing we do know is that Mike was convicted and Kobe's case never went to trial. For some reason *the court of public opinion* has things reversed, and we all know the reason why. The color of the accuser is the reason why. The *court of public opinion* said fuck the Criminal Justice System, and then *tried* and *convicted* Kobe, just like the *20th Century Southern Lynch Mobs.* The Media also took justice into their own hands, just like the *20th Century Southern Lynch Mobs.* Mr. Tyson's accuser voluntarily went to his room, and in *the court of public opinion,* she had it coming to her. *The court of public opinion* had the opposite opinion in the Kobe Bryant case. Mr. Bryant's accuser voluntarily went to his room, and as a hotel employee, she was savvy enough to know that she should sneak up to his room (*if an autograph is all you seek, then why in the world would you need to sneak*). Why the *different* opinions? The color of the accuser is the reason why. Like I said, we don't know what happened in that Colorado hotel room, but we do know what didn't happen in the Colorado courtroom. No trial, and no jail time. I'm sure White America wasn't too pleased seeing Kobe walk into that Colorado courtroom with a White Female attorney either. I wonder how much *Hank Aaron-type* fan mail she received. There's no doubt the negative Media coverage has helped to shape the present day negative image of Kobe Bryant. The negative Media coverage has occurred even though Mr. Bryant has always treated the Media with respect. And of course, *"Race has nothing to do with it."*

I'm sure Race had nothing to do with the fact that *22* out of *125* sports writers left Kobe Bryant completely off of their 2006 MVP ballots. These ballots allow writers to list their choices for the league's *top five* players in numerical order. Mr. Bryant led his team to a playoff berth, led the league in scoring, and was also selected to the NBA's all-defensive team. Despite these accomplishments, nearly *one* out of every *five* voters decided that Kobe wasn't *one* of the *top five* players in the league. These writers exhibited the classic signs and symptoms of **Small-Poleons Complex.** Many of these same writers also get the opportunity to voice their opinions on television, and of course on the radio. Many of these writers ensure that **"Hate Nigger**

Radio" is alive and well. Many of these writers are currently moaning in agony about the falsely accused Duke Lacrosse players. I continue to hear these writers and commentators state that these poor kids will never get their names or reputations back. **Give me a motherfucking break.** I'm sure they won't be damaged for life, and I'm sure they won't lose one single job opportunity. If they're uncertain about what the future holds, they can get some post-rape accusation advice from William Kennedy Smith, who appears to have survived. These young men are not the Scottsboro Boys, but I'm sure the Scottsboro Boys would've appreciated some of the concern that these young men are currently receiving. The bottom line is, I'm sure these poor kids won't be joining Mr. Bryant in the ranks of *America's Most Hated.*

By comparing the Kobe accusation to the Tyson conviction it's obvious that many of this country's Racial attitudes have never changed. Ask yourself: **"Would Kobe Bryant be as Hated if his *accuser* was Black?"** I'd be willing to bet the accusation would have quickly been forgotten. Ask yourself: **"Would Mike Tyson's *conviction* be forgotten if his victim was White?"** Hell, Mr. Tyson might still be in prison if his victim was White. What we learn when we compare the two situations is: *"The accusation of raping a White Woman is more damning than being convicted of raping a Black Woman."*

Color Trumped Conviction. The great Racial Divide remains intact, and thanks to entities such as the Media, **Devaluation** lives on.

Chapter 3
"The Great American Déjà vu"
(The Till & Simpson Trials)

Def: Déjà vu- *"A feeling of having been in a place or experienced something before"*

September 23rd 1955 (The Emmett Till Verdict)

"Forty Years and Ten Days later"

October 3rd 1995 (The O.J. Simpson Verdict)

About every *40* years there's a Racial earthquake which exposes America's great Racial Divide. These Racial earthquakes always create a huge crevice that finds Blacks standing on one side and Whites standing on the other. Since I may not be around for the next Racial earthquake, I'm going to savor the one that occurred during my lifetime, the O.J. Simpson Trial. I certainly don't mean that as disrespect to the victims. I'm just saying the O.J. Simpson Trial was a historical event and I feel fortunate to have seen it unfold. I know I'm not the only one, because when the verdict was read the entire nation came to a standstill. The reading of the verdict became the most watched event in the history of television, with an estimated *150* Million viewers. The O.J. Simpson Trial established careers, produced numerous books, and formally introduced the nation to the **Race Card.** The O.J. Simpson verdict was without question a Racial earthquake. In this chapter, I'm going to compare the 1995 Simpson verdict to the previous Racial earthquake, the 1955 Till verdict. There have been Racial tremors between the major quakes, things like riots and assassinations, but the Race-quakes seem to be on a *40* year cycle. You've got a toss-up between *Jack Johnson winning the Heavyweight title* in 1910 (*and the nationwide Race riots that followed*) and the release of D.W. Griffith's **Birth of a Nation** in 1915. 1877 gave us the end of **Reconstruction,** and 1831 gave us the infamous *Nat Turner Revolt.* Each of these events exposed the great Racial Divide, and also had a profound impact on Race relations and Race perceptions during their respective time periods. I'm kind of superstitious, so I believe in things like *'karma'*, and I also believe in all of those boring clichés:

"Life is too short to Hate"

- The more things change, the more they stay the same.
- History has a way of repeating itself.
- What comes around goes around.

You may not believe in *'karma'*, but after this chapter the year 2035 just might pique your curiosity. Here are a few similarities between the *Emmett Till Trial* and the *O.J. Simpson Trial.*

Pre-Trial Opinions

Till- Pre-Trial Opinions- Local stores, gas stations, dry cleaners, and other businesses collected *$10,000 DOLLAR$* in counter top jars, to fund the defense for Roy Bryant and J.W. Milam. That's a lot of money considering this was 1955 rural Mississippi. The majority of Whites felt Roy and J.W. were innocent. The majority of Blacks felt Roy and J.W. were guilty.

Simpson- Pre-Trial Opinions- The majority of Whites felt O.J. was guilty. The majority of Blacks felt O.J. was innocent.

Rallying beyond your 'socio-economic' Base

Till- Rallying Beyond Your 'socio-economic' Base

"People of the *socio-economic* level of the two defendants in this case (Roy and J. W.) were obviously looked down on by the more aristocratic Whites...almost with the same disdain that they looked down on Blacks...But they were still White Folks, *and when push came to shove the White community rallied in support of them...*against a young Black person for whom they had even greater disdain."

William Winter
Former Governor of Mississippi
From the PBS Documentary
The Emmett Till Story

Simpson- Rallying Beyond Your 'socio-economic' Base- The one thing many Whites still fail to understand is why so many of Black American's rallied to O.J.'s defense. After all, *99 %* of Blacks in America had nothing in common with O.J. *socio-economically.* Blacks still rallied to O.J.'s defense and celebrated when he was acquitted, even though *socio-economically* O.J. had left us long ago. The bottom line is that he automatically became one of us once he became embroiled in the Criminal Justice System. It was never about his guilt or innocence. Privately most Blacks admit that O.J. (*at the very least*) had something to do with the murders. This certainly isn't meant as a show of disrespect to the victims (*unlike those who supported Roy and J.W.*). All of the disrespectful things I've heard about the victims have come from Whites. I've heard many Whites imply that Nicole deserved to be killed for marrying outside of her Race (*that's obviously code for marrying a Nigger*). Blacks immediately rallied to O.J.'s defense once it became obvious that Whites felt he was guilty well before the trial even started. White Folks are innocent until proven guilty, and Black Folks are guilty until proven innocent. Black Folks want the same **presumption** of innocence that White Folks receive, *Nothing More and Nothing Less*. When push came to shove, O.J. was a Black Man on trial in America. Black contempt for the Criminal Justice System trumped the *socio-economic* divide that separated O.J. from the rest of us, just like White contempt for Blacks trumped the *socio-economic* divide that separated many of them from Roy and J.W. Blacks weren't necessarily rooting for O.J.; Blacks were definitely rooting against the Criminal Justice System.

The Prosecution's Case

Till- The Prosecution's Case- Several eyewitnesses, including Emmett's uncle Mr. Mose Wright, personally identified Roy Bryant and J.W. Milam as the men who came into the house and took the *14* year-old boy. Can you imagine that? Two motherfuckers just walk into your house at night and take your kid. Mr. Wright was able to identify Emmett's mutilated/decomposed body because **Dumb and Dumber** (Roy and J. W.) forgot to remove Emmett's ring. The ring had the initials ***L.T.*** engraved on it for Louis Till, Emmett's deceased father.

Simpson- The Prosecution's Case- The prosecution started off by focusing on the ***Domestic Abuse*** evidence and then moved into the Blood evidence. There was also hair and fiber evidence. The jury didn't buy O.J.'s performance when he tried on the gloves, so this hilarious debacle scored no points for either side. Everyone admits the prosecution could've done a better job, but what did the experts have to say?

In Vincent Bugliosi's book **OUTRAGE: The Five Reasons Why O.J. Simpson Got Away With Murder,** he stated: **"if the prosecution** had given an *'A+'* rather than a *'D-'* performance the verdict most likely would've been *different.*" Wow, a fucking *'D' minus.* Isn't a *'D-'* a mere pubic hair above an *'F'?* I've been out of school for a while, but from what I can remember *'F'* stands for *Failure.* The Prosecution Team put in over a year of hard work and according to Mr. Bugliosi, they were only a mere pubic hair better than complete *Failure.* Who can argue with Mr. Bugliosi? No one, after all Mr. Bugliosi put the Manson family behind bars for life. Mr. Bugliosi is a graduate of U.C.L.A. Law School and was also the president of his graduating class. His book **OUTRAGE** credits him with winning *105* of *106* felony jury trials as a prosecutor for the L.A. County District Attorney's office. Actor Robert Conrad patterned himself after Mr. Bugliosi in the television series **The D.A.** If Mr. Bugliosi says the Simpson Prosecution Team gave a *'D-'* performance, there aren't too many people on this planet who are qualified to argue with him. Wow, a fucking *'D-'.* That's a pubic hair above not even showing up.

Law Enforcement & The N-Word

Till- Law Enforcement & The N-Word
Sheriff H.C. Strider stated before the trial:
"I'd like for the NAACP or any Colored organization anywhere to know that we are here giving all parties a free trial... and intend to give a fair and impartial trial... and we don't need the help of the NAACP... and we don't intend for them to help us. We never have any trouble.... until some of our Southern *'Niggers'* go up North and the NAACP talks to them, and they come back home."

Simpson- Law Enforcement & The N-Word

Detective Marc Furman, from the *Furman Tapes:* **"You see a *'Nigger'* in a Porsche and he doesn't have a $ 100 dollar suit on, then you stop him because he has probably stolen the car."**

The Defense's Case

Till- The Defense's Case
The foundation of the Defense's case was the body found in the Tallahatchie River was not Emmett Till. The Defense even went as far as accusing Civil Rights organizations of robbing a grave, throwing a body in the river, and claiming that it was Emmett. Sheriff H.C. Strider stated: **"It (*the body*) was in mighty bad shape....The skin was slipping off the**

entire body. If one of my sons had been missing...I couldn't have told it was him. All I could tell it was a human being."

If there was anything else I could mention on behalf of the Defense I certainly would.

Simpson- *The Defense's Case*

The foundation of the Defense's case was that O.J. was framed by the L.A.P.D. For those of us in the real world, a guilty man was framed. What many of us in the real world selectively forget is that:

* The *court of public opinion* may determine guilt or innocence, but
* The *court of law* requires the state to prove its case beyond a **Reasonable Doubt.**

White America has a tough time swallowing this when it comes to the Simpson verdict. Their Racial *outrage* clouds their sensibilities. Their *outrage* is certainly Race based when you consider the complete *lack of outrage* over the Robert Blake acquittal. Don't give me that bullshit excuse **"O.J. killed two people and Blake only killed one."** If a waiter had run out to the parking lot to return a forgotten item to Ms. Bakley, there would've been a second body. The lack of a second body should not equate to the complete *lack of outrage* on the part of White America. There was more *outrage* over Michael Jackson's molestation acquittal than Robert Blake's murder acquittal. **Reasonable Doubt** is the threshold that must be cleared, and each and every American expects that threshold to apply to them if they were on trial. The facts are:

* Blood was found on the back gate that had the preservative EDTA in it. This suggests it was previously in a tube, and therefore was planted on the back gate. **The Discovery Times Channel** featured a show in October of 2005 entitled **The Case of O.J. Simpson.** The lone spokesman for the prosecution team was Deputy District Attorney Bill Hodgman. When asked about the blood on the back gate that contained EDTA, Mr. Hodgman stated:

"I saw nothing to suggest the reality of an L.A.P.D. conspiracy...so with that premise, then the effort becomes...how do we reconcile the presence of EDTA with the known results? Perhaps the EDTA came

from another source...I have to speculate about that. Intuitively I know there's a way to reconcile that...*I simply can't explain what it is."* The jury couldn't reconcile that either, which equals *Reasonable Doubt*. There was a gallon of blood in other places that didn't have EDTA in it, but if your ass was on trial you'd want an explanation for that one drop that appeared to be planted, wouldn't you (*that's not a question, because we all know the answer*).

* Barry Scheck put L.A.P.D. Chief Criminologist Dennis Fung on the witness stand for *6* days and absolutely destroyed him. Mr. Scheck got Mr. Fung to admit:
- There were blood drops in places that were blood free after the murder.
- The evidence chain of custody was compromised.
- His staff was inexperienced.
- There was a strong probability of blood evidence being contaminated due to improper storage (*blood was left in a hot vehicle instead of refrigerated*). This continued to create a cloud of *Reasonable Doubt* over the blood evidence.

* The Furman Factor. I'm not talking about whether he planted the *Bloody Glove* or whether Furman is a Racist. I'm talking about the credibility of a key witness. In the **PBS** documentary **The O.J. Verdict**, U.C.L.A. and Columbia University Law Professor Kimberle Crenshaw put it like this:

"Let's think about it? What was monstrous about a defense...that suggested one of the key officer's...that found key evidence...linking the defendant to the case...was an officer who manifested Racial bias...particularly against Inter-Racial relationships...had claimed on more than one occasion that he did manufacture evidence, and had subscribed to a whole range of extra-legal punishments that he thought would be appropriate for African-Americans...It would be *malpractice* not to introduce evidence to undermine the credibility of this officer."

After the introduction of the Furman Tapes, Mr. Furman pleaded the *5th* Amendment when questioned about his usage of the N-Word. Here are *two* more questions Mr. Furman pleaded the *5th* to:

- **QUESTION – "Have you ever falsified a police report?"**
- **ANSWER- "I wish to assert my 5th Amendment privilege."**

- **QUESTION- "Did you plant or manufacture any evidence in this case?"**
- **ANSWER- "I wish to assert my 5th Amendment privilege."**

Pleading the *5th* Amendment is not an admission of guilt, nor is it a denial, but if you're a key witness for the prosecution because you found a key piece of evidence, and you have to plead the *5th* in the middle of the trial, it looks pretty fucking bad. The threshold is **Reasonable Doubt**, and there's no doubt Mr. Furman damaged the prosecution's case. Mr. Furman's baggage was well known before the trial, and the prosecution didn't need him or the *Bloody Glove* to win the case. I've actually had White Guys tell me that it *didn't matter* if Furman was a Racist cop. I remind them that just because it doesn't matter to them, it certainly matters to me. The bottom line is that professionals are expected to leave their personal prejudices at home and perform their duties with complete impartiality. Mr. Furman's credibility was destroyed **NOT** because he's a Racist, but because he brought his Racist attitudes to work. This made him fair game for the defense.

Similar Evidence

Famous Hand-wear
The Ring was the only way Emmett's body could be identified, thus making it *The Bloody Glove* of its day. Why is the *Ring* the *Bloody Glove* of its day? Because the *Ring*, like the *Bloody Glove*, was a key piece of evidence that created a critical linkage, but didn't sway either jury.

Not-so Famous Footwear

Till- **"For three hours that morning we had a big old fire in the yard. Damn if that Nigger didn't have crepe sole shoes. Do you know how hard they are to burn?"**
This is from J.W. Milam's confession to **Look** magazine which detailed how he and Roy *destroyed* evidence.

Simpson- **"I don't have any ugly ass shoes like that."**
This was O.J.'s *denial* of owning a key piece of evidence. Pictures of O.J. wearing the Bruno Magli shoes (*that matched foot prints at the crime scene*) would later surface during his Civil Trial.

The Judge's Performance

Till Judge- Was considered to be pro Defense Team.

Simpson Judge- Was considered to be pro Defense Team.

The Jury's Performance

Till- The Jury's Performance- There were problems finding impartial jurors from the onset because:

• Prospective jurors were related to the Defense Attorneys.
• Prospective jurors obviously lived in close proximity to the crime.
• Many prospective jurors had contributed to a defense fund for the defendants.

They eventually found *12* impartial White Male jurors. We know what the results were. I seriously doubt if any of the jurors were surprised when they read Roy and J.W.'s confession in **Look** magazine, just *4* months after their acquittal. I wouldn't have a problem with their decision if someone could point out one shred of *Reasonable Doubt.*

Simpson- The Jury's Performance- The majority of the *outrage* over the Simpson verdict has been directed towards the jury. The Simpson Jury consisted of *9* Blacks, *2* Whites, and *1* Hispanic, and *10* of the *12* were women. This is the type of jury the prosecution wanted because they were playing the *Domestic Abuse Card.* Right or wrong, the jury didn't want to hear about *Domestic Abuse*, and for some reason this really peeved a lot of legal experts and Media members. If the jury was *over-focused* on the murder charges, then it was the prosecution's responsibility to show why *Domestic Abuse* was so important to the case. With the right presentation, you can sell anything.

Example: The Bush Administration consistently implied that Iraq and Sadaam Hussein were involved in the attacks on September 11th 2001. Polls consistently showed that *60 %* of the American people actually believed that bullshit, so obviously the presentation was successful. The Bush Administration did such a great job of selling *only* the small picture (*Sadaam Hussein*); the American people failed to make a connection to the big picture (**Oil**). The presentation was flawless, thanks to the help of a Media that feared being branded as liberals or unpatriotic. The Prosecution Team did such a poor job of selling the small picture (*Domestic Abuse*); the jury was unable to make a connection to the big picture (**Murder**).

It's all about making the right kind of presentation, and giving your audience the right blend of information to paint the specific picture you desire. The prosecution team needed a Karl Rove. The prosecution's presentation failed to convince the jury that *Domestic Abuse* was important to this case. Is this the jury's fault? In the eyes of White America apparently it is the jury's fault. When *99 %* of the evidence is damning, White America has every right to expect justice. The only problem is that in America justice is often determined by factors that outweigh the importance of good evidence.

If *99 %* of the evidence is damning and *1 %* is not only questionable, but appears to have been planted, what do you do? In America that question is answered by *two* additional questions:

 # 1 What color is the victim?
 # 2 What color is the accused?

Those *two* questions can be broken down into *four* **Racial Combinations**:

 # 1 Black on White crime
 # 2 Black on Black crime
 # 3 White on White crime
 # 4 White on Black crime

Now take the *four* **Racial Combinations** I just listed, apply the Simpson evidence (*99 %* good and *1 %* questionable) and imagine an All-White jury. Now ask yourself who's more likely to walk, and who's more likely to get convicted?

An All-White Jury which receives evidence that is *99 %* good and *1 %* questionable would:

 # 1 Black on White crime = Conviction
 # 2 Black on Black crime = Conviction
 # 3 White on White crime = consider the *Reasonable Doubt*
 # 4 White on Black crime = consider the *Reasonable Doubt*

As you can see, this shit is damn near pre-determined. The *two* main reasons it turned out *different* for O.J. were:

 # 1 He had the money to buy a Defense team that could point out the questionable *1 %*.

 # 2 He had a jury of his Racial peers willing to consider the ***Reasonable Doubt*** created by that questionable *1 %*. He received the same ***Reasonable Doubt*** that White juries have always given White defendants.

They didn't let him walk just because he's Black, they let him walk because they were willing to accept the questionable *1 %* as sufficient ***Reasonable Doubt***. White juries do that shit everyday or do the complete opposite, and convict a Black Man when *99 %* of the evidence is questionable and only *1 %* is good. If the victim is White, *100 %* of the evidence can be questionable and a White jury will still convict a Black Man. On the flipside, if O.J.'s victim was Black, he'd still be playing golf at California country clubs.

The Simpson jury has been called all of the ***Stereotypical*** names that Black Folks know quite well. This was to be expected, and this *overshadowed* the hypocrisy and the irony of the event. A Black jury was supposed to do something that White juries have consistently failed to do. Take Race out of the equation. A Black jury was supposed to do something that White juries have consistently done. Convict a Black Man even though the prosecution presented a '*D-*' case.

I repeat, '*D-*' is a pubic hair above not presenting a case at all. Whites still insist the Simpson jury should've reached a guilty verdict. Why? The color of the victim (*White*) and the color of the accused (*Black*) is the reason why. Of the *four* **Racial Combinations** I listed, Black on White crime scores the highest on the *Outrage Scale*. The Racial *outrage* over the Simpson verdict clouds the judgment of the best legal minds in this country. When you hear the Nancy Grace's and Jeffrey Toobin's of the airwaves talk about the Simpson verdict, you can feel their *outrage*. Their true feelings about Race clouds their legal judgment; this tells us the great Racial Divide hasn't gone anywhere. In the Simpson case Color trumps the lack of a Conviction. I mentioned Mr. Bugliosi's book **OUTRAGE**, and I want to share with you a few wonderful examples of how Racial *outrage* clouds legal judgment. Mr. Bugliosi gives *5* reasons why the case was lost, but also stated that the *5* reasons could be distilled down to *2* reasons:

 # 1- The jury could hardly have been any worse, and
 # 2- neither could the prosecution.

That's pretty direct and very damning. The jury could hardly have been any worse. Damn! This was on pg. # 6. Why was the jury so fucked up? They must've been Racially biased, pretty damn dumb or both, right. Exactly *16* lines down the page from his *"could hardly have been any worse"* comment, Mr. Bugliosi ruled out Racial bias when he wrote:

"And in listening to the Simpson jurors in post-trial interviews, and reading a book jointly written by three of them, my feelings in this respect have been strengthened. I got *no* sense at all from them that they didn't care if Simpson was guilty or not, *no* sense that their state of mind back in the jury room had been:

Even though O.J. is obviously guilty we like O.J., so let's give him two free murders or,

Even though we know O.J. is guilty, Blacks have been discriminated against by Whites for centuries, so let's pay Whitey back and give O.J. a couple freebies.

I *didn't sense* that, nor do I *believe* it for one moment."

That negates *one* of White America's most popular charges. The charge that the jury let O.J. walk because he's a fellow Black. Mr. Bugliosi didn't see it that way. The other popular charge is the jury was a bunch of dumb ass Niggers who didn't have the *Intellectual* capacity to process the mountains of evidence against O.J. This is the typical White perception of Blacks and Mr. Bugliosi easily fell into this bigoted mindset, and then a few lines later he fell out of this bigoted mindset. Here's what Mr. Bugliosi said about the *dumb* jurors on pg. # 7:

What I did see, however, were jurors who:
(1) clearly did not have too much *intellectual* firepower, and
(2) were biased in Simpson's favor, most likely from the start.

Previously on pg.'s # 6 and # 7, he explained that he *didn't sense* or *believe* they were biased, but for some reason he had to revisit the *bias* theory. Is he confused? Mr. Bugliosi is considered *one* of the greatest prosecutors in our nation's history, so I certainly wouldn't make that charge. Exactly *8* lines down the page from his *"not too much intellectual firepower"* comment Mr. Bugliosi had this to say about the same jury:

"And this *jury wasn't quite as dense* as some have felt. In post-trial interviewing, nearly all have proved to be *fairly articulate*, two having *college degrees*. The only kind of juror you can't turn around would be one who was determined to let Simpson get away with these murders even if he or she had no doubt at all Simpson was guilty. But it would be an extremely rare occurrence for even one juror to have this outrageous and unconscionable attitude, much less all twelve."

Are they *biased* or not Vince? Are they *dumb* or not Vince? Mr. Bugliosi's Racial **OUTRAGE** trumped his legal judgment and that's why you end up with complete contradictions on the same fucking page, just a few lines apart. If this man can't put his legal judgments above his personal Racial *outrage*, then it's no wonder Black Folks usually get fucked in *the court of law*, as well as *the court of public opinion*. Mr. Bugliosi confirmed how Racial *outrage* trumps legal judgment on pg. # **387** when he writes about the all-White jury in the Rodney King Trial:

"To the Simi Valley jury, the man on trial was Rodney King, and the main lawyer arguing on his behalf, the prosecutor, was another Black Man. Assisting the Black Man was his co-prosecutor, who is Jewish. To many hidebound White conservatives, Jews are liberal, left-leaning ACLU types who deep down are really on the side of the criminal. The four White defendants, on the other hand, had four White, Christian, God-fearing lawyers defending them."

When you consider the actions of the Simi Valley jury, as well as many other all-White juries that Blacks have faced in the past, maybe Black Folks deserve a couple freebies. But I would never say that, because that would be acknowledging the Simpson jury didn't reach the appropriate verdict. Let's just say, the Simi Valley jury was willing to accept the *1 %* of questionable evidence, and overlook *99 %* of the good (i.e., *videotaped*) evidence. Remember the *four* **Racial Combinations?** Oh, that's right, *"Race had nothing to do with it."*

The prosecution did not prove its case beyond a **Reasonable Doubt**. When the Prosecution doesn't reach the threshold of guilty beyond a **Reasonable Doubt** in *the court of law,* a Black defendant is entitled to an acquittal, just like a White defendant, regardless of what verdict *the court of public opinion* reaches. Mr. Bugliosi inadvertently made it very clear what kind of justice is appropriate for Black Folks. I realize very few cases are an '*A+*' or *100 %* airtight, but if the threshold to execute a Black Man is a '*D-*', what does that say about the system? It says **Devaluation**, that's what it says. There's a lot of Brothers locked up because of *'D-'* evidence, or a *'D-'* eye witness, or a *'D-'* investigation, or a *'D-'* public defender, or a *'D-'* jury, or a *'D-'* prosecution, or a *'D-'* judge. O.J. was merely a groundbreaking exception to that historical rule.

Closing Arguments of The Defense Team

Till- Closing Arguments of The Defense Team

"I want you to tell me where...under God's shining sun.... is the land of the free and the home of the brave? *If you don't turn these boys loose...your forefathers will absolutely turn over in their graves!***"**
Defense Attorney J.W. Kellum

"There are people in the United States who want to destroy the customs of Southern people...They would not be above putting a rotting, stinking body in the river in the hope he would be identified as Emmett Till. *I'm sure that every last Anglo-Saxon one of you has the courage to free these men in the face of that pressure!***"**
Defense Attorney John W. Whitten Jr.

Simpson- Closing Arguments of the Defense Team

"Furman wants to take all Black people and burn them. That's genocidal Racism. Maybe this is one of the reasons we're all gathered together here this day. Maybe there's a reason for your purpose? Maybe this is why you were selected? There's something in your background or in your character that helps you understand this is wrong. Maybe you're the right people, at the right time, at the right place, to say *No More!***"**
Defense Attorney Johnnie Cochran

Length of Jury Deliberations

Till- Length of Jury Deliberations

67 minutes. One of the jury members stated: *"It would've been even shorter but we stopped to drink some pop."*

Simpson- Length of Jury Deliberations

210 minutes.

Post Trial Comments

Till- Post Trial Comments

"What I saw was a shame before God and man. The way the jury chose to believe the ridiculous stories of the defense attorneys…I just can't go into detail to tell you the stupid things, the silly things that were brought up as probabilities, and they swallowed it like a fish swallows a hook. Just anything…any excuse…to acquit those two men."

Mamie Till

Simpson- Post Trial Comments

"He (Johnnie Cochran) suggests that Racism ought to be the most important thing that any one of us ought to listen to in this court. That anyone of us in this nation should be listening to. And it's because of Racism we should put aside all other thought, all other reason…and set his murdering client free!"

Fred Goldman

Post Trial Reactions

Till- Post Trial Reaction

"There was a huge celebration outside the courthouse when the *Not Guilty* verdict was announced. Shot guns were fired in the air like it was the 4th of July."

Mamie Till

Simpson- Post Trial Reaction

There were camera's positioned on Whites and Blacks across the nation. The nation got to see Black Folks celebrate like it was the 4th of July. The nation also got to see the shock and sorrow on the faces of Whites. The shock and sorrow on the faces of Whites was eerily similar to the shock and sorrow on the faces of Blacks who attended Emmett's open-casket funeral.

The Second Trial

2*nd* *Till* **Trial**
Six weeks after the acquittal a Grand Jury was convened to consider the evidence to charge Roy and J.W. with kidnapping. After all, they strolled into Mr. Wright's home in the middle of the night with pistols and flashlights and removed the *14* year-old. In less than *20* minutes, without hearing from *one* eyewitness, the Grand Jury concluded there was insufficient evidence to charge Roy and J.W. with kidnapping. A *second* trial has yet to occur, and it looks like *no one will ever pay* for this crime.

2*nd* *Simpson* **Trial**
The Civil Trial featured a predominately White jury, a lower burden of proof, and newly introduced evidence (most notably the Bruno Magli shoes, the Bronco chase, and O.J. babbling on the witness stand). The jury found O.J. liable and ordered him to pay *33.5* Million *DOLLAR$*. As of now, no payments have yet to occur, and it looks like O.J. will *never have to pay* for this crime.

The Defendants

Till- **The Defendants**
Roy and J.W. sold their confessions to **Look** magazine, and were subsequently shunned by their community and also by their state. An entire state had claimed the two men were innocent, and claimed that communist or the NAACP had staged the whole event. The **Look** magazine confession made the entire state of Mississippi look like a bunch of _____
_____(*feel free to fill in the blank with whatever you like*). Both Roy and J.W. ended up divorced. Both ended up broke. Both had time to reflect on their lives because they died from the slow death known as cancer. Both died in their early 60's.

Simpson- **The Defendant**
O.J. lives an isolated life but still has a few friends. He seems to be handling single-parenthood very well, other than occasionally butting heads with a teen-age daughter, which is normal. He's not broke, but he does play on public golf courses now. Until O.J. sells his confession to a major publication, many Black Folks will continue to say that he's Not

Guilty. As history told us in the Till case, Not Guilty doesn't mean your innocent. O.J. may seem like he's much better off than Roy and J.W., but he's not. O.J. faces his crime everyday when he faces his children. He sees his deed in his children's eyes, because he can see Nicole's eyes in his children's eyes. He knows what look was in her eyes when she gasped her last breath. That's not cancer; it's a much slower death than cancer. But if I was him I'd still be getting my prostate checked regularly.

The Victims

Till- The Victim
Emmett Till's death ignited a movement which eventually led to Civil Rights legislation.

Simpson- The Victim
Nicole Simpson's death ignited a movement which eventually led to new Domestic Abuse Laws across the nation, saving countless lives.

The Aftermath

The great Racial Divide is still here, and when it's exposed, Blacks and Whites still stand on their respective sides of the crevice. The divide was recently exposed during Hurricane Katrina. Hurricane Katrina may have seemed like a full-blown Race-quake at the time, but in many ways it's already been forgotten. Hurricane Katrina was barely mentioned in President Bush's 2006 State of the Union address, and the liberal Media barely even noticed the omission. So I'd say Katrina was just a tremor or maybe an aftershock. For those of you who make it to the next Race-quake, which is due in the 2030's, just remember this verse from the **Crosby, Stills, Nash, and Young** song **Déjà vu:**
"And I feeel like I've been here befooore"

Chapter 4 "*TOM*FOOLERY"

I hope it doesn't seem like I've got something against Mr. Bugliosi because I don't. But I would like to take issue with one more comment from his book **OUTRAGE**. Mr. Bugliosi had a theory on how the prosecution could've turned the predominantly Black jury against the Black defendant, O.J. Simpson. Mr. Bugliosi felt the prosecution should've subpoenaed Hall of Fame football player Jim Brown to come in and testify that O.J. Simpson was an Uncle *Tom*. When I read this (on pg. #193) I laughed my ass off. I'm not a legal expert, so I'm sure Mr. Bugliosi has some reasonable explanations for the inconsistencies I noted in the last chapter. I am a "*Tom*foolery" expert, because as a Black Man who has to function in White society, you have to be. As an expert in *Tom*foolery, I have no problem saying Mr. Bugliosi doesn't know what the fuck he's talking about. As someone who has been called an Uncle *Tom*, and as someone who has called fellow Black Men Uncle *Toms*, I, like most Black Men in my shoes, have mastered a game that White Men will *never* know and *never* understand. The ability to function in White society without giving off the '*Tom*' vibe requires great skill. The Uncle *Tom* Game is the Black Man's game and only the Black Man's game. White Men need not apply. White Men don't understand the *Tom* Game, can't feel the sting of the *Tom* Game, and only make the *Tom* Game worse. The *Tom* Game is basically Blacks playing the **Race Card** against Blacks. I don't know if Mr. Brown would've testified that O.J. was an Uncle *Tom*, only Mr. Brown can answer that question. I do know what the ramifications would've been had Mr. Brown done so:

> **# 1** Most Blacks probably do feel that O.J. was *Tommin'* it back then, but if Mr. Brown had given testimony to help send a fellow Brother to Death Row, he would've lost all street cred (*credibility*). He would've been deemed untrustworthy by most Black Men on the street. Mr. Brown is one of the few high-profile Black Men who gets in the trenches of the Black community and provides guidance to those who've gone astray. The reason Mr. Brown is so effective in his mentoring endeavors is because he's so well respected. If he were to testify against O.J. he would've jeopardized that respect. It's true that O.J. lived in a White world, but he wasn't an outspoken *Tom* or an *anti-Black Tom*. Men like Ward Connerly,

Shelby Steele, Thomas Sowell, Armstrong Williams and of course Justice Thomas, now that's a *different* story. Those men are *anti-Black Toms* because they publicly *Jack-Off* White Men and embrace *anti-Black* policies (See **Terms & Def's** for *Jacking-Off*). It would still be hard to walk into a courtroom and send a fellow Brother to Death Row on behalf of *The Man*. Especially when that Brother did absolutely nothing to you personally.

 # 2 There is a good chance Mr. Brown's testimony could've backfired. The predominantly Black jury could've easily resented Mr. Brown's actions, resented the prosecution's effort to pit Black against Black, and therefore resented the entire episode. The result of trying to play the *Tom* Card could've created the complete opposite effect of its original intent. As for Mr. Brown, he would've risked being considered a sell-out for selling-out a man who was already widely perceived as a sell-out.

As you can see, the nuance of the *Tom* Game is something that Whites will never truly understand. Mr. Brown is on record as saying O.J. exhibited *Tom-like* behavior, but sitting on the witness stand and testifying against him is a whole new ballgame. What would a Black Man look like testifying on behalf of *The Man* against another Black Man? He'd look like an Uncle *Tom*. Testifying on behalf of *The Man*, even against an Uncle *Tom*, is a plantation game that I just don't see Mr. Brown playing. If you're subpoenaed you have to testify, but my guess is Mr. Brown's testimony would've been useless. Mr. Brown certainly would not have perjured himself, and certainly would've testified that O.J. had very little contact with the Black community. Other than that information, I have a hard time believing Mr. Brown would've helped to send a fellow Black Man to Death Row, when the Black Man in question never did anything to Mr. Brown personally. After all, he's had way more run-ins with the Criminal Justice System than O.J., so he definitely understands how the game is played. I could be wrong, but I doubt it. The Uncle *Tom* Game is the Black Man's game, period. White people do not understand it, do not understand the nuance of it, and have no place in it.

When a Black Man gets called an Uncle *Tom* by another Black Man, it's a serious charge that can only be addressed by the Brother on the receiving end. The absolute, *100 %*, last thing a Black Man needs, is for a White Man to come running to his rescue when the *Tom* Charge has been made. This shit cracks me up, and it tells you just how fucking clueless Whites are when it comes to the *Tom* Game. When Whites run to the defense of a Black Man because he was called an Uncle *Tom*, it confirms the *Tom* Charge in every Black person's mind. Why does it confirm the *Tom* Charge? The fact that White Folks never run to the defense of a Black Man any other time confirms it. This would raise an automatic Red Flag, or in this case an automatic *White Flag*. All the Black Folks would say **"Damn, he must be an Uncle Tom because White Folks don't run to our defense any other time."** The truth is, there are only *two* times when Whites will run to the defense of a Black Man:

1- When it's a Black athlete in trouble.

Obviously, the Race of the victim plays a major role in how vigorous the White defense will be. We see Black athletes get away with shit at every level because Whites are willing to give them breaks that are usually reserved just for Whites. Athletes are spoiled and coddled, regardless of Race, but Black athletes get away with shit that normal Black Folks don't. Whites are willing to help them, give them the benefit of the doubt, and even give them a second chance. We've seen it time and time again. An *18* year-old Black Male gets busted for retail theft, and an *18* year-old White Male gets busted for breaking into dozens of cars. Guess which one usually ends up being charged as a *felon* (*which basically means fucked for life*)? The Black Man, right. Wrong, if he's great ball player. Look at how many opportunities Lawrence Phillips got. If Ray Lewis wasn't a great football player he'd be in jail right now. If Ray Lewis had to utilize a public defender he'd be in jail right now. His employer stood by him and was willing to wait until the incident was finalized by the Criminal Justice System. Any other Black Man, in any other occupation would have been suspended without pay or fired. I'm certainly not implying Ray Lewis got away with any crime whatsoever. I'm saying there's a lot of Black Men in prison for bullshit, and if they were athletes they'd be on the street. If Rae Carruth hadn't fled and got busted hiding in a trunk, the Carolina Panthers would've stood by his side until the verdict was read (*this is obviously dictated by the victim's color*). The bottom line is Whites will defend Blacks when it will benefit them down the road. They're basically protecting an investment. I'm certainly not complaining. All I'm saying is this is *one* of the *two* times you'll see Whites rush to the defense of a Black Man.

2- When the Uncle *Tom* Charge has been made.

This one is also a matter of protecting an investment. Whites that defend Blacks when the *Tom* Charge has been made are doing so because they need that Black person in their corner. As long as that lone Black face is in their corner, they can fend off any charges of Racism. You're beginning to see this more than ever because you've got a handful of Black Conservatives who always seem to be on display. It's a hilarious spectacle because conservatives fail to realize it's their actions that give the appearance of Racism. Parading out perceived *Toms* doesn't mitigate the appearance of Racism, it enhances it. Conservatives say *"You can't call me a Racist, after all:*

"Clarence *Tom*as agrees with me"
"*Tom*as Sowell agrees with me"
"*Tom*-strong Williams agrees with me"
"Ward *Tom*merly agrees with me"
"Kenneth *Tom*well agrees with me"
"*Tom* C. Watts agrees with me"
"*Tom* 'Cock-eye' Christie agrees with me"
"*Tom-Al*an Keyes agrees with me"
"*ToM*ichael Steele agrees with me"
"*Tom*by Steele agrees with me"
"Rev. *Tom* Watkins agrees with me"

Black Conservatives receive most of the *Tom* Charges nowadays and it's well deserved.

If you're going to ride with the party that employs the divisive **SOUTHERN STRATEGY** to win elections, then you better be ready to defend yourself against the *Tom* Charge.

If you're going to ride with the party that coddles the *Confederate Flag*, then you better be ready to defend yourself against the *Tom* Charge.

If you're going to ride with the party that caters to *Racists*, and therefore receives the majority of the *Racists Vote*, then you better be ready to defend yourself against the *Tom* Charge.

If you Love to yell about the ills of *Welfare*, but don't say shit about *Corporate Welfare*, then you better be ready to defend yourself against the *Tom* Charge.

If you Love to yell about the ills of *Affirmative Action*, but only whisper when the subject is *Legacy Admits (i.e., family members are alumni) or Development Admits (i.e., family members are wealthy)*, then you better be ready to defend yourself against the *Tom* Charge.

If you're going to ride with the party that is LOADED with men who voted against the Martin Luther King Holiday, then you better be ready to defend yourself against the *Tom* Charge.

If you're going to ride with the party that was on *Vacation* while your people were drowning during Hurricane Katrina, then you better be ready to defend yourself against the *Tom* Charge.

If you're going to ride with the party that has a *2 %* approval rating among Blacks in this country, then you better be ready to defend yourself against the *Tom* Charge.

The Bush Administration's *2 %* approval rating among Blacks was earned, not given (*or as conservatives say*: **It's based on *Merit***). I'm not saying all White Conservatives are Racist. I'm saying many of them openly cater to Racist elements. One could easily make the argument that catering to Racists has put conservatives in the majority. The *SOUTHERN STRATEGY* is the cornerstone of their movement because its effectiveness is automatic. The *SOUTHERN STRATEGY* unites more conservatives than abortion, gay marriage, and the religious right combined. There were many hands involved in the creation of the *SOUTHERN STRATEGY,* but there's no doubt who its founding father was. That would be the rapist from the great state of South Carolina, Sen. Strom Thurmond (see *RANT:* **"Lifestyles of the Rich & Rapists"** in **VOLUME I**).

Sen. Thurmond created a new party (*the Dixiecrats*) and then switched parties (*Democrat to Republican*) just so he could cater to Racists. Eventually nearly every Senator from the South would follow suit. The basic goal of the *SOUTHERN STRATEGY* is to make Race a wedge issue. Race has been a social divider in this nation from its inception, so it was relatively easy to convert the Racial fear and Racial contempt into political fear, and therefore political reward. The Brown Decision and the passing of the 1964 Civil Rights Act created the fear. Conservatives then developed terms such as *Welfare Babies* and *Welfare Queens* in order to create the much needed contempt. Pres. Nixon then unknowingly gave conservatives the crowned jewel of the *SOUTHERN STRATEGY.* The introduction of Affirmative Action to the political arena created both fear and contempt.

There's no doubt the fear and contempt created by Affirmative Action has mobilized more White Male voters than Roe *v.* Wade and Gay Marriage combined. Generations of politicians from coast to coast quickly learned that the *SOUTHERN STRATEGY* delivers election victories. The Brown

Decision and the Civil Rights Act were *mini-Race-Quakes* that shook the nation; the *SOUTHERN STRATEGY* is an ever enduring tremor. The *SOUTHERN STRATEGY* is like Jessica Tandy in the movie **Driving Miss Daisy.** Like Miss Daisy, the *SOUTHERN STRATEGY* serves as the backseat driver of the Republican Party. It tells the party where to go and what to do. The *SOUTHERN STRATEGY* has been allowed to sit in the backseat and give orders because the so-called liberal Media has failed to expose it, even though this *STRATEGY* plays a major role in who becomes President of the United States. After all, no self-respecting Southerner would dare vote for a Northerner, because Northerners only want to give everything to them damn worthless Niggers. If you're a Black Man and these are the bedfellows you've chosen, then you better be ready to defend yourself against the *Tom* Charge.

To pretend this attitude doesn't exist is nothing more than pretending to not see the backseat driver. The common bond of the *Red States* has always been its attitudes on **Race.** *Religion's* ascent to the front seat of *Red State* politics is a fairly new phenomenon, but *Religion's* attitudes are old news. *Religious* attitudes and **Racist** attitudes often walk *hand-n-hand*, and even though many will claim that *Religion* and **Racism** are not bedfellows, we mustn't forget that in America, Sundays are the most segregated day of the week. In the *Red States* the front seat passenger (*Religion*) rarely disagrees with the directions of its backseat driver (**Racists**). Bob Jones University was the embodiment of these *two* **non-competing** forces for decades. The wedge issues that rally the *Religious Right* often walk *hand-n-hand* with the wedge issues that rally the **Racists.** Therefore, the *SOUTHERN STRATEGY* becomes the Big Tent that Republicans are really singing about. The attitudes within this Big Tent are the attitudes of Hate and Intolerance (which have always walked *hand-n-hand*). Inside of this Big Tent, the attitudes towards Homosexuals *are eerily similar* to the attitudes towards Blacks. This tells us the front seat rider and backseat driver are on the same page. And of course, the role of Morgan Freeman (*the driver in* **Driving Miss Daisy**) is happily played by Black Conservatives.

The *SOUTHERN STRATEGY* is not only a major determining factor in who will become President of the United States, it is also the underlying factor in the current climate of partisanship. The *SOUTHERN STRATEGY* doesn't just cater to angry White Males; its objective is to create angry White Males. The *SOUTHERN STRATEGY* became the line in America's political sand, because it forced White politicians to become Liberal or Conservative, and nothing in between. This distinct line in the sand facilitated the *extinction* of politicians who were known as Liberal Republicans and Conservative Democrats. The end result of this divisive

STRATEGY is the *extinction* of moderate politicians who were willing to cross the isle and vote their conscious. Their *extinction* made things like non-partisan, bi-partisan, compromise, common ground, and middle ground, *extinct* as well. These were political virtues that improved Race relations and improved Race conditions. Without those political virtues, the Racial Divide has grown before our eyes. When the Racial Divide grows, Black Folks automatically lose, because we also *Economically* lose. If you're a Black Man, and you support the people who created the political divisions that have stymied your people's progress, then you motherfuckers better be ready to defend yourself against the *Tom* Charge.

There are certainly times when the *Tom* Charge doesn't have merit. Black Men who don't work, Love to make the *Tom* Charge against Black Men who do work. I actually had a Black Friend say to me: **"Man, I can't believe you gonna go to that place and work for the White Man,"** and I explained to him: **"The White Man you're referring to helps me pay my bills, and your sorry ass on the other hand costs me money because you can't afford a fucking beer."** End of conversation, and end of the *Tom* Charge. When you're hit with the *Tom* Charge, you and only you can defend yourself. When Muhammad Ali used to call Joe Frazier an Uncle *Tom*, Mr. Frazier didn't want and didn't need any White Men to come to his rescue. He answered the *Tom* Charge personally, in the ring. Even though he lost *two* of his *three* fights against Mr. Ali, there's no denying the physical damage he inflicted. There's also no denying the psychological damage Mr. Ali inflicted. Mr. Frazier is an extremely proud Black Man, and to this very day he still harbors resentment towards Mr. Ali because of the *Tom* Charge. The *Tom* Charge is the Black Man's game, Whites need not apply. Many times you don't have to respond to the *Tom* Charge, because people will *consider the source.*

Another time the *Tom* Charge is made is when a Black Man is involved with a White Woman. What you do in your bedroom has nothing to do with who you are out of your bedroom. It's your actions outside of the bedroom that will determine how you're judged. Charles Barkley is married to a White Woman and no one would ever dream of calling him an Uncle *Tom*. If Justice *Thom*as did anything remotely helpful for Black Folks, no one would say one word about his White Wife. His actions on the bench are the foundation for the *Tom* Charge, not his White Wife. His White Wife becomes the icing on the cake when the *Tom* Charge is made, that's all. There's a ton of Black Men out there with White Women and they don't let it diminish who they are or where they came from. I've always felt that a White Woman on the arm of a Black Man is our version of the ***Stars and Bars.*** It's **kryptonite** to the **Confederate Flag waivers,** which is quite alright with me. If it makes their blood boil, then obviously they have some Hate in their veins. Remember the definition of Hate is **Small-Poleons Complex**. It always ties together in one nice neat package doesn't it? Black Men with White Women is *not* the **true essence** of *Tom*ism, but it can certainly become an *element* of *Tom*ism, if you let it. Before identifying the **true essence** of *Tom*ism (i.e., *what makes someone an* **Uncle Tom**), maybe we should take a quick look at the history of *Tom*ism.

For those of you who don't know, the term 'Uncle *Tom*' comes from Harriet Beecher Stowe's 1852 novel **Uncle Tom's Cabin**. One of the inspirations for the novel was the autobiography of a Black Slave named Josiah Henson. The novel paints a brutally honest picture of Slavery, and is considered one of the stepping stones to the Civil War. The main Black character in the novel is a Black Male Slave named *Tom*, and it's *Tom's* *"Yessuuum Maaasa"* relationship with his White master that spawned the term Uncle *Tom*. There's no doubt the term Uncle *Tom* is often thrown around without merit, but throughout history there have certainly been Black Men who've earned the title. The Black Slave Josiah Henson gave us the definition of *Tom*ism well before the term Uncle *Tom* came to be. In 1825 Mr. Henson was given the responsibility of transporting *18* Black Slaves and his wife and *2* children, from his master's farm in Maryland, to his master's brother's farm in Kentucky. While traveling through Ohio, a free state, Mr. Henson was told repeatedly by Blacks and Whites that they could remain in Ohio, and would therefore be considered free. Mr. Henson refused to be deterred by talk of freedom and *Stayed the Course*. Mr. Henson completed his mission and later wrote:

"I had promised that man to take his property to Kentucky, and deposit it with his brother; and this only, I resolved to do."

When I picture this event I get chills. Like I said, the Uncle *Tom* game is the Black Man's game, Whites need not apply.

<u>What is the **true essence** of *Tom*ism?</u>

• Acting White is *not* the **true essence** of *Tom*ism. Acting White is only an *element* (*or a small part*) of *Tom*ism. It's not about acting; it's about your actions.

• Leaving your people behind is *not* the **true essence** of *Tom*ism. Moving on is only an *element* of *Tom*ism. If you've got crazy-ass family members who don't want to act right, you just might have to leave their asses behind. That doesn't make you an Uncle *Tom*. Turning your back on your people is only an *element* of *Tom*ism. It's what you do after you've moved on that makes you an Uncle *Tom*.

• Black Men who *Jack-Off* White Men to get ahead is ***not*** the **true essence** *Tom*ism. Black Men *Jacking-Off* White Men to get ahead is only an ***element*** of *Tom*ism. It's the results of their *Jacking-Off* that will determine if they're an Uncle *Tom* or not.

The **true essence** of *Tom*ism is when Blacks move on and then help create ***barriers*** that hold other Black Folks back. Moving on and then putting up ***barriers*** so no one else can move forward is the **true essence** of *Tom*ism. ***Benefiting*** from Affirmative Action and then ***denouncing*** Affirmative Action after you've gotten your slice of the pie is the **true essence** of *Tom*ism. Doing shit like aiding and abetting the Ignorance of Whites by singing that *'pull up your bootstraps'* bullshit, without pointing a finger at those who intentionally hide the boots, is the **true essence** of *Tom*ism. Mr. Henson could've taken his wife and kids to Kentucky and freed the rest of the Slaves, but he chose to hold them back. That's the **true essence** of *Tom*ism.

When Blacks tell other Blacks to get their shit together, it comes from true concern. When Blacks tell Whites that Black Folks need to get their shit together, it creates a lack of concern. The Blacks who do this shit are usually just blowing their own horn at the expense of the Blacks they left behind. The ***"I'm not one of them"*** attitude encourages Whites to have disdain for ***them.*** Many Whites have always believed the line from the movie **The Godfather:** ***"They're (Blacks) animals anyway, so let them lose their souls."*** What Black Conservatives often do is affirm this belief for White Conservatives. Black Conservatives unknowingly tell Whites ***"They're animals anyway, but I'm not one of them."*** Black Conservatives enable those corrosive attitudes, and enabling those corrosive attitudes is just another way of restricting those who you've turned your back on. Those corrosive attitudes are an ***external barrier*** for Black America, and when you consider the number of ***internal barriers*** that Black America faces, it doesn't look good for the home team. Present day there's a fierce debate going on within the Black community. The debate is over how to stop the downward spiral of Black America. There are a number of *different* factions and theories, but still no progress. What I find *encouraging* is the fact that there is genuine concern from most of the factions, and most of the theories have merit. What I find *discouraging* is the fact that some of those theories come from Black Men who side with men who have no genuine concern. What keeps Black Conservatives under the cloud of *Tom*ism is the company they keep.

There's only one Black Conservative who's proven that he wants to uplift his people and not hold them back. Colin Powell is the only Black Conservative who is pro-Affirmative Action, and Colin Powell is the only

Black Conservative who consistently acknowledges the playing field is *not* level. It's *not* his stance on Affirmative Action that makes him unique among Black Conservatives. It's his acknowledgement that the playing field is *not* level that makes him unique among Black Conservatives. Affirmative Action is merely a policy. Race relations are a reflection of our attitudes, and it just so happens our policies are also a reflection of our attitudes. When attitudes change, our policies will change accordingly. When Blacks choose to become conservatives the only attitudes that get changed are their own. The result is the same old *'pull up your bootstraps'* song and dance. Meaning, I got mine, the rest of you Niggas' is on your own.

Even though Sec. Powell is a truly unique Black Conservative, he's still criticized by many Blacks. Sec. Powell was called an Uncle *Tom/House Nigger* by Harry Belafonte and once again White Conservatives came running to the rescue. Just imagine how much faster the federal response would've been if it was Hurricane *'Tom'* that hit New Orleans instead of Katrina. When the word *'Tom'* is mentioned White Conservatives show immediate concern for Black Folks (*all 2 %*). Sec. Powell basically dismissed Mr. Belafonte's *Tom* Charge, and applied the *"consider the source"* defense. That still wasn't good enough for White Conservatives. Mind you, many of these same White Conservatives made it very clear a few years ago that they would **never** support a Powell Presidential bid. These are also many of the same White Conservatives who gladly watched Sec. Powell leave the Bush Administration. Now it turns out that Sec. Powell's voice was the only voice of reason inside the Bush Administration. Just imagine how sound and coherent our foreign policy would be if Iranian mullahs had called Sec. Powell an Uncle *Tom*. Or what if N. Korea's Kim Jong-Il had called Sec. Powell an Uncle *Tom*? Or what if Venezuela's Hugo Chavez had called Sec. Powell an Uncle *Tom*? Or what if the Communist leadership in China had called Sec. Powell an Uncle *Tom*? Conservatives would've rushed to his defense, and who knows, maybe our policies towards those countries wouldn't be so *pussy-like*. I'm sorry, just a little wishful thinking. What if the Racist *"Black Sambo"* postage stamps sanctioned by Mexico's Vicente Foxx had said *"Uncle Tom Powell"* across the top of them? Would Conservatives have kicked back and enjoyed the commotion, like they did with the *"Black Sambo"* stamps? Where were Black Conservatives during the *"Black Sambo"* postage stamp commotion? No *Tom* Charge, no concern (*they take no offense to being called "Sambo" because they're used to it*).

Bernard Goldberg was so incensed by Mr. Belafonte's remarks, that he listed him at **# 79** in his book entitled **100 People Who Are Screwing Up America**. Mr. Belafonte was given this ranking nearly *two* years before his recent comments about Pres. Bush being a terrorist. With all the polluters, White collar thieves and crooked politicians in this country, I find it hard to believe that Harry Belafonte is on Mr. Goldberg's list just for calling another Black Man an Uncle *Tom*. That shows you just how important it is for White Conservatives to defend Black Conservatives. If you want to know why so many White Conservatives are considered bigots, just thumb through Mr. Goldberg's list of the *100* people who are screwing up America. Mr. Goldberg proudly wears his bigotry on his sleeve, and his list is a reflection of that bigotry. Let us start near the top of the list, shall we. To rank Rev. Jesse Jackson at # **4** and Rev. Al Sharpton at # **17**, tells you everything you need to know about Mr. Goldberg's views on Race. Trust me, I'm not a Jesse Jackson or Al Sharpton apologist. I don't like a lot of the stuff on their resumé, and I know they're not going to care too much for this book, so the feelings will be mutual. But like I said in the *Stereotypes* chapter, there's a lot of White Folks out there who prefer two kinds of Black Folks, *Dumb* or *Quiet*, and preferably *both*. Mr. Goldberg is definitely one of those White Folks who prefers all of the above. By the way, do you think there were any outspoken White Conservative multi-Millionaire televangelists on his list? You know which ones I'm talking about, the Commercial Christians. I'm talking about the Christians who preach Intolerance, and have openly wished death on others, called for the death of others, or stated the death of others was God's way of punishing them. Mr. Goldberg listed Jimmy Swaggart, but you know I'm not talking about Rev. Swaggart. I'm talking about the Millionaire Televangelists who got rich by spreading Fear, Hatred and Intolerance. There was no mention of them. I found that odd considering these televangelists pray every evening for the Second Coming, which in their view would bring about the destruction of Mr. Goldberg's Jewish Brothers and Sisters. I guess Color Trumped Faith.

Instead of talking about who isn't on the list, I'll mention *two* names that are on the list. A full *41* places behind Rev. Jackson, at # *45* is Ken Lay, the former head of Enron. A man who marched with Dr. King, and has also helped get our servicemen out of captivity is considered worse for America than a man who robbed thousands of his employees of their pensions. I guess in Mr. Goldberg's world Color Trumps Greed (*no big surprise there*). Tyco thief Dennis Kozlowski came in at # **44**. Mr. Goldberg assigned *3 ¼* pg.'s to Rev. Sharpton and *3* pg.'s to Rev. Jackson. He assigned *1* page to Mr. Kozlowski and *½* a page to Mr. Lay. Being an outspoken activist in America is tantamount to screwing up the nation, and robbing people of their retirement gets you honorable mention. Mr. Goldberg also had two additional chapters in the book which more than summed up his Racial views. In his chapter entitled **White-Collar Thugs** he made a *half-assed*, *3* paged attempt to further condemn the ENRON gang. I found it admirable that he feels White collar criminals should be sent to *Attica-like* prisons or hung, but I don't think he genuinely means it. After all, he preceded the **White-Collar Thugs** chapter with a chapter entitled **Racial Enforcers**. This chapter was *6* pg.'s long and went right back to the Uncle *Tom* game. This time Mr. Goldberg felt the need to run to the rescue of Shelby Steele, Clarence *Thom*as, and Ward Connerly. For those of you scoring at home, pages dedicated to *'outspoken'* Black Men outnumbered pages dedicated to White collar thieves *12* to *4*. A book entitled **100 People Who Are Screwing Up America,** placed more emphasis on *'outspoken'* Blacks than White thieves. I had to keep looking at the cover because it seemed more like a David Duke publication than something from a Jewish journalist. By the way, Mr. Duke, the Hate-spewing Klansman, came in at **# 66** on Mr. Goldberg's list. You would think that a man who would like to see Jews and Blacks eliminated from the face of the earth, might have been ranked a little higher, but in Mr. Goldberg's world outspoken Black activists pose a much greater threat than Hate-spewing Klansmen. Color Trumps Hate. Like I said, he wears his bigotry on his sleeve, and when you take into account the fact that he's also doubled as a sports journalist, suddenly everything adds up (refer to **"Hate Nigger Radio"** if you don't remember).

I'm sure if Mr. Goldberg was questioned about his obvious bigotry he would be quick to play the persecuted Jew Card. The problem with the persecuted Jew Card is that it doesn't work in America. In America, you are ***"whatever you check on a job application."*** Since Mr. Goldberg checks the box next to the word **CAUCASION**, persecution doesn't apply to him in the good old U.S. *of* A. This makes him no *different* than any other bigot regardless of his faith. Mr. Goldberg spent more time telling us about the people who exercise their right to speak, than he spent telling us about the people who are fleecing the American Middle Class through corporate thievery. Thievery obviously doesn't appeal to Mr. Goldberg. In Mr. Goldberg's world, Ludacris singing about *bitches* and *ho's,* or Randall Robinson singing about *reparations*, is a much greater threat to the American way of life, than the countless White collar thieves and crooked politicians he left off of his list. In Mr. Goldberg's world running to the rescue of Black Conservatives who've been called Uncle *Tom* is a matter of National Security. If White Conservatives like Mr. Goldberg want to participate in an Uncle *Tom* debate, I'll tell you exactly where to start. Why don't you start within the Republican Party?

RANT: "Uncle Tonya's Log Cabin Republicans"

The great thing about being a Black Conservative is that they are truly needed. No one wants to be called a Racist in today's society, and this is why Black Conservatives are so dearly needed by White Conservatives. To put it mildly, Black Conservatives make great window dressing. They're scarecrows in three-piece suits. They scare away those of us who crow Racism, so the fields of bigotry can continue to flourish. Racist policies can be passed, Racist actions can be practiced, and as long as no Racist terminology is attached to those policies or actions, all is Lovely. Then with the help of Black Conservatives, any and all accusations of Racism can be easily deflected. Being called a Racist is nothing but rhetoric unless there's something for the charge to stick to. It's tough to make those charges stick nowadays, because it's tough to distinguish Racism from Indifference. Black is synonymous with poor, but Black Folks aren't the only poor folks; so quite often you can't tell Racism from Indifference. No one wants to be called a Racist, but the Racist charge is still relatively easy to deflect. That is, unless someone's words or actions are blatant. What cooked Trent Lott's goose was the fact that he had a voting record and a history that matched his *Dixiecrat* rhetoric. In America, there is one thing and only one thing worse than being called a Racist, and that's being called a liberal. This charge is thrown around a hell of a lot more, and seems to stick much easier. Anyone who doesn't march in 'lock-step' with conservatives is branded a liberal. *Oooooooh, spoooky.* The Media is so scared of being called liberal, they let conservatives do as they please and no one says more than a peep. The so-called liberal Media will ask a question a few times, get no answers, and then move on like shit never happened. No *'Blue Dress'*, no dogged pursuit of the story. I could point to about *10 different* examples of the Media failing to ask tough questions, but if I exposed their failures, it would piss off Sadaam Hussein, and he would then order his men to crash passenger jets into my home, like he did on *9/11.*

The subject that most exposes the Media's spinelessness, and also exposes the hypocrisy of conservatives, is the subject of Uncle *Tonyas.* Uncle *Tonyas* are Homosexuals who have moved on politically and ideologically, but undermine the pursuit of equal rights by their gay Brothers and Sisters. To move on is an individual's choice, but to actively support policies and policy makers who chop your Brothers and Sisters off at the knees is the **essence** of *Tom*ism, or in this case *Tonya*-ism. The Republican Party is loaded with Homosexuals who fight against the rights of Homosexuals. Conservatives are the biggest homophobes, and conservatives seem to really enjoy persecuting all Homosexuals, except those within their ranks. This is not about outing someone because of their personal Sexual preference; this is about policies and hypocrisy. White Conservatives have no problem sticking their noses in debates between Blacks when the issue is Affirmative Action, because Affirmative Action is a policy. When the President talks about a Constitutional Amendment banning Gay marriage, it then becomes a potential policy that's open for national debate. Gay Republicans should have to answer why they oppose gay marriage when so many of their Brothers and Sisters support it. I'm *not* talking about the Log Cabin Republicans. **I'm talking about the Uncle *Tonyas* in the party.** I'm *not* talking about the hypocrites who've been exposed, like the late-Mayor of Spokane, Washington, Jim West. I'm talking about the hypocrites who should be exposed, the same way Blacks expose Black Conservatives for their *Tom*-like behavior. I'm talking about *top* officials in the R.N.C., powerful Republican congressmen from the state of California, Senate staffers, House staffers, and well known conservative radio personalities who've had to pay settlements to men for Sexual harassment (*I won't even get into family members of many prominent conservatives*). All of these blowhards sing about the ills of Homosexuality or support an administration that sings about the ills of Homosexuality, but practice **Brokeback** policies when the lights go out. The Media gives these conservatives a free hypocrisy pass because they don't want to be branded as liberals. This has to be the reason why, because I've yet to understand how a **Gay Male prostitute** can run around in the White House and the story just fades away. I guess since there was never a *Smoking Gun* or a *Blue Dress* (*that we know of*) there was no need to pursue the story.

When the Media fails to ask tough questions about issues of National Security for fear of being labeled liberal, our nation is in trouble. This story is definitely about National Security, because from February of 2003 to February of 2005, a **Gay Male prostitute** could enter the White House at will, using a fake name, and was running around in the wee hours of the morning disguised as a *journalist*. At a time when honor and integrity were supposedly being restored in the White House, we were treated to a spectacle eerily similar to ***street ho's*** referring to themselves as ***Precious*** or ***Luscious***, and being disguised as *crossing guards* or *meter maids (in the wee hours of the morning)*. But let's get back to matters of National Security, shall we.

NOTE: In October of 2005 a U.S. Marine of Philippine decent was charged with espionage because he E-Mailed classified documents from the Vice President's office. The sensitive documents were sent to a group that was trying to stage a coup in the Philippines.

If you can't trust a U.S. Marine, you damn sure shouldn't trust a *former* U.S. Marine who's also a **Gay Male prostitute** using a fake name? This is a National Security issue because regulations were broken so a **Gay Male prostitute** could have unimpeded access to the White House. James Guckert aka Jeff Gannon aka Bulldog is a **Gay Male prostitute** who attended a *two*-day seminar for journalism, worked for a phantom news agency called Talon, and then suddenly found himself as a member of the prestigious White House Press Corps. James Guckert stated that he's a '*former*' **Gay Male prostitute**, but placing the word '*former*' in front of **Gay Male prostitute** doesn't justify or explain unimpeded access to the White House. Mr. Guckert is also a *former* U.S. Marine, so I have the utmost respect for him as a man, and I've stated throughout this book that I'm not a Homophobe, but I am a National Security-*phobe*. That said, I'm also a dumb country boy from Ohio, but I'm not stupid. Jeff Guckert is a **Gay Male prostitute**, and he should be considered a **Gay Male prostitute** until he produces the following:

1- Pictures or gifts from his prostitution retirement party.
2- Some form of retirement papers that state: *"I ain't a-ho-no-mo."*

Until he provides one of the above, I'm inclined to believe he's still a *working guy*.

Folks, this shit isn't **Pretty Woman;** Mr. Guckert wasn't swept away by some wealthy White House official, and then swept into retirement (*that we know of*). Comedian Andrew Dice Clay once theorized **"Either you suck *Dick* or you do not suck *Dick*, there is no in-between."** My guess is the same theory would apply to selling ass: **"Either you're selling ass or you are not selling ass, there is no in-between."** So if both theories are correct, that would explain why Mr. Guckert's on-line **Gay Male prostitute** profiles remained active during his *2* years in the White House Press Corps. It's been reported that Mr. Guckert could be found on Hotmilitarystud.com and Militaryescorts4m.com. The fact that Mr. Guckert is a Homosexual or a prostitute is irrelevant; it's the National Security violations that make this story relevant. The fact that he's an Uncle *Tonya* who was working for other Uncle *Tonyas* in the Bush Administration makes this story doubly-relevant. The Talon News Agency was nothing more than a web-site and Mr. Guckert had the nerve to post articles that stated John Kerry might be the first Gay President because he supported the pro-Gay agenda. Mr.

Guckert was well known for asking soft-ball questions that were obviously planted. Whoever was planting the questions could've E-Mailed them to him or just telephoned him, but for some reason Mr. Guckert's presence was continually required at the White House. The fact that Mr. Guckert worked for a bullshit news organization and asked soft-ball questions is also irrelevant. The fact that he had unlimited access to the White House makes this story relevant.

White House logs show that Mr. Guckert stayed overnight at the White House on many occasions. White House logs show that Mr. Guckert stayed overnight even when there were no press conferences scheduled. Mr. Guckert visited the White House nearly *40* times, even though there were no press conferences scheduled. On *14 different* occasions the Secret Service had **no record** of Mr. Guckert's *entry* or *exit* times. When did Mr. Guckert *enter,* or more importantly, where did Mr. Guckert *enter?* Perhaps the *rear?* Why was Mr. Guckert's presence repeatedly required? Hmmm? I'd like to give a fellow Marine the benefit of the doubt and assume that Mr. Guckert was there on business, but that's the problem, he was probably there on business. Was it his supposed *'former'* business, or was it his sham of a new business? With no *Blue Dress*, there was no dogged pursuit of the story, so we'll never know. As a Marine, I've visited many strip clubs and I've heard all of the stories about girls who were working their way through college by *stripping, hooking* or whatever. I'd like to believe that Mr. Guckert **hookered** his way through journalism school, and was saving for his retirement like Jamie Lee Curtis in **Trading Places**, but that's probably not the case. Who completes a *two*-day journalism seminar and becomes a member of the White House Press Corps? No one, that's who. Mr. Guckert's very *first* journalism job was as a member of the prestigious White House Press Corps, and he even got to ask Pres. Bush a question. It would be easy to say this was just another example of the Bush Administration appointing cronies, but to say that would be acknowledging that Mr. Guckert was truly a journalist. I'm trying to give him the benefit of the doubt, but reality says no way. Even if you acknowledge that Mr. Guckert was a journalist, can you honestly acknowledge that being a journalist was his primary job? **Hell No!** His numerous suspicious visits to the White House remind me of one of my old platoon sergeant's favorite sayings: *"You can't turn a 'ho' into a housewife."* Meaning, you can't turn a **Gay Male prostitute** into a journalist, even if he completes a *two*-day journalism seminar, and even if you feed him the questions. What makes this episode so sad is the fact that the Log Cabin Republicans continually have to deal with Uncle *Tonyas* who undermine all of their efforts from the inside. Log Cabin Republicans are brave men and women who've come out of the closet, and already have to deal with continuous public ridicule, and then also have to deal with disingenuous support from the Republican Party.

The hypocrisy of Uncle *Tonyas* and the hypocrites who enable them should be exposed. The Media stayed on the Guckert story for about a week and then let it die. Had they kept harping on this story and demanded some answers, they would've been branded with the dreaded *'L'* word, liberal. The biggest hypocrites of the Guckert incident were not the people who failed to ask tough questions. The Media may have been a bunch of pussies but they were not hypocrites. The biggest hypocrites were the people who *didn't demand answers.* All of the outspoken homophobes of the conservative movement were strangely silent. The homophobic Commercial Christians were strangely silent. The White Conservatives who Love to stick their noses in the Uncle *Tom* debate were strangely silent. Conservatives *busted ass* (*no pun intended*) to make this story go away, but I guarantee you their attitude would've been much different had this occurred during the Clinton Administration. The Commercial Christians would've demanded Congressional hearings, and there's no doubt their demands would've been met. Instead, there were no such demands, and they chose to employ a strategy of silence. In the future, maybe conservatives should apply the same silent strategy when a Black Man levels the *Tom* Charge against another Black Man. Conservatives should stop trying to defend what they don't understand (i.e., **the *Tom* Charge**), and start addressing what they know exist among them (i.e., **Uncle *Tonyas***).

B.T.P.

The rallying cry of Black Conservatives is the *bootstrap theory*. Hey, *pull up your bootstraps* and make it happen, I did. I also believe in the *bootstrap theory*, but you can't hide the boots from people and then tell them to *pull up their straps*. On **Meet the Press** in 1967 Dr. Martin Luther King was asked why some Negroes succeed and some don't, and his answer was as follows:

"Some succeed and not others because the system is stacked against the Negro…and it's alright to say to people to lift yourself by your own bootstraps, but it's cruel to say to a bootless man that he ought to lift himself by his own bootstraps…and the fact is that Millions of Negroes have been left bootless as a result of poverty… as a result of illiteracy caused by inadequate education ….and the real lack of educational opportunities….and as a result of centuries of neglect and hurt. And

I think the government, and everybody must see the Negro can't do this job by himself."

Obviously a lot of things have changed in the last *40* years, but many things have also remained the same. I won't go as far as Dr. King, and mention the 'G' word (Government), but I'll repeat what I've said throughout this book: ***"Black Folks want the same as White Folks, Nothing More and Nothing Less."*** This is not about Affirmative Action or Welfare; this is about the attitudes that create the need for Affirmative Action and Welfare. Fair access to employment and educational opportunities would negate the need for Governmental assistance in most cases. These attitudes are a societal epidemic that has permeated every walk of American life. I personally recruit minorities for the fire service, and I'm appalled at how many bright young Black and Hispanic Males I have to turn down because they have a bullshit felony on their record. These young men are fucked for life over some stupid shit that usually amounts to nothing more than community service for young White Males. It's not just a matter of better legal representation; it's a matter of these young men being considered worthless, and therefore **Devalued** by the system. It's amazing how lenient a judge can be when he's told that the young man deserves a second chance because he can shoot a basketball. The young man who can't shoot a basketball also deserves a second chance, but he's often considered a drag on society. That's about attitudes, not policies. The disparity is due to **Devaluation**. The true sentence of that felony charge is a life on welfare, a life of crime, or both.

Public education is another area that's become an absolute joke in this country. Why are inner-city schools so inadequate? The reasons are numerous and the lack of accountability is an embarrassment. Standardized tests only measure what these children don't have, *not* what they don't know. These test scores reflect under-paid teachers, and over-paid administrators. These test scores reflect dilapidated schools that lack the technology of suburban schools that are often just a *15* minute drive away. These test scores reflect the overall lack of concern by all involved. The parents, who many times don't know any better, still bare much of the responsibility. The over-paid poor teachers and the under-paid good teachers certainly bare some responsibility, because they're supposed to have the skills and the willingness to communicate with inept parents. The administrators, who often measure progress in terms of test scores and budgets, also bare much of the responsibility. Measuring the enthusiasm of teachers and students will tell you more about progress than test scores ever will. A school that teachers and students are proud of is a school that will bring out the best in the teachers, who in turn will bring out the best in their students. A dilapidated school will give dilapidated results. These problems always seem to reside in communities that are predominantly Black. This disparity is due to **Devaluation**, and the true sentence for failure is a life on welfare, a life of crime, or both.

These disparities don't require you to connect the dots to see the results. Legacy and Development college admissions don't require you to connect the dots to see the results. Any school that allows Legacy/Development admissions should have Affirmative Action, period. Nepotism in the hiring practices of government institutions doesn't require you to connect the dots to see the results. All public sector/government entities should be a reflection of the communities they represent. Instead, there is usually rampant nepotism and not a peep from the *bootstrap* advocates.

The White *'bootstrap'* advocates always seem to forget they were born wearing fishing waders. Even Whites born in poverty can find a pair of boots to put on, if they choose to. A *400* year head start doesn't leave a lot of boots lying around, and quite often, the boots that are left lying around always seem to find their way into a pair of White hands. You only have to go back *60* years to find the biggest free boots giveaway in this nation's history. White veterans were able to slip on a new pair of boots right after W. W. II. White veterans were the recipient of the largest Affirmative Action policy in this nation's history, the G. I. Bill. The G. I. Bill was created to help the millions of W.W. II vets get off to a good start when they returned home. Ira Katznelson's book **When Affirmative Action was White** details how the G. I. Bill reached *8* out of *10* White Men born in the 1920's, and therefore uplifted an entire generation of Whites by giving them the opportunity to:

- **buy property with no money down and low interest rates**
- **start their own businesses with small-business loans**
- **go to college**

The *Economic* advantages that grew from the G. I. Bill were passed down to the children of the recipients. Whether it was a house, a small business or an education that evolved into a good job, there was a continual trickle down effect. A house purchased for *$13,000 DOLLARS* could turn into a *$400,000 DOLLAR* investment by the end of a lifetime. A small business can obviously be passed down through the family. A college degree can get you a good job that will afford you the opportunity to send your children to college. The G. I. Bill was written by Southern legislators who intentionally made it difficult for Black veterans to cash in their chips.

The Bill was written so control would be at the local level. This allowed:

- **banks to deny Blacks loans for property**
- **banks to deny Blacks loans for creation of small-businesses**

Denying Blacks the opportunity to own property and start businesses was meant to keep them in positions of menial labor. It was designed to keep a cheap unskilled workforce on hand. Blacks were supposed to continue to fill the bill that illegal aliens fill today and nothing more. Many Black veterans were *welcomed home* from the war with beatings while standing at bus stops in uniform. A man can accept an ass kickin', because ass kickins' usually don't last too long. Restricting Black veterans from fair access to the G. I. Bill kicked the asses of several generations of Blacks. Blacks were kicked in the ass with the very *boots* they were denied access to. It would be quite miraculous (*and painful*), to pull up the *'bootstraps'* when the boots are in your ass.

There's no doubt that denying access to the G. I. Bill and restricting educational opportunities enabled hopelessness to permeate several generations of Blacks. That said, there have certainly been many good White Folks who realized that America is a chain, and a chain is only as strong as its weakest link (i.e., the *bootless* poor). Today, America is like a man with a *new boot* on one foot, and *no boot* on the other foot. We're just hobbling along, one foot warm and secure, and one foot blistered and bloodied. The question America will eventually face is: **"What will happen when the blistered and bloodied foot has had enough?"**

This **SECTION** was not meant to be the traditional *"Wo is me, us po Black Folks can't get a break"* song and dance, so I hope no one took it that way.

This **SECTION** was meant to remind *all* of the *bootstrap* advocates of Racial disparities in the Educational System, in the Criminal Justice System, and the Media.

This chapter was meant to remind *all* of the *bootstrap* advocates not to overlook the **History** of the hidden boots.

This chapter was meant to remind Black Conservatives that luck played a role in their ascent, because no matter how good you are, you still need someone White to judge you on your *Merits* and not your skin color.

The Black Conservatives that preach the *bootstrap* theory often preach the right message, but they choose to preach to the wrong choir. When you're sitting with people who openly support a state's right to fly the **Stars and Bars,** you've abdicated any and all rights to preach to Black Folks about anything, period. Black Conservatives, I suggest you find a mirror and start preaching the *jockstrap* theory, but I guess *you gotta have a pair* before you'd need a *jockstrap.* In *140* years of freedom, Black Americans have had less than *20* years of sound leadership (1955 to 1968), and to see some of our brightest minds actually work against the *struggle* is quite sad.

They don't have to work for the **Cause,** but they damn sure don't have to work against it either. Working against the **Cause** is the **true essence** of *Tom*ism, and only a Black Man can make that Charge. Only a Black Man can make the *Tom* Charge, and only the accused Uncle *Tom* can refute the *Tom* Charge. Anything else is mere **"*TOM*FOOLERY."**

SECTION VII Closing The Divide

"People are people…strike them and they will cry; cut them and they will bleed; starve them and they will wither away and die. But treat them with respect and decency, give them access to the levers of power, attend to their aspirations and grievances, and they will flourish and grow, and if you will excuse an ungrammatical phrase, join together to form a more perfect union."

Justice Thurgood Marshall

"In life things are rarely Black and White. I like to think of life as an inch of Black on one side, an inch of White on one side, and a mile of Gray in the middle. Those of us who acknowledge the Gray's existence tend to handle the peaks and valleys of life a little better than those who only see life in terms of Black and White or Right and Wrong.

What the *RANTS* allow me to do is stray off topic and briefly explore the Gray areas of life. When it comes to Race, Religion, Politics and Sex it's all Gray anyway."

That's the definition for *RANT* in the **Terms & Definitions** chapter. I'm sure it seems like I've strayed way off topic many, many times, but actually I haven't. If you've judged this book solely by its cover, then yes, I've strayed off topic. One of the goals of this book was to show people just how trivial our *differences* really are. If you're still judging this book by its cover, then I've failed to enlighten you. For that I apologize. The deliberate madness of **White Men Can't Hump** was:

•   To bring Black Men out of the Sexual gutter created by centuries of White Male Fear-Mongering. Why is Sexual equality so important? Because when you belittle and degrade someone's Sexuality, you also belittle and degrade them as human beings (*just ask Homosexuals*).

•   To bring Racist and Greedy White Men down to size, because the *Economic* playing field will never be level, unless the Racial/social playing field is level. The bottom line is, America's Racial Divide has no chance of being closed until America's *Economic* Divide is closed.

White Men Can't Hump is like Marine Corps boot camp because it tears you down and then challenges you to better yourself. **White Men Can't Hump** specifically targeted Racist White Men and Greedy White Men because they're responsible for widening America's Divide. I targeted

Greedy White Men because they widen the *Economic* Divide. I targeted Racist White Men because they widen the Racial Divide. **Small-Poleons Complex** was my dedication to the *Racists*, and **Limpbaugh Syndrome** was my dedication to the *Greedy*. I truly believe that all men are created equal, so in order to bring the *big boys* down to *size*, a good kick in the groin was required. I guarantee you there are plenty of White Men who've read this book and weren't bothered by one single page. These are probably the White Men who know how to handle their *bizzness* inside the bedroom, and have no petty animosities outside the bedroom. The good White Folks are beyond the silliness and judge people as they present themselves. The Sex in this book was meant to show that even though we're all *different*, we're all still human beings. The Sex in this book *links* us all. Our past and our present continue to be linked by Sexual perceptions, and the importance of Sexual perceptions in our society cannot be overlooked. I'm sure many will Deny the Sexual component of this book, but until someone can give me a reasonable explanation as to *why*:

• A Love story featuring Halle Berry and Russell Crowe would make up to *200* Million *DOLLAR$*.

• The same exact Love story, featuring Halle Berry and Denzel Washington, would only make *50* Million *DOLLAR$?* (from **VOLUME I**)

The answer to the above question resides in America's Sexual perceptions of Black Men. Those Sexual perceptions are the Cornerstone to Racism against Black Men in America. As absurd as my little theory may sound, its plausibility resides in the fact that Racism itself is absurd. To despise someone because of the amount of melanin in their skin may be the greatest absurdity that man has ever perpetrated against fellow man. **It doesn't make sense.** On the other hand, it makes perfect sense to despise someone because they can please a woman better than yourself. Throughout history, man has despised his fellow man for things far less important than Sex. Racism towards Black Men in America has always been about **Fear of the Black Penis,** and has **never** been about *Fear of Black Pigmentation.* The Fear that has been sold to the masses is all about Sex, not skin color. The *castration* rituals that accompanied the thousands of lynchings of Black Men had nothing to do with skin color, and everything to do with Sex. The *anti-Miscegenation Laws* that were passed by legislatures from coast to coast had nothing to do with *Race Mixing*, as long as it was a White Penis doing the *mixing*, and not a **Black Penis.** The Tuskegee Experiment (i.e., *observing Black Men rot inside and outside with syphilis*) had absolutely nothing to do with skin color, and everything to do with **Fear of the Black Penis.** The manufactured

Fear of the Black Male rapist and the Black Male pimp is all about Sex, and not skin color. Why is all of this so important? Because you can't kick an addiction (drugs, alcohol, or **Fear of the Black Penis)**, unless you're aware of the fact that you have an addiction. And you can't overcome an addiction, if you continue to Deny its existence. Whites will Deny, Deny, Deny, but their actions don't lie. If factories were packin' up and moving to the inner-cities of America (*instead of China*), and were only hiring Black Folks, Whites would make their outrage known. Instead, we only hear a whimper. If Whites were being forced out of their jobs and forced to train Black American replacements (*instead of Indians from India*); the outrage would be loud and clear, and legislation would soon follow. No one pushes the White Man's Hate-Button like Black Men, and until I hear a reasonable excuse for this, **Small-Poleons Complex** will more than suffice.

The bottom line is, **Black Men who are _un_educated, _un_employed, or _incarcerated_, pose *no* Sexual threat to White Men. Black Men who are educated and employed are far more *Sexually Appealing*, and *do* pose a threat to many White Men. I call that a *Million Miles of Motive*, my friends.**

The truth is, man's instincts are still very primitive, which means men still have *two* very primitive priorities:
- *Kickin' Ass (physically, and/or financially)*
- *Gettin' Laid*

As long as those *two* primitive instincts remain high priorities, White Men know they have only *one* true rival, and his initials are **Black Men** (*woops*). The Racial Divide will never be closed if people are in Denial about its origins. Hopefully this book will add some clarity for the future. Closing the Divide is about unifying us as a species, and eliminating dividers such as Race, religion, and politics. Closing the Divide is about putting our commonalities first and our *differences* a distant second. Religion and politics are what you believe and Race is what you see on the surface. One would think the Racial Divide would be the easiest divide to close. In a perfect world Race would not be a divider, it would serve as nothing more than an identifier.

The evidence that Race doesn't have to be a divider has been seen time and time again. Sports, the military, and any field that requires teamwork to survive, serves as proof that we can peacefully coexist, and peacefully flourish together. Thus proving that we all have more in common than not. There has been amazing progress on many fronts, but many old injustices have remained intact. I may have been a little tough on Black Conservatives, but there's no doubt I'm proud when I see Sec. of State Condoleezza Rice and former Sec. of State Colin Powell, and I applaud

President Bush for giving them the opportunity. I'm proud that they were appointed to those positions based on so-called *merit*. At the same time, I don't have a problem with token appointments like Justice *Thom*as either. Once a token appointment proves they can do the job, most people forget the person was a token appointment. Token appointments only become an issue when it's a person of color or a woman. White Men make token appointments everyday in the forms of nepotism and cronyism, and no one seems to notice. These are the **barriers** that are the toughest to break through, and for Black Folks to Close the Divide, these are the **barriers** that must be broken. It's a slow gradual process that can only be encountered *one* step at a time. For Black Folks, the key to Closing the Racial Divide is to Close the *Economic* Divide.

Chapter 1 Closing the Economic & Racial Divide

I don't remember where I heard this phrase: "When White America sneezes, Black America catches the cold, and when White America catches a cold, Black America gets pneumonia," but unfortunately it's quite true. There's a lot of *different* ways to interpret that phrase, and I think the best way to sum it up is *uneven unity*. The bottom line is, we're all in this great experiment called America together. Some people believe America is their country and the rest of us are just visitors. Those people are dead wrong and I dedicated much of this book to bringing those people down to *size*. The Racists and the Greedy obviously have voids in their lives that desperately need filled. I wish them luck and I hope this book motivates them to take a long look in the mirror. I've had in-depth discussions with many Racists in my lifetime. Some of them made a strong case for disliking an individual, but none of them ever made a strong case for Hating an entire group of people. Being a White Supremacist while at the same time being a Michael Jordan fan is just one of the many kinds of contradictions you can usually draw out of these people during a friendly conversation. When you ask these people to list their grievances, skin color is rarely mentioned and *Economics* is always mentioned in some way, shape or form. Words like: Lazy, Jobs, Affirmative Action, Welfare, and Entitlements are all just code words for *Economics*. So it doesn't take a genius to realize *Economic* security is one of the keys to Racial harmony.

NOTE: Obviously, those infected with **Small-Poleons Complex** have *internal* issues that will be much tougher to overcome.

Economic security certainly doesn't guarantee Racial harmony, but one thing we know for sure is *Economic in-security* certainly doesn't help. *Economic* insecurity magnifies our *differences*, agitates our *differences*, and creates many of the petty jealousies that lead to disharmony. Blacks have been told for years that the key to the American dream is *Economic* independence. *Economic* independence only comes to members of the American Upper Class. Since you've got to crawl before you can walk, the obvious key for Black America is to make it to the Middle Class.

A growing American Middle Class needs a strong White Middle Class. I know there are segments of the Black population who don't want to hear that shit but it's true. It is what it is. Black America, *just like the rest of the world*, needs a strong White Middle Class. What's going on today doesn't make for a strong Middle Class of any Race. Black Folks only make up *13 %* of America's population, but probably deal with *50 %* of the turmoil. That *13 %* is without question a **VERY LOUD 13 %,** but we like to let people know when *we're in the house.* We may be in the house, but right now we're still buried in the basement. We have very little financial capital, and we have very little future capital (*50 %* of Black Males are dropping out of high school). There's still a thriving Black Middle Class, but unfortunately they're the *silent minority.* The Black Middle Class is the *silent minority* because they'll never be heard until they become the *overwhelming majority* of the Black community. That's not fair but it should be taken as a challenge. I've heard all of the wonderful arguments about the need for Black entrepreneurs, the need for Black owned businesses, and the need for Black *Economic* empowerment. I agree with all of those needs wholeheartedly. Those are all just *different* paths to the same destination, the American Middle Class. Education is also a path to that same destination, and in my opinion it's the most important path to that destination. You can't experience the wonderful wealth of Upper Class America, unless you first become entrenched in Middle Class America. The wonderful rags to riches stories are not the norm. The parents who bust their asses to send their children to college with the hope that their children find even greater success than themselves is the norm. It's a *one* step at a time process, and it's always been the foundation of this nation. That foundation is under assault right now, and that doesn't bode well for Black America. It's tough to move from the Lower Class to the Middle Class when the Middle Class is *struggling* and shrinking. When the American Middle Class is strong, it's much more receptive to all Americans. A strong and vibrant American Middle Class closes the Racial Divide. A weak American Middle Class brings out the worst in all of us. When the American Middle Class *struggles*, the dreams of a Middle Class life become a distant desert oasis for America's poor. *Economic* aspirations serve as our tree of hope and *link* us, in spite of our *differences.* Black Folks in particular, need a strong White Middle Class for psychological reasons, as well as *Economic* reasons. When shit gets fucked up, the psychological impact has a stronger affect on Whites than Blacks. Black Folks are used to shit being fucked up; White Folks tend to blame everybody but White Folks when shit gets fucked up. White Folks blame illegal aliens instead of blaming the Whites who hire them. White Folks blame India for outsourcing instead of blaming the Whites who outsourced the jobs to India. White Folks blame China and big business for factories packing up and moving to China, instead of blaming the White politicians (*regardless of party*) who created the environment for this to happen.

"Put yourself in the author's shoes"

The Black Middle Class, like the rest of the American Middle Class, and *just like the rest of the world*, needs a strong White Middle Class that doesn't have its head buried in the sand. Whether you like it or not, we're all in this great experiment called America together (**Sorry, but it's worth repeating**). As long as we allow ourselves to be distracted by *singular* issues like abortion and Gay marriage, which are issues that affect individuals, we do a disservice to the population as a whole. These distractions cause us to lose sight of the *plural* issues like health care, jobs, and poverty, which one way or another impact all of us. Some girl in some distant town who wants to get an abortion doesn't affect me or you one damn bit.

When people don't have health insurance, they call for an ambulance and get their treatment in the emergency room. This affects the community because an ambulance is out of service for some bullshit that a family physician would normally treat. This affects all of us because the uninsured drive up health care cost for all of us. If you're one of the thousands who just lost your job at Ford or GM, you probably don't give a fuck about whether or not some young girl on the opposite coast needs an abortion. It may matter to you when your job is secure, but in today's America no one's job is secure, and that's why we as a people can no longer afford to be distracted. Some Homosexual in some distant town who wants to get married doesn't affect me or you one damn bit.

How important is Gay marriage, if you've just found out the company you've given your life to has reneged on its obligation to pay your pension? The pension that you've contributed your hard earned **DOLLAR$** to for the last *30* years. Thousands of people are losing their pensions because of corporate greed. This will surely increase the rolls of the uninsured, and also increase the number of elderly people living in poverty. These are issues that affect the masses, and to focus on the *singular* issues only diverts our attention from the things that truly matter. It's no coincidence that the most outspoken opponents of the *singular* issues are usually Millionaires. They've got their piece of the pie, so now they can spend their free time telling everyone else what to focus on. Why don't the Commercial Christians (the Millionaire televangelists) ever talk about poverty, corporate corruption or corporate greed? Why is their focus always on the *singular* issues? Hey, when your pockets are fat you can do that. These people thrive on keeping us divided over the *singular* issues and distracted from the *plural* issues. We can't demand accountability if we're divided and distracted. If you're a Millionaire televangelist, you've already got good health care, so you don't want rant and rave about that bullshit. If you're a Millionaire televangelist, you've already got a pretty decent retirement plan, so this gives you plenty of time to raise hell about abortion and Homosexuality. If you're a Millionaire televangelist, you've got a strong ally in the corrupt politician. You've both got the same agenda (*create wedge issues*), and you both employ the same methods (*divide, distract, and frighten the masses*). What exactly do the *people* get for their much valued support? Do the Millionaire televangelists and corrupt politicians put food on your table? Do Homosexuals and abortion doctors take food off of your table? Those questions can't be answered until a large segment of our population takes its head out of the sand.

What's going on in America's *bedrooms* is old news; it's the same shit that human beings have engaged in since the beginning of time. The only problem is the lack of discretion and privacy. Everyone likes to openly discuss matters that were once considered private. This problem has nothing to do with the *bedroom*, and everything to do with our willingness to openly discuss it. That said, our willingness to openly discuss what's going on in America's *bedrooms* is not a threat to our way of life. What's going on in America's **boardrooms** is a threat to our way of life. What's going on in America's *bedrooms* has no effect on anyone's:

- Health care premiums being increased.
- Pension plans being reduced.
- Wages being frozen, while the cost of energy, the cost of education, and the overall cost of living continue to skyrocket.

What's going on in America's *bedrooms* has no effect on any of the above, but what's going on in America's **boardrooms** is the primary reason for all of the above. And it's the American Middle Class that continues to suffer, thanks to all of the above.

The only *people* on the planet who do *not* admire the American Middle Class are those who voluntarily live in a *Theocracy*. The American Middle Class gives the planet hope that *Man* can peacefully co-exist under mutually agreed upon laws. It hasn't always been peaceful but we are where we are, and America is still the sweetest deal on the globe. There are obviously a few folks out there who don't care for our way of life, and unfortunately, the only folks who are considered a threat to our way of life are the ones who fly airplanes into buildings. There are other threats out there, but unfortunately many of our leaders are blinded by Greed. There's currently a new emerging enemy, and this new enemy poses a much greater threat than the nuclear armed former Soviet Union. The nuclear armed Soviet Union was *Economically* defeated. The new enemy has learned from the former Soviet Union's mistakes, and has skillfully attacked our strength (i.e., **our economy**). The new enemy is *Economically* smarter than the old enemy, and at the same time, many of the same *Ideological, Strategical,* and *Military* threats still remain. For some reason, the largest Communist country in the world is considered a friend (*China*), and the smallest Communist country in the world is considered a threat (*Cuba*). The new enemy is like a vampire and corporate America is shaking hands with it neck first. The bottom line is, the short-term money grab we're seeing today by Greedy White businessmen is doing long-term *Economic* damage to the American Middle Class, and is also doing long-term damage to our National Security. The good old **Short-Sighted Formula** continues to just hum along.

The *Economic* crisis we currently face is bound to worsen because we have the same attitude towards the largest communist country in the world that we also have towards the largest democracy in the world (*India*). This shows us that our foreign policy is not based on ideology, it's based on greed. The *Economic* crisis we currently face is bound to worsen because we also continue to fall behind China and India *Educationally.* Annually, China and India graduate *five times* as many young people with degrees in science, math, and engineering than we do. Many people obviously point to China and India's huge populations, and say it's no Big Deal. I would be inclined to agree with those people, if Chinese and Indian graduates *competed* against other Chinese and Indian graduates in their respective homelands. Instead, Chinese and Indian graduates are *competing* against each other for American jobs, or being *handed* jobs that were once the backbone of the American Middle Class. We then helplessly watch our jobs go to China, as entire factories pack up and move. We then helplessly watch our jobs get outsourced to India, so Greedy White businessmen can pocket extra profits that would've been earmarked as healthcare or retirement benefits for an American worker. Then our President has the fucking nerve to tell us we don't have enough skilled workers, even though skilled workers are being laid off by the thousands. We then helplessly watch the businesses that have remained cut its employee's benefits, or hire illegal aliens because they don't have to pay them shit or provide any benefits at all. Then our President has the fucking nerve to say illegal aliens are needed because no other Americans want those jobs, even though Americans would gladly shovel shit for a decent wage and benefits. Then when you complain, our government calls you a protectionist. If wanting to protect the American Middle Class makes us protectionists, then so be it, we need more protectionists. The only people who cry protectionism are the people who profit from the lack of it. Yet somehow the American Middle Class still remains the envy of the world, even though it's currently a victim of domestic abuse. Take, take, take and no one gives anything in return. Having a business in America used to be considered a privilege and an honor, but nowadays our government gives tax breaks to businesses so they'll remain here. I say fuck em'. I say take your ass overseas, and by the way, you're not selling your bullshit to the American consumer. Being able to sell your products in America is an honor, but for some reason hiring Americans has become a dishonor. What's left for the American Middle Class? It was recently reported that *One* out of every *Four* jobs in America pays less than a poverty-level-income. That's what's left and that number is growing thanks to you know who. Greedy White businessmen have been given the *Green Light* to create this environment and the truth is they could care less. It would be nice to say pack your shit and go to China, but as long as we allow them to sell their shit right back to us why bother. The Greedy White businessman has been given the *Green Light* by his partner in crime, the corrupt politician. The end result is the bi-partisan sodomization of the American Middle Class. We as a people are screwed, and the politicians know this and use this against us. The politicians know that the American people have nowhere else to go and they take full advantage of this. As an individual, where can you go if you're Pro-Life and Pro-Gay Rights? As an individual, where can you go if you're Pro-Choice and Anti-Gay Rights? While you internally grapple with those *singular* issues, you're unknowingly getting raped *Economically* by those whom you voted for.

Until the American people stand up and say *"No More"* this *Economic* prison rape will continue. The American people should demand that every trade agreement be torn up and re-written to ensure *100 % fair* trade. If we can arbitrarily invade another country and replace its government, then we can damn sure pull out of every trade agreement that rapes the American Middle Class. The loss of jobs in this country can be traced right to the trade deficit, and the trade deficit can be traced right to China. Isn't it funny how our strategy for ending Communism in China is the exact opposite of Pres. Reagan's successful strategy that ended Communism in the Soviet Union? It's all a matter of applying *pussy-diplomacy* in the quest for profits, at the expense of the people. In other words, it's all about whose *gettin' paid*. The defense sector got paid during the Cold War, and continues to get paid because we're currently fighting *two* wars. Now it's corporate America's turn to *get paid*, and it's the American Middle Class that's getting screwed. The problem is no one told Communist China the Cold War is over. China's relationship with the U.S. is like the relationship between a *Pimp* and his *Ho*, and it's getting embarrassingly worse. China's President came to the U.S. in April of 2006 and treated Pres. Bush like a **Bitch**. China's President met with the head of Microsoft (*Bill Gates*) and met with executives from Boeing before meeting with anyone from the Bush Administration (*this was basically a diplomatic Bitch Slap*). China was merely keeping its **Ho** in check, like an up and coming **Pimp** is supposed to do. Many still refuse to acknowledge America's decline, but you can't Deny the *two* following facts:

1 **When Pres. Reagan left office, the U.S. was the *lone* super power.**
2 **When Pres. Bush leaves office, there will be *two* super powers.**

One super power will be on the rise, and thanks to the present leadership, one has peaked and begun its decline. It happened to the Roman Empire, the British Empire, the French Empire, and every other Empire of the past. To think that America is immune to decline, is merely displaying the same kind of arrogance that's gotten us into this mess.

Like I've said throughout this book, it's not your label that matters, it's your actions. The same applies to foreign policy. It's not how tough you talk, it's your actions. Most of our foreign policy problems and most of our *Economic* problems could be solved if someone in our government had the *"Balls"* (*or even just one testicle*) to deal with China. Dealing with China harshly on the *Economic front* is the best way to deal with Iran, and the best way to deal with N. Korea. Dealing with China harshly on the *Economic front* is the best way to avoid dealing with them on the *Militaristic front* in the future. It should come as no surprise that every country we consider a geo-strategic problem is friendly with China. I know it sounds like I'm stuck in the Cold War but I truly fear for our future. Americans better start teaching their children to speak Chinese, and better start explaining to their children what *"Jim Chow Laws"* are (See **VOLUME I, The United States of Communist China**).

That said, National Security and a shrinking American Middle Class obviously doesn't mean shit to Greedy White businessmen. Greedy White businessmen would sell their mothers if it strengthened the quarterly profits they live for. National Security and a shrinking American Middle Class obviously doesn't mean shit to corrupt politicians either. They'd sell their mothers if it guaranteed re-election, and some more of that tasty lobbyist money they live for. We're all in this together, and if the White Middle Class refuses to demand accountability then all of America's in trouble. When Black Folks complain it's considered whining, so it's up to the majority to start complaining. Don't complain on behalf of Black Folks; complain on behalf of yourselves, because when this Titanic strikes the iceberg that's in our horizon, we're all going down together. As the *Economic* Divide continues to grow, we're starting to see more and more Whites standing on the *'have not'* side of the crevice with Black Folks, but they're still clinging to the *singular* issues. My only hope is that these people eventually realize that abortion rights and Gay marriage don't put any food on anybody's table except the people who use it to divide us. Preserving the American Middle Class is not just about preserving the American way of life, it may be the key to preserving the species we call ***Man.***

Chapter 2 Closing the Human Divide

What usually divides us as human beings is petty in the *Grand Scheme of Things*. What is the *Grand Scheme of Things?* The *Grand Scheme of Things* is the survival of the human species. Without getting into religion or the end of the world and all of that gloomy stuff, we're still just a species merely trying to survive. We're trying to survive in spite of our efforts to the contrary. We're still evolving and still adapting biologically. Physically, we're bigger, stronger, and faster than ever, and we're living longer than ever. Psychologically we're still intolerant of others, and we're still as resistive to change as we've been for thousands of years. We continue to advance technologically, and we seem to be regressing harmoniously. We also still choose to resolve our *differences* through violence, and we continue to see *Cultures* impose their will on other *Cultures* through the use of force. This always backfires because the human spirit prefers to evolve on its own, instead of by gunpoint. To survive as a species, each and every one of us has to choose to make a positive *difference*. **To survive as a species, each and every one of us must be aware of what we pass on to our children, because that is our truest Legacy.** My old platoon sergeant used to ask us during our miserable *10* mile runs: **"What do you want your Legacy to be?"**; **"Do you want to be remembered as a quitter?"** We all should be asking ourselves: **"What do I want my Legacy to be?"** If you're a person of *faith* do you really believe the petty issues of today, will matter in the *Grand Scheme of Things?* Do you really believe that when you meet your maker, trivial bullshit like: low taxes, less government, and whatever it is that Democrats stand for, will matter? Just picture it: **"Lord, God, My Savior, I stood for low taxes, less government, and guns for everyone."**

More and more people are dedicating their life to shit that only endangers our species. I'm sure that's great news for those who pray every day for the end of the world to come. On the other hand, some of us think *life on earth* is pretty cool, and we're in no hurry to see it come to an end. Some of us want to enjoy life, and embrace life, and not be reminded of impending spiritual doom on a daily basis. It sure would be nice to see a little more focus on the problems here on earth. To deal with the problems on earth, we've got to ask ourselves: **What do I want my Legacy to be?** It's quite sad that so many people choose to leave a Legacy of Hate behind.

Hate and Intolerance create an undue stress that takes years off of your life, and therefore waste much of the precious time you've been given. Greed, Hate and Intolerance are the worst Legacies you could possibly pass on to your children. Greed is like a drug and unfortunately America is hooked. Living only to *get paid*, and living only to spread Hate and Intolerance, is living a Life of irrelevance in the *Grand Scheme of Things.* Passing these attitudes on will only ensure that the gap between the *haves* and *have nots,* and the Tolerant and Intolerant, continues to grow. Relevance comes from making everyone's Life better, not worse. In Life we can make a positive *difference* that can far outlast the few precious seconds that we're given on this beautiful planet. In Life, some choose to make a negative *difference* that further erodes the *Grand Scheme of Things,* and will eventually Deny others a few precious seconds on this beautiful planet.

Greed is somewhat understandable because it has an intoxicating effect, and it appeals to our primitive survival instincts. Hate and Intolerance on the other hand, are baffling in the *Grand Scheme of Things.* Medical science should've made Hate and Intolerance obsolete years ago. If you have a child or family member who needs a blood transfusion, or a new heart, or a new liver, or a new kidney, do you really give a fuck what color the donor's skin is? Do you really give a fuck what Sexual preference the donor is? We still find ourselves divided over things that are petty in the *Grand Scheme of Things.* **So what do you want your Legacy to be?**

In the *Grand Scheme of Things* the only concern should be the welfare of your fellow man. If your true concern is for your fellow man, your policies would reflect those concerns, but as we all know, that's wishful thinking. If you're about greed, and wealth, and fuck everybody else, then just remember, death is the greatest equalizer. In death's eyes we're all Niggers. Death doesn't discriminate. You can think *your shit* don't stink today, and then find yourself in a *piss-smelling* nursing home tomorrow. Our lives are nothing but a *Blip* in the *Grand Scheme of Things.* Each and every single one of us is on the clock at birth, and each and every single one of us will spin **The Death Wheel.** Where will **The Death Wheel** stop when it's your turn to spin? Will the Wheel stop at Heart Attack or Cancer or Traffic Accident or will you be Murdered by your fellow Man? Can you make it to *20* years old, or *40* years old, or *60* years old, or can you sneak by to *80*. Does it matter? *How* and *when* we depart is an irrelevant consolation prize that every single one of us will receive. *How we Die* is irrelevant in the *Grand Scheme of Things,* but *how we Lived* carries a ton of relevance. Death is our truest common bond, but it's Life that carries relevance, so why can't Life also be a common bond? Deep down inside we all want the *same things.* Why can't we respect the fact that many of us choose *different* routes to find that *same thing?* **The only two ways we can truly bond in Life, is to show a mutual respect for one another, and show a mutual concern for what we leave behind.**

So what do you want your Legacy to be? We've seen throughout **History** that *individuals* can make a *difference.* We've also seen throughout **History** that *individuals* can make a negative *difference.* **99.9 %** of everything we'll ever *say, see* or *do,* we'll *never* even remember. This means that all of recorded **History** is based on the *.1 %* of what we do remember, yet look at the *.1 %* we often choose to be remembered for. It's pretty sad when you think about it. In today's *Culture* of Greed, Hate and Intolerance, we find ourselves short of *individuals* who are willing to step up and make a positive *difference.* In the **Grand Scheme of Things** this doesn't bode well for the future of the human species.

Ask yourself:
"Will human beings be here **One Hundred Years from now?**"
"Will human beings be here **One Thousand Years from now?**"
"Will human beings be here **One Million Years from now?**"
"Will human beings **Sleep with the Dinosaurs?**"

As *individuals,* we can't answer the above questions until we first answer this question:
What do I want my Legacy to be?
P.S. A good place to start your *Legacy* is at the bottom of this page.

DEDICATION

This book is dedicated to those who choose Love over Hate and those who seek Progress for all, instead of the status quo for the fortunate few. For us to survive as a species we must reach for the unreachable, and search for a place that will never exist. That place is known as Utopia, and though its existence will never come to fruition, it is the search that will sustain our existence. *What we choose to search for will make us, and what we choose not to search for will break us, it's that simple.*

Embrace each Day,
Each Hour,
And every single Minute,
Because you'll never get them back.
T.W.

For those of you who missed the first leg of this journey, **VOLUME I,** here's the **Table of Contents**, so you can see what you've missed.

VOLUME I RACE & SEX IN AMERICA
Table of Contents

SECTION I Opening
Chapter 1 Opening Pandora's Box
Chapter 2 About the Author
Chapter 3 Terms / Definitions / Miscellaneous Information
   RANT: "The N-Word"
   *RANT: Inside of **RANT**: "I am not an African-American"*

WARNING: FOR MY WHITE READERS

SECTION II History
Chapter 1 Where it all Began
Chapter 2 Slavery: What is the true Legacy?
Chapter 3 The Devaluation Triangle (H 2 I)
   Sub-Chapter 'A' Hate
   RANT: "America's New Niggers"
   Sub-Chapter 'B' *Indifference*
   RANT: "The United States of Communist China"
   Sub-Chapter 'C' *Ignorance*
   RANT: "Lifestyles of the Rich & Rapists"

SECTION III Hollywood
Chapter 1 "White Men Love Them Some Brown Sugar"
   RANT: "Bi-Racial = Race Neutral"
Chapter 2 "America's Most Neutered"
   RANT: "Quentin 'FRANKEN BERRY' Tarantino"
   "The King of Black Sexploitation Films"

Chapter 3 Sex Symbols: "Black Men Need Not Apply"
   RANT: *"Ho-in's Alright, When the Pimp is White"*
Chapter 4 PUNCH LINE: "Hollywood and the Black Penis"

SECTION IV W. M . D .
Chapter 1 W.M.D. = ***White Man's Dread***
= "Fear of the Black Penis"

Sub-Chapter 'A' LYNCHING PSYCHOLOGY 101

   RANT: *"The first time ever I saw his Face"*

"Emmett Till and the Summer of 1975"
Chapter 2 W.M.D. = ***Weapon of Mass Destruction***
= "Misuse of the Black Penis"

   RANT: *"The Busta Test"*

   RANT *Inside of a* ***RANT:*** *"No Busta Test For You!"*

Sub-Chapter 'A' The *50/50* Proposition

   RANT: *"Survival Tips for D.W.B. (Driving While Black)"*

   RANT *Inside of a* ***RANT:*** *"Survival Tips after getting pulled over for D.W.B."*

DEDICATION

Table of Contents for VOLUME II